Legal Rights and Mental-Health Care

Legal Rights and Mental-Health Care

Stanley S. Herr
University of Maryland
Law School
Stephen Arons
University of Massachusetts
at Amherst
Richard E. Wallace, Jr.
White & Case

LexingtonBooks
D.C. Heath and Company
Lexington, Massachusetts
Toronto

Library of Congress Cataloging in Publication Data

Herr, Stanley S.
Legal rights and mental-health care.

Includes bibliographical references and index.
1. Mental health laws—United States. 2. Insanity—Jurisprudence—United States. I. Arons, Stephen. II. Wallace, Richard E. (Richard Edward), 1954- . III. Title. [DNLM: 1. Patient advocacy. 2. Informed consent—Legislation. 3. Community mental health services—United States—Legislation. WM 33 AA1 5L]
KF3828.H47 1983 344.73′044 81-47823
ISBN 0-669-04910-7 347.30444

Second printing, August 1984

Published simultaneously in Canada

Printed in the United States of America on acid-free paper

International Standard Book Number: 0-669-04910-7

Library of Congress Catalog Card Number: 81-47823

To Raquel Schuster-Herr; the memory of Albert Cole, M.D.; and Anne Secor Wallace

And to the clinicians and advocates who preserve the rights and dignity of mental-health clients

Contents

Foreword

Historically, the rights of the mentally ill have been the concern of only a few lawyers, mental-health professionals, and citizens. Legal advocates especially have tended to emphasize the rights of inpatients rather than outpatients; the individual patient rather than those who may be affected by him; freedom rather than treatment; the right to hospital treatment in emergencies rather than care in community settings; the right to refuse treatment rather than the right to alternative treatment; and the right to treatment in the least restrictive environment rather than the most therapeutic one. But many of these emphases are changing, and this book chronicles some critical shifts both in the law and in the methods and objectives of legal advocates.

In 1955, when deinstitutionalization began in this country, it was propelled by many forces, of which legal advocacy was but one. Well-meaning lawyers, psychiatrists, and mental-health administrators promoted deinstitutionalization as a means of ending the age-old scandals of institutional life. For lawyers, the primary objective of deinstitutionalization was to end the needless deprivations of liberty without treatment, the risk of brutality in institutions, and the use of hospitals as agents of social control. For psychiatrists, it was to place chronic patients in more normal surroundings where their disabilities could be better addressed, and to minimize the risks of institutionalization for those never hospitalized. For some administrators, it was the desire to provide less-expensive but equally effective treatment and care; others were motivated by a desire to transfer the social costs of caring for the inept from the medical to the welfare system.

In retrospect, attempts to implement deinstitutionalization in this country seem naive and narrowly focused. Freedom without services proved to be no freedom at all; exchanging one institution for another (nursing homes for state hospitals, for example) was zip-code therapy at its worst; and good community care turned out to be no less expensive than hospital treatment and traditional aftercare together—in fact, more expensive during the transition period when it is necessary to fund two systems simultaneously. Finally, whereas all the medical, psychiatric, dental, housing, social, vocational, and like needs of the severely and chronically mentally ill had been met under the umbrella of a single institution, no such integration existed in the community. Rather than relating to one institution, no matter how badly run, patients now had to contend with dozens, in what one expert has dubbed a "scrounging system."

It was fine for advocates of inpatients to call for treatment and care in the community. The resultant deinstitutionalization should have been beneficial. Unfortunately, the result was not *deinstitutionalization* but *depopulation* of the state hospitals and *transinstitutionalization* into nursing homes and board and care facilities. Now, some twenty-eight years later, we are beginning to realize that most advocacy efforts were too narrow and too rash: too narrow in that they focused on ending inpatient care rather than creating outpatient care, and too rash in that they pushed depopulation ahead without sufficient community preparation, without adequate social consensus for the necessary programs, and without a plan for deinstitutionalizing dollars and services along with patients.

Released patients found few advocates to assist them in obtaining needed services. Mental-health clinicians and administrators were seen as self-serving when they called for greater funding of community services; lawyers were seen as predominately interested in securing freedom for inpatients rather than services for outpatients; and families, until the emergence of the National Alliance for the Mentally Ill, were too stigmatized and fragmented to lobby at state or national levels.

Now, however, things are beginning to change. First, community support programs, sponsored by both federal and state governments, coordinate the disparate services needed by the chronically ill. Core service agencies serve as umbrellas under which patients find diverse programs tailored to individual needs. Second, legal-service and family advocates are beginning to work together to secure community services.

This is not to imply that all is peaceful among clinicians, attorneys, and family members. Clinicians still feel that service advocacy is more crucial than legal advocacy; lawyers still feel that the client's freedom outweighs all else; and family members still feel that it is too difficult to get adequate inpatient or outpatient care. All three groups legitimately feel that they represent the patient/client/relative, but their points of view are so different as to make clashes inevitable. What is interesting is not the inevitability of a clash, but the promise of coordination of efforts. Common cause has been forged through efforts to secure the right to treatment in the community, and common energies have been expended in the recent battles to halt the destructive effects of funding reductions.

This book offers the reader an exciting look into the development and current state of thinking on the full range of legal-rights issues that involve the mentally ill. By presenting them in exquisite detail, it reveals not only the legal underpinnings of and precedents for each issue, but provides a fascinating glimpse at how lawyers resolve the dilemmas they face daily. In addition, a parallel emerges between clinical and legal professionals struggling with many of the same problems. A few examples may illustrate the point.

Psychiatrists, seeing the legal advocate pursue a client's stated objectives with no apparent regard for that client's impaired reality testing or the consequences of his choices may assume that the lawyer is ignorant of pathology or unconcerned with the client's psychiatric needs and mental condition.

The lawyer, seeing the psychiatrist administer services in which every patient walks or is pushed lock-step through the same daily program, may question the psychiatrist's ability to see each patient as someone with different needs, abilities, and disabilities. By explaining the basis and purpose of the legal advocate's singular focus and unyielding pursuit of the client's stated wants, as distinct from the client's needs or best interests, the book imparts a better understanding of the differences between legal and psychiatric professionals and lays the foundation for collaboration between them.

Parallels are also apparent in the conundrums faced by lawyers and psychiatrists alike. The chapter on advocacy, for instance, raises a host of knotty dilemmas: must the patient always come first—before the public welfare, family feelings, and social sensibilities? What is the lawyer to do upon learning of a delusion, unknown to the clinical staff, before a commitment hearing? And how do we reconcile the right to protection from harm, which is far easier to ensure in institutions than in the community, with the right to treatment in the least restrictive alternative?

Both clinicians and lawyers are torn when it comes to effecting care in less restrictive alternatives. One case manager recently expressed to me her dismay at being asked to link up patients with community services when there were none. How do lawyers ensure that their clients receive less restrictive care when there are an inadequate quantity and quality of options?

Finally, how do we all deal with a world in which societal and cultural forces beyond our control hamper the efforts of both lawyers and clinicians? At a time when society seems to care less and less about its vulnerable, infirm, and disadvantaged, it is difficult to fight just one battle at a time.

The fields of psychiatry and law both have inherent problems. Psychiatry's knowledge is murky, law's status ever changing. Advocacy for both groups has been polarized: psychiatry's toward service provision, the law's toward patients' rights. The real future of both advocacy efforts may be determined less by internal forces than by such external factors as fiscal constraints, and the people who will suffer if we do not succeed will be the mentally ill.

We have come a distance in both fields from the 1950s and 1960s, and their interface has also been the site of shifting emphases. Disagreements will always occur, but this intelligently written, highly articulate, and intensely thoughtful book brings us all together. We may not agree on what to do, but we do have a common client, and with knowledge of the reasoning behind patients' rights, we can move from clashing to cooperating and communicating.

John A. Talbott, M.D.
Professor of Psychiatry, Cornell University Medical College;
President, American Psychiatric Association;
Associate Medical Director, The Payne Whitney Psychiatric Clinic, The New York Hospital

Acknowledgments

This book is a guide to the process of mental-health legal advocacy and the rights of persons receiving mental-health care. It grew out of a project supported by the Center for Mental Health Services Manpower, Research and Demonstration Division of the National Institute for Mental Health (NIMH). The purpose of that effort was to make the basic legal principles in this field accessible to a wider audience of mental-health professionals, advocates, and scholars. To Dr. Samuel Silverstein of NIMH, we offer our appreciation for recognizing that need.

This work was nurtured within, and stimulated by, the Mental Patients Advocacy Project. Based on the grounds of Northampton State Hospital in western Massachusetts, that project has brought together a remarkably dedicated and talented group of advocates, clinicians, and academics. We are grateful for this encouragement of our effort to improve awareness and understanding of the rights of those receiving care and treatment in the mental-health system. Special thanks are due Steven J. Schwartz and Robert D. Fleischner for their generous advice and consultation.

Dr. Spencer Eth, assistant professor in the Department of Psychiatry and the Behavioral Sciences at the University of Southern California School of Medicine, and assistant director, Child and Adolescent Psychiatric Outpatient Department, Los Angeles County-U.S.C. Medical Center, served as our clinical consultant. We have greatly benefited from his suggestions and valuable critiques.

Of the many people who aided us in providing references and reviewing particular chapters, we are especially indebted to: Eugene Martin-Leff, National Employment Law Project; Julia Springs, Columbia Law School; Courtenay Harding, Yale School of Medicine; Cathy Costanzo, Mental Patients Advocacy Project; and Steven Krugman, West Rock Park Community Mental Health Center.

The typing of the manuscript for this book, in its many drafts, was done with great skill and cheer by Nancy Kane, Susan Fritz, and Caroline Service.

To those to whom this book is dedicated, we owe debts of inspiration too numerous to detail.

Part I
Guiding Principles

1 Introduction

This society is involved in a profound reshaping of its laws and attitudes regarding the rights of mental patients. Until recently, action to secure the enforceable legal rights of consumers of mental-health care was almost nonexistent. The rights bestowed on the vast population of hospital patients and on those living in the community proved largely symbolic. Members of the legal profession shunned those prospective clients. Even the consumers themselves faced too many obstacles—external as well as internal—to risk the assertion of their rights. In the wake of the civil-rights movement of the 1960s and the growth of public legal services in the 1970s, these patterns began to change.

Mental patients, following the path of minorities, poor persons, women, institutionalized persons, and students, increasingly sought legal protection of their rights. Through the time-honored method of asserting interest-group claims as legal rights, this disenfranchised minority gained visibility and public support. Legislative reforms and court decisions accelerated the release of patients from large mental institutions, tightened procedures for admission or commitment, and enunciated patients' rights by setting minimum standards of care and other remedies.[1] As a result, the focus inevitably shifted to those legal rights and advocacy systems that can sustain and support mentally disabled persons living in the community.

This book reflects that new focus. It is intended to serve as a concise introduction to an area of the law that is undergoing rapid transformation. Although written primarily for an audience of mental-health practitioners, it will prove useful to other mental-health professionals, clients, advocates, and interested citizens.

This project provides a summary of basic legal theories and client rights in the mental-health system. Not only is this law in a state of flux, but its content also varies between the several states, between federal and state law, and between the law in the books and the law as it is applied. Because of both the change and variance, the law on mental health is far from uniform.

This guidebook, obviously, cannot be a substitute for legal representation of individual clients. It is, instead, an attempt to explain some basic legal principles affecting mental patients across the country, thus reinforcing the efforts of clinicians to safeguard the rights of a particular client or group of clients. One of our aims is to dispel some of the confusion concerning the nature of those rights and the misunderstandings about legal advocacy.

Typically, mental-health professionals and paraprofessionals have only limited knowledge about patients' legal rights.[2] Although lack of familiarity or mistaken ideas about the law can have grave implications, clinicians rarely receive sufficient guidance or training in identifying specific legal issues or in recognizing when or how to summon an advocate's assistance. By exploring the advocacy role in the community mental-health system and by sensitizing clinicians to some basic rights within that system, we hope to encourage that training.[3]

Language reveals other signs of transitions. For reasons of convenience, we have resorted to abbreviating some terminology. *Clinician* is used throughout to refer to a mental-health professional, although we are well aware of the heterogeneity of the core professionals, including social workers, therapists, nurses, psychologists, psychiatrists, teachers, and other professionals and paraprofessionals who staff community mental-health programs. Similarly, *advocate* is used in a broad sense to include lay advocates, paralegals, citizen volunteers, and lawyers involved in client-directed or client-oriented advocacy. This concept recognizes the client as the source of the advocate's power, with the advocate obligated to be a partisan for the client's objectives. *Patient* and *client* are terms used interchangeably to denote the recipient of mental-health services or care.[4]

More than ever, we believe there is a necessity for an exchange and sharing of the knowledge of the differing perspectives of clinicians and advocates. Advocacy systems will bring clinicians into greater contact with advocates and legal-rights issues in their professional lives. As community-based programs develop, the need for cooperative efforts among various professionals and concerned citizens also becomes more acute. To combat discrimination and indifference to the plight of patients and expatients, our efforts must be cooperative and concerted.[5] For example, neighborhood resistance to community group homes and other living arrangements requires coordinated responses, such as public-information campaigns by clinicians and zoning test cases by advocates. Cuts in government spending at the state and national levels imperil efforts to maintain decent community mental-health services. Mentally disabled persons will bear a disproportionate share of those cuts unless they and their allies can protect their interests from society's unconcern. Such persons face an even riskier and uncertain future if federally ensured rights to educational, residential, vocational, advocacy, and financial services are repealed or diluted. In this political atmosphere, advocates and clinicians will find compelling reasons to work together in defending their mutual clients' claims on society for rights, not charity.

Knowledge can yield some accommodation as well as clarify areas of disagreement, but sometimes there will be conflict and tension at the interface of law and community mental-health services. This may be because of clashes of professional value systems and lack of understanding between workers in the legal and the community mental-health enterprises.[6] But the conflicts are often overstated. Lawyers, for example, have been portrayed as narrow courtroom adversaries concerned solely with civil liberties and individual rights, and psychiatrists have been seen as interested in helping people "without expressing particular concern for their legal 'rights.'"[7] Although these images have had some validity, they fail to capture the rich diversity of professional relationships among advocates and clinicians.

Concern for the rights of mental patients should not be the monopoly of any single profession. Both clinicians and advocates can endorse the human and legal rights of disabled persons generally and mentally disabled persons specifically. This commonality of purpose has already been incorporated in various national and international statements of equality. It is embodied in the United Nations Declaration on the Rights of Disabled Persons and other international documents to which the United States subscribes.[8] It is increasingly incorporated in national law in this country and abroad. According to the World Health Organization, many countries have recently enacted statutes considerably strengthening the rights of mental patients: in particular, their rights to treatment, liberty, and due-process safeguards.[9]

The development of mental-disability law in this country is consistent with this trend, adopting the view that mental patients are citizens first and are therefore entitled to at least the rights and protections guaranteed to all citizens.[10] Plainly, one does not relinquish basic constitutional and statutory rights solely because of admission to a mental-health facility or program. This doctrine of equal citizenship has been consistently reaffirmed by the courts with respect to the exercise of autonomy in a wide variety of contexts.[11]

However, courts and legislatures alone cannot be the sole protectors of principles of equality. Those receiving or seeking mental-health care depend on the conscience, good faith, and law-abiding character of clinicians to be their first line of defense. Professional associations also acknowledge that they and their members have an obligation to uphold the primacy of individual rights and client dignity. An abundance of position papers, task-force reports, and friend-of-the-court briefs reflect this sensitivity to the protection of the recipients' human and legal rights and to the guarantee of freedom of choice as a core principle of society.[12] But, as this book demonstrates, reform is far from complete, backlash is evident, and the injustices that elicited these responses still exist.

Recipients of mental care are not only entitled to be treated as equal citizens, they are also entitled to exercise the freedom of choice attendant to that citizenship. And to the extent that a disability renders an individual incapable of exercising such choice, then that person is guaranteed a substitute decision maker, in the form of a friend, advocate, or guardian, to express his or her preferences. The contract model of services, with its implication that persons with disabilities are capable of and should be encouraged to negotiate acceptable services, offers a means to put these principles into practice. This model, common to medical and educational services, is familiar to many in the mental-health field, particularly those who stress the therapeutic alliance between patient and clinician. The President's Commission on Mental Health, endorsing this approach, stated:

> Each client or patient must have the maximum possible opportunity to choose the unique combination of services and objectives appropriate to his or her needs. This must include the option of preferring no services as well as the option of selecting particular services in preference to others.[13]

In many settings, implementing this model has barely begun. However, as special-education laws have proven, even large public agencies can incorporate elements of client choice, direct or surrogate participation, and negotiation between client and professionals in the planning and provision of individual programs.[14] Similar processes are authorized under progressive state regulations, such as the individual-service-plan requirements of the Massachusetts Department of Mental Health.[15] By guaranteeing client involvement and choice in that planning, these regulations offer a partial counterweight to the unequal bargaining power of participants and a departure from the take-it-or-leave-it approaches of the past. Whether these gains are realized will depend on the extent of staff comfort with the virtues of client participation, a greater degree of partnership, and a premium placed on voluntarism. This contract model promotes client dignity and self-esteem, instead of passivity, dependence, and lack of responsibility for choices, and by so doing assists the therapeutic process. It advances the desire of human beings for a self-mastery, described by Sir Isaiah Berlin as a:

> wish to be a subject, not an object, to be moved by reasons, by conscious purposes, which are my own, not causes which affect me, as it were, from outside. I wish to be somebody, not nobody; a doer—deciding not being decided for, self-directed and not acted upon by external nature or by other men as if I were a thing, or an animal, or a slave incapable of playing a human role, that is, of conceiving goals and policies of my own and realizing them.[16]

This book identifies advocacy approaches and legal rights that can augment these principles of autonomy and social integration. Part I describes the nature of advocacy in mental-health systems and the interrelated issues of competency, consent, and client participation. Part II sets forth rights in the mental-health treatment process, including the right to treatment, the right to refuse treatment, the principle of the least restrictive alternative, and the rights to privacy, confidentiality, and access to records. Part III discusses rights to community services, including some special problems and rights of children, guardianship and other protective services, and nondiscrimination and the promise of equal opportunity. The final chapter describes ways in which clinicians can assist those they serve to exercise their rights and opportunities.

Securing these legal principles in practice will require effort from many corners. Enabling clinicians to become familiar with this law is plainly a critical first step.

Notes

1. President's Commission on Mental Health, Report to the President 3 (1978).

2. *See, e.g.,* Laves & Cohen, *A Preliminary Investigation into the Knowledge of and Attitudes toward the Legal Rights of Mental Patients*, 1 J. Psychiatry & L. 49 (1973); J. Wilson, The Rights of Adolescents in the Mental Health System 6 (1978).

3. For example, clinicians using this guidebook as a foundation could form study groups and enlist specialists to present localized training materials. Given increasing emphasis on community-based services, this training could also deal with some of the outside services and agencies that affect the mental-health professional's work and the client's rights and welfare.

4. As a matter of respect for the individuality of the participants in the mental-health system, we are uncomfortable with any monolithic labeling. References to mental patients do not imply that we subscribe to a medical model, they simply reflect the common usage of that term by others.

5. Without these alliances recent gains will be eroded. See *Mental Health Needs a Boost*, N.Y. Times, March 29, 1980, at 22, col. 1.

6. For a discussion of the paradigms of mental-health advocacy and mental-health treatment, see chapter 2, *infra*.

7. A. Brooks, Law, Psychiatry and the Mental Health System 1 (1974).

8. For an analysis of these declarations and their impact, see Herr, *Rights of Disabled Persons: International Principles and American Experiences*, 12 Colum. Human Rights L. Rev. 1 (1980).

9. Harding & Curran, *Mental Health Legislation and Its Relationship to Program Development: An International Review,* 16 Harv. J. Legis. 19, 37–42 (1979).

10. *See* Rogers v. Okin, 478 F. Supp. 1342, 1361 (D.Mass. 1979). For the subsequent history of that case, see chapter 5, *infra*.

11. *E.g.*, Rennie v. Klein, 462 F. Supp. 1131 (D.N.J. 1978), *aff'd in part, modified in part, and remanded,* 653 F.2d 836 (3rd Cir. 1981), *vacated and remanded,* 458 U.S. 1119 (1982) (right to refuse treatment, discussed in chapter 5, *infra*); People *ex. rel.* Drury v. Catholic Home Bureau, 34 Ill. 2d 84 (1966) (right to consent to adoption).

12. *See, e.g.*, American Psychological Association, Task Force on Patient Advocacy for Mental Patients (Phase One Report, August 1979); American Psychiatric Association, *Position Statement on the Right to Adequate Care and Treatment for the Mentally Ill and Mentally Retarded*, 134 Am. J. Psychiatry 354 (1977).

13. President's Commission on Mental Health, *supra* note 1, at 42.

14. *See* Education for All Handicapped Children Act, 20 U.S.C. §§1411-1420 (1980).

15. "Standards for Individual Service Plans," Mass. Admin. Code tit. 104 §21.00 (1980).

16. I. Berlin, Four Essays on Liberty 131 (1969).

The Nature of Advocacy

Several years ago a state mental-health commissioner and the director of an advocacy project found themselves on the same speaker's platform at a conference. The commissioner, a psychiatrist who had recently taken up his post, indicated in his speech that he saw advantages to being sued by mental-health advocates. He reasoned that advocates shared goals with him and that the state bureaucracy was difficult to move by traditional means. The advocacy director, an attorney, assured the commissioner that he would soon find himself in court. The commissioner set everyone in the hall laughing when he replied that the only question was "whether you can sue me before I commit you."

Beneath the banter, this exchange between psychiatrist and attorney reflects the general tension that is present when members of the two professions are found working with the same clients. There is a recognition that both advocates and clinicians are attempting to help the same persons, and there is agreement about many of the changes needed in mental-health systems and public services. But there is also a certain degree of professional skepticism about the other's ability to understand or deal with the real needs of the client. There is a clash of professional outlooks, priorities, and methods of working.

The warinesss of advocates and clinicians about each other's work is the result of two very different approaches to understanding what it means to help another person, of two different paradigms of personhood and society. The aim of this chapter is to aid the clinician in understanding the professional and ethical requirements that are imposed on the mental-health advocate. By acknowledging that differences in approach to clients will inevitably lead to some conflict between the professions, it may be possible to minimize those misunderstandings and apprehensions that stand in the way of cooperation between clinicians and advocates. This book demystifies advocacy by discussing the actual development of substantive patients' rights by courts, legislatures, and administrative agencies. This chapter attempts to give an insider's view of the nature of mental-health advocacy—its basic attitudes and obligations—in the interests of realism and mutual respect between clinicians and advocates.

Describing the attributes of mental-health advocacy can be controversial, especially given the great variety of types of advocacy and advocates who labor at this work. Mental-health advocates may be lawyers or laypersons;

they may be well-trained recent college graduates, experienced community members, ex-patients, or trained members of other professions. The training and supervision available to them and the forums in which they can advocate on their clients' behalf vary enormously from state to state and from advocacy project to advocacy project. In terms of personal commitment, aggressiveness, craftsmanship, and personality, advocates provide a spectrum no less broad than clinicians. Yet through all the differences in advocacy there are fundamental principles that must be maintained if advocacy is to be true to its own ethics and useful to its clients.

Sole Loyalty to the Client

The cardinal principle of mental-health advocacy, as of other forms of legal advocacy, is that the advocate's sole loyalty is to his or her client. The absolute adherence to this principle in practice as well as appearance is essential to maintaining the client's trust; yet it often arouses the mistrust of employees of the mental-health system, who must balance their loyalty to their clients with bureaucratic demands, programmatic responsibilities, and professional judgments that what the client wants may not be what the client needs.

The advocate's sole loyalty to the client may require that points of view be presented by the advocate that no clinician or mental-health administrator would consider reasonable, desirable, or even sane. Still the advocate must take the position that the client requests, whether it be in negotiations, discussions, or hearings. The advocate must adopt the client's point of view and make it as forceful and convincing as possible before any and all decision makers.[1] This loyalty is as crucial as it is hard to maintain, especially when the advocate is employed by the mental-health system or some related governmental agency. The advocate must remain aware of the possibility that managers may put pressure on the advocate to avoid certain positions or problems because of the allegedly disruptive effect they might have on the mental-health system. Clinicians may also regard the advocate on occasion as acting counter to a client's therapeutic needs by articulating a client's so-called unhealthy wishes or reinforcing a client's instability or pathological tendencies. In spite of these possible reactions, the advocate can never forget that any betrayal of the client's position without the client's informed consent will irrevocably damage the relationship of trust between client and advocate, not only for this advocate and client but for other advocates and clients as well. It may be expected that a person labelled mentally ill, whose liberty, reputation, and dignity are so much in the hands of a government agency, will place enormous reliance on an advocate to redress the imbalance of power. Trust is an essential element of this relationship; and the advocate's sole loyalty to the client is the basis of this trust.

At some point, the client's desires or demands must certainly be balanced against the resources of the institution or service agency, the judgment of the clinicians, and the requirements of society as set out in law and regulation. But this balance cannot be legitimately accomplished by turning the advocate into a double agent. Perhaps the hardest part of this loyalty is for advocates to avoid substituting their own judgments for those of their clients.

The clinician will probably recognize that although therapy and advocacy often differ, the ethics of both require sole loyalty to the client. Yet the reality of clinical practice in government agencies is to place the clinician under divided loyalties to the patient and the state. The advocate must avoid this situation, not only in attitude and self-image but also in the structures under which advocacy takes place.

The mental-health advocate, like any other legal representative, cannot serve two masters. All the considerations of sole loyalty to the client are reflected in the principle that the advocate must be independent of any administrative, political, or financial control by the mental-health system. To the degree that the advocate is dependent on that system for salary or resources, policy or priorities, the client's interests may be compromised and the quality of advocacy limited and distorted. All such conflicts of interest, real or apparent, must be avoided or reduced whenever possible; and mental-health personnel should not be surprised to find advocates acting on a presumption of independence that some of their colleagues may not enjoy. Advocates can be expected to seek funding independent of the mental-health system and to accept the cooperation and facilities of that system only when such assistance cannot be capriciously withdrawn.

Conflicts of interest are by no means limited to directives, threats, or dismissals of advocates for contradicting the policies of mental-health systems or the preferences of mental-health personnel. Everything from the political tone of a mental-health agency to the amount of paperwork required by that agency may enable that system to curb an advocacy office dependent on it. Moreover, the extreme scarcity of resources available for mental-health systems in general and for mental-health advocacy in particular increases the risk that the advocate will be asked to sacrifice independence as the price of support. The advocate will require some kind of a buffer between mental-health system and advocacy project (for example, a contract to an independent legal-services agency for purposes of evaluation and supervision). The support of clinicians for such buffers may depend on their understanding that in the state-run mental-health system sole loyalty to the client is a principle fundamental to competent advocacy.

Confidentiality

Closely allied to the principle of sole loyalty to the client is the obligation of maintaining confidentiality of communication between client and advocate.

A similar privileged relationship is protected by the law of most states for doctors and patients, priests and penitents, and husbands and wives.[2] A privileged relationship requires that in the absence of the client's waiver of confidentiality the professional party to the relationship cannot legally be compelled or permitted to reveal communications between the parties. Subject to narrow statutory limitations, which vary from state to state, this protection holds regardless of how much the disclosure of confidences may seem to be in the interest of the client or the public. Various requirements of confidentiality may lead advocates to violate personal ethics by refusing to reveal critical and damaging facts. Yet it is just at this point that confidentiality is most important to maintaining professional ethics. If the client fears that the advocate may reveal confidential communications, the flow of information to the advocate will diminish, and the advocate will be unable to represent adequately the client's interests.

An example drawn from the experience of a mental-health advocate working in a state hospital may illustrate the problems inherent in the principle of confidentiality. The client in question had been a civilly committed resident of the state hospital for over twenty years following an act of extreme violence committed against a family member. The advocate was assigned to represent the man, under the supervision of an attorney, in an upcoming commitment review in which the man's freedom might be granted. After talking with ward staff and hospital clinicians, the advocate discovered that the client had been a model resident for years and was viewed by all as healthy enough to be released. The client had been involved in no violent incidents according to staff reports and records, and no clinician was prepared to testify that the client exhibited significant mental illness. The night before what seemed to be a straightforward hearing leading to release, the advocate held a final conversation with the client to prepare for the hearing. Toward the end of the conversation the client revealed to the advocate an elaborate delusional network. The client described himself as under the control of one of the characters of the delusion and indicated that if this character ordered him to kill someone he would have to do so. No clinician had indicated any awareness of these delusions or evaluated the seriousness of any potential instability or violence by the client.

The advocate's dilemmas were legion. Should the delusion be revealed to a clinician who might testify at the hearing? Should the delusion be revealed after the hearing to the clinician who might then seek to treat the patient's psychosis? Should the advocate continue to represent a client who might commit an act of violence without warning? Should the client be allowed to testify and possibly undermine his case before the judge? If the client's therapist already knew about these delusions and sought to testify at the hearing, will that jurisdiction's law permit the advocate's successful objection to the testimony as a breach of a privileged relationship between therapist and client? Even if the advocate can secure her client's freedom, should she try to counsel the client to seek voluntary or outpatient help?[3] The loyalty and confidentiality principles provide clear ethical answers to this advocate's problems of representation, but they do not alleviate the personal anguish that the ethics of advocacy impose in such a situation. The client wishes to be released from the hospital. The advocate must act consistently with this wish, using whatever tools are legally available and leaving to a neutral third party the responsibility for deciding the case.

The Presumption of Client Autonomy

In addition to sole loyalty and confidentiality, a third principle, client autonomy, marks the relationship between advocate and client. The presumption of client autonomy has two parts: following the expressed wishes of the client and regarding the client as a person possessing all the legal rights of a full citizen. This two-part presumption is generally at odds with the paradigmatic view of personality used by clinicians and entrenched in mental-health systems. It is a difference of approach and understanding between advocates and clinicians that is extremely difficult to bridge.

Unless the client has been legally declared incompetent and a guardian has been appointed, the advocate's job is to assist in achieving that client's expressed wishes. Although others may seek to probe the latent content of client communications, the only definition of the client's best interest on which the advocate may act is that expressly given by the client.[4] This may seem especially incongruous because the advocate is representing a person who has been labelled mentally ill and may have become dependent on others for direction and support. But if the advocate were to act on the best interests of the client as interpreted by an institution, a clinician, or even the advocate's own understanding of the latent content of the client's communications, the usefulness of the advocacy role would be threatened. The client must be treated by the advocate as a legal person—presumed to be rational and the best judge of his or her own self-interest—even when circumstances indicate otherwise.[5]

Thus the advocate operates on the explicit wishes of the client, presuming the client to be a full legal citizen, and basing the relationship of advocate and client on the client's strength rather than weakness or pathology. The advocate treats the client as a citizen of equal worth and equal legal rights to all other citizens, and the advocate presumes that in the absence of clear evidence of the client's legal incompetence, the government, court, and mental-health system will do the same. This presumption of autonomy sustains the advocate's role as one of assisting the client to achieve the dignity, the particular rights, and the autonomous status that law and society accord the individual.

The existence of clients' legal rights and, even more fundamentally, the presumption that clients are persons whose standing in society is equal to that of any citizen, are of primary importance to the advocate. In order that mentally troubled persons not lose their standing as citizens and persons of moral worth, it is essential that persons labelled mentally ill not lose their legal rights by virtue of any mental disability other than one that renders them legally incompetent. Mental-health systems and institutions are not empowered to grant or deny rights. They must instead recognize legal rights as a sign of the undiminished status of their clients. The advocate's presumption of client autonomy does not regard rights as ends but as the most direct means to preserving the status and worth of the client in a system that often reinforces the stigmatization of those labelled mentally ill.

The emerging experience of mental-health advocacy has indicated that ethical and professionally responsible behavior of mental-health personnel is significantly improved by the presence of advocates acting to advance the primacy of clients' legal rights. Such rights may be the client's firmest link with the mainstream of social life. Certainly the focus on these rights is central to competent advocacy and an important tool for scrutiny of mental-health systems.[6]

The implications of the primacy of clients' legal rights are far-reaching because the emphasis on rights and autonomy highlights the different professional paradigms of advocate and clinicians. The advocate frequently helps to resolve legal problems for the client with the support and appreciation of clinicians and administrators. But on occasion an adversarial relationship arises between advocate and mental-health system. When this happens it may feed on the conflict of philosophies held by two professions that identify themselves as helping the client but that derive their ideas of what is helpful from very different understandings of personality, social structure, and professional work. At its worst, this tension may create a hostile atmosphere in which the mental-health professional accuses the advocate of legalizing the therapeutic relationship and ignoring or damaging the client's welfare, while the advocate accuses the mental-health professional of ignoring or destroying the client's humanity through paternalism, stigmatization, and coercive treatment. Such potential conflicts between the professionals do not lessen the preeminence of the client's legal rights for the advocate nor reduce the validity of therapeutic interventions as far as clinicians are concerned. They do point to the need for care in the way each profession appraises the motives of the other and for mutual trust based on an understanding of differences in professional orientation.

Professionalism toward Mental-Health Staff and Systems

There is a great risk that areas of potential cooperation between advocates and clinicians could be overlooked as a result of even minor misunderstandings of the nature of advocacy. This risk is much greater in state institutions, where the two professions are more likely to confront one another in adversary proceedings due to coercive treatment or substandard conditions. In community-based systems of care, opportunities for cooperation between advocate and clinician in solving a client's legal problems should be better and should reduce the likelihood of the two professions working at cross-purposes. In either situation it is important that mental-health advocates develop a constructive approach toward mental-health systems and place responsibility for harmful conditions on systems rather than individuals.

One of the most common experiential conclusions of advocates is that total institutions can and do inflict harm to human beings. To the extent that a mental-health system relies on institutionalizing its clients, that system itself will be suspect in the eyes of many advocates. In reacting to this perception of harm it has served advocates well to understand that effective advocacy minimizes individual blame and focuses on the reform of structure and the redistribution of power. Although some advocates, driven by a sense of moral outrage, have been successful in serving their clients, tempered approaches have been more consistently effective.[7] In fact, skillful advocacy calls for a considerate relationship with the people who control such a large part of the clients' lives. Individual responsibility for cruelties and mistreatment cannot be excused, but there are seldom obvious villains to pillory. There are, on the other hand, many harmful structures, inappropriate policies, and maldistributions of power.

Certainly an experienced advocate knows that a strongly expressed negative attitude toward the system, even if it does not focus on individuals, may threaten personnel at the institution. Despite the advocate's respect for the staff, individual staff persons may not feel respected, and hostility toward the advocate and the client represented by the advocate may result. Such hostility can undermine clients' rights and the advocate's ability to be of assistance to all other clients. It can also precipitate a struggle over the validity of advocacy in general. At the same time, vigorous advocacy on behalf of clients cannot be sacrificed simply because hostility ensues. An excessive concern for the maintenance of cordial relationships between advocates and staff at an institution can erode the independence of the advocate and harm clients by elevating etiquette above the duty to the client. Advocates who work in hospitals must be particularly sensitive to the danger of becoming co-opted and losing their effectiveness.

Developing an approach toward the mental-health system that effectively minimizes hostility, secures competent representation for the client, honestly reflects conditions at the institution, and maintains respectful relations among persons, even when they are adversaries, is an enormous challenge. Shunning personal blame in favor of institutional analysis and systematic change seem important starting points if the relationship of the advocate and clinician is to be constructive.

Access to Clients

Regular and dependable physical access to clients is essential for competent mental-health advocacy. Those labelled mentally ill are traditionally among the most underrepresented of any group whose rights require protection through advocacy. The underrepresentation is in part related to the conditions within state hospitals and the isolation and dispersion of potential clients in the community. In state institutions many residents are confined to locked wards or to restricted areas of the hospital. Advocates frequently have either no office on the grounds or an office that is so far removed from residential units that its location discourages potential clients from seeking the help of an advocate.

The advocate may tend to rely on the personnel of the mental-health facility to refer clients, or the advocate may simply wait for the clients themselves to identify and seek help for their legal problems. As a result of this lack of communication between advocate and prospective clients, the legal problems of those labelled mentally ill are frequently either misperceived or underestimated. The client, the institution, and the public may believe that there are few problems; or the limited available energy for correcting problems may be misdirected because patterns of significant difficulties are not perceived.

The advocate's lack of physical access to clients is aggravated considerably when dealing with persons who have been institutionalized for so long that they have become exceedingly passive. Such persons either do not seek out help or cannot successfully identify problems amenable to legal solutions. Only aggressive outreach appears capable of providing any real benefit to them. Even when the potential client is not enmeshed in the institution, it remains true that neither the client nor the staff members of the institution are trained to recognize those problems that have legal components or are capable of solution through advocacy. The result is that there remains a significant number of residents with legal problems that are neither identified nor resolved.

Because isolation of clients and the masking of their legal problems are characteristic of the conditions in which most mentally disabled persons live, advocacy programs must maintain physical presence at institutions and other major service centers. This requires regularly open and accessible offices, branch offices, and outreach activities. It is essential that the accessibility of the advocate to the client be left free of institutional barriers. Obstructions, such as lack of on-site offices, lack of access to locked wards, and unnecessary restrictions on client-authorized access to personal records, have hindered the effectiveness of advocates.

It should be noted that physical presence and the dissemination of information about client rights do not constitute solicitation of clients. The traditional legal rules regarding solicitation do not apply in institutional contexts when nonprofit legal advocacy groups communicate with clients.[8]

The presence of the advocate at the site of the mental-health facility and the free access of the advocate to institutionalized persons have on occasion been resisted by administrators or others who believe that such a presence encourages conflict and interferes with the smooth running of the institution. Yet attempts to deny such access may be contrary to constitutional and statutory law, such as statutes providing for a client's rights to receive visitors, to obtain the services of an advocate, or to gain representation in such proceedings as civil commitment, periodic reviews, or authorization of voluntary admission.[9] Even where legal authority exists for access, it does not guarantee that such minimum access will be provided. The experience of advocacy projects is that physical access to clients is essential; without access a false sense of harmony, a substantial infringement of patients' rights, and a distorted sense of advocacy priorities are all likely results.

Pursuit of the Full Range of Remedies

A fundamental attribute of mental-health advocacy is the advocate's freedom to seek any suitable remedy for a client in any forum within the mental-health system or the legal system. The range of forums in which the rights of a patient may be vindicated is broader than many people imagine, and a number of classifications of advocacy have arisen (such as internal and external advocacy) that are based on artificial restrictions about which forums the advocate and client may use. Within a single institution or administrative unit, whether a residential or outpatient facility, there may be an ombudsman; a human-rights committee; a system-employed fact finder operating under the misnomer of advocate; a series of legislatively, administratively, or professionally mandated interdisciplinary teams that review patient status, treatment plans, or client privileges; case managers; and an administrative chain of command.

Outside the mental-health system lies an even broader array of settings in which to be heard. There are hearings and judicial reviews in matters such as civil commitment, competency determination, appointment of guardians, and receipt of legislatively created entitlements and benefits. There may also be court orders for system or facility reform that set out procedures for airing patient grievances or correcting patterns of problems revealed by patient complaints. Through litigation, the state and federal courts can vindicate the rights discussed in this book or enforce state and federal constitutional guarantees that apply to all citizens. Access to all these forums ensures that the client is given the full benefit of being a citizen, reinforces the presumption of client autonomy, and reduces the possibility that the advocate may compromise the client's interest because of lack of ability to pursue a complaint in a forum that has the power to fashion a remedy.

Ensuring access to all forums for conflict resolution is critical in preserving the client's trust and vindicating the client's rights. From the advocate's point of view this access also acts to increase the leverage of advocacy within the mental-health system. The ability to seek judicial review, for example, strengthens the efficacy of informal modes of advocacy. In most instances the advocate will participate in negotiations and in the so-called internal forums on the assumption that the mental-health system will function according to administrative regulation and formal law. But the experience of advocates as well as clinicians is that the mental-health bureaucracy can be systematically resistant and even vindictive toward those who seek to change it. The advocate must therefore be able to bring an issue before a neutral outside agency that has the power to correct abuses of patients' rights and to order administrative compliance with legal standards.

The systems to protect rights established in some states may hinder access to external forums and thus cripple their staffs' ability to represent clients. This lack of access contributes to a distrust of advocates by clients and reduces the effectiveness of advocacy so greatly that it may exist only in name. The creation and labelling as advocacy of such exclusively internal systems serve mostly to protect the mental-health system from public scrutiny and neutral judicial review. This development will co-opt patients and advocates by channeling their energies into ineffective actions. It may also force conflict over patient rights into adversarial proceedings, thereby reducing the chance for cooperative change.

At bottom, access to the entire range of forums for the resolution of conflict helps rectify the imbalance of power between the client and the bureaucracy. The ability to pursue a client's rights in any forum distinguishes true mental-health advocacy from other useful but more limited roles such as ombudsman, human-rights committees, or internal advocacy. The significant increase of patient rights and the movement to restore the dignity of citizenship to the mentally ill did not take place until the organs of formal law began to address the problems of those labelled mentally ill. There is, therefore, a need for advocates to maintain the possibility of resort to the courts. This need should not, of course, obscure the areas of significant cooperation among advocates, clinicians, internal investigators, and others concerned with human rights within mental-health systems.

Clinician-Advocate Cooperation

The goals of clinicians, clients, and advocates are often the same, especially outside the state hospital. Differences in professional approaches should not hinder cooperation here. Many clients are the victims of social and economic discrimination based on their status as mental patients. In areas such as housing, voting, medical services, public benefits, and jobs, those labelled mentally ill are often deprived and unable to fend for themselves. The effect of this coerced isolation of clients from the mainstream of society is often to aggravate any emotional or mental problems a client may suffer. A clinician's attempt to help a client adjust to the requirements of normal life can often be thwarted by this isolation and deprivation; and it is here that clinician and advocate can work together to identify and remedy client problems. Securing welfare or disability payments and resisting housing discrimination are prime examples.

Progressive treatment for patients within the community often encounters neighborhood hostility and public misunderstanding, or it may become unavailable because of legislative resistance based on alleged community opposition. The combined skills of clinicians and advocates hold the potential here for securing the necessary treatment and facilities for the client, while respecting the community's legitimate concerns and avoiding the so-called dumping of patients. As deinstitutionalization becomes more common, more conflicts are likely to arise in which the rights and status of clients in the community can be advanced by advocacy.[10] The availability of adequate treatment in the community may become a central issue in which the advocate's role may be to ensure that the mental-health system makes the clinician's services available to the client to avoid reinstitutionalization. Whether it involves arranging social-security benefits, opposing housing discrimination, overcoming zoning restrictions, or protecting the jobs of clinicians in the community, the deinstitutionalization of the mentally ill presents increasing numbers of cases in which problems with clinical repercussions are amenable to legal remedies.

Within institutions, especially large residential institutions, a central problem is eliminating unethical practices to secure the confidentiality, professional independence, and trust that are essential to quality treatment and patient dignity. Here too advocate and clinician may find they can work together toward a common goal of creating more professionally responsible conditions of work and life in mental hospitals. Cooperation can also arise where the complex regulations governing periodic reviews, diagnostic staffings, isolation and restraint, medication, and consent to risk-laden treatments are subject to legal as well as clinical interpretation. Clinician and advocate will have an interest in ensuring that regulations and procedures are clear and lawful, do not obstruct useful treatment, and do not undermine client dignity.

There is a great potential for both conflict and cooperation between clinicians and advocates as mental-health advocacy becomes pervasive. The rights of patients are being created and recognized at a rapid pace, and mental-health systems are increasingly subject to public scrutiny and legal judgment. At the same time, daily contacts among advocates, clinicians, and other mental-health personnel are becoming commonplace. The more the relationship of clinicians and advocates is built on such daily contact and work, and the less it is built on ideological or paradigmatic differences, the healthier the situation will be. Some conflict between advocates and clinicians is inevitable given their differences of approach to clients. But cooperation will increase if it is recognized that both professions have distinct ethics and that conflict, if properly handled, can be constructive.

Notes

1. Loyalty to the client may involve taking a position that the client requests regardless of whether such request is in the client's best interest. *See* Schwartz, Fleischner, Schmidt, Costanzo, Gates & Winkelman, *Protecting the Rights and Enhancing the Dignity of People with Mental Disabilities,* 14 Rutgers L.J. 541, 570–72 (1983). *See also* Cihlar, *Client Self-Determination: Intervention or Interference,* 14 St. Louis U.L.J. 604 (1970); Schwartz, *The Professionalism and Accountability of Lawyers,* 66 Calif. L. Rev. 669 (1978).

2. See chapter 7, *infra,* for a discussion of confidentiality in these privileged relationships in general, and between clinician and client in particular.

3. On the controversial question of legal expertise and moral responsibility in such context, see A. Stone, Mental Health and Law: A System in Transition 235 (1976).

4. *See generally*, D. Rosenthal, Lawyer and Client: Who's in Charge? (1974). *Compare* Eth & Eth, *Can a Research Subject Be Too Eager to Consent*, 11 Hastings Center Report 20-21 (August 1981) *with* Edgar, id. at 21 ("We presume adults' statements are legitimate signs of their preferences over a vast domain of activity. . . . Similarly, we act on the words they say recognizing that people often do not say what they mean or mean what they say").

5. See chapter 3.

6. *See* S. Schwartz, O. Fowlkes, S. Arons & R. Fleischner, Representing Mentally Disabled Persons: Models for Institutional Advocacy and Paralegal Training (Final Report of the Mental Patients Advocacy Project, NIMH Grant No. 5-T21, Aug. 13, 1979).

7. For an empirical study on program effectiveness as measured by client outcomes and perceptions, see Government Studies and Systems, Evaluation of Models of Advocacy Programs for the Mentally Ill and Developmentally Disabled: Final Report (NIMH No. 278-79-0047, Dec. 17, 1980).

8. *See In re* Primus, 436 U.S. 412 (1978); Herr, *The New Clients: Legal Services for Mentally Retarded Persons,* 31 Stan. L. Rev. 553, 596–97 (1979).

9. *E.g.*, Cal. Welf. & Inst. Code §5325 (h)(West Supp. 1982) (right to see and receive the services of a patient advocate); 42 U.S.C. §9501 (1)(M)(Supp. 1982).

10. For examples, see *Suit on Homeless Mental Patients Asks New York State for Housing*, N.Y. Times, May 21, 1982 at A1, col. 1, and chapter 11, *infra*.

Competency and Consent

The enjoyment of virtually all individual rights is conditioned by the law on an individual's competency to properly exercise those rights. Similarly, the lawful administration of treatment or therapy is conditioned on competent consent to the treatment. As a result, the twin legal issues of competency and consent are of central importance in mental-health law. And it is because these issues pervade the entire area that we begin the presentation of substantive mental-health law with this chapter on competency and consent.

Competency

Stated most simply, legal competency is a measure of ability, specifically, of ability to exercise certain basic legal rights. Conversely, legal incompetency signifies an inability that requires legal intervention in the form of protective services. Incompetency represents a formal, judicial determination that an individual, in the interest of his own protection, is to be deprived to some extent of the basic right of self-determination, of freedom of choice.

These rights are the very foundation of a free society and therefore are guarded closely by the law. As one notable court opinion stated, "Anglo-American law starts with the premise of thorough-going self determination."[1] Furthermore, in the now-famous words of the late Supreme Court Justice Louis Brandeis, "the right to be let alone [is] the most comprehensive of rights and the right most valued by civilized men."[2] One essential safeguard of these rights is the legal presumption of competency.

The Presumption of Competency

In the law's view, all persons are presumed competent unless and until the contrary is proven in a court of law. Much like the presumption of innocence in criminal law, this presumption of competency is a legal doctrine that guarantees personal freedoms against unwarranted restrictions. The import of this doctrine is that all individuals retain full control of their own bodies and are free to make all personal decisions in accordance with their own judgment, unless determined to be incompetent by judicial proceedings.

The presumption is not defeated by a psychiatric diagnosis, nor by one's status as a client in the community mental-health system.[3] Rather, mental-health clients are entitled to the same right of self-determination, the same "right to be let alone," that all other legally competent persons enjoy. They are free to make purchases and gifts, contracts and wills, and even mistakes. And within the mental-health system itself, the presumption of competency requires that all clients not judged legally incompetent be free to make their own choices and decisions regarding treatment. Some exceptions to this general rule are set forth in detail in chapter 5, but the exceptions permit nonconsensual treatment of voluntary clients only in extreme emergencies or following judicial determinations of incompetency.[4]

One court, in upholding a mental patient's right to decline medication, explained the heart of the presumption of competency: "If the law recognizes the right of an individual to make decisions about her life out of respect for the dignity and autonomy of the individual, that interest is no less significant when the individual is mentally or physically ill."[5]

The Standards and Tests of Competency

Clinicians are frequently required to assess client competency. Courts look to clinicians for evaluations in guardianship, conservatorship, and other proceedings in which competency is adjudicated. Relatives and friends of clients often seek clinical advice prior to initiating judicial proceedings of this sort. Finally and most importantly, clinicians must consider client competency whenever seeking consent to treatment. For all these reasons and more, the practicing clinician must be familiar with the relevant factors and standards that determine competency.

"The search for a single test of competency is a search for a Holy Grail"—so stated a group of leading commentators, and quite rightly.[6] No single test will do, because competency is a relative term with significantly different meanings in different contexts. As a measure of a client's ability, the threshold of competency varies depending on the purpose for which it is being determined. A leading court decision in this area illustrates the point well. In *Kaimowitz* v. *Michigan Department of Mental Health,* the consent of an involuntary patient to undergo experimental psychosurgery was challenged on the grounds that he was incompetent—or more precisely, that he lacked the requisite "capacity"—to give that consent.[7] The court ultimately held that involuntarily confined mental patients, although generally competent to consent to "regular surgical procedures" and even to "accepted neurosurgical procedures," are incompetent to consent to experimental psychosurgery which is "dangerous, intrusive, irreversible, and of uncertain benefit to the patient and society."

One lesson of the *Kaimowitz* decision is the relativity of competency. As *Kaimowitz* demonstrates, legal competency is not an abstract, absolute measure of one's cognitive abilities; rather it is a measure of one's ability to meet given demands, to provide for one's own protection and best interests. Hence, legal competency depends on a wide variety of factors bearing on one's need for protection. In *Kaimowitz,* it was in large part the experimental and dangerous nature of the proposed surgery that rendered the patient incompetent to consent to that surgery. For purposes involving less danger—consenting to "regular" forms of surgery, for instance—the same patient was considered competent.

The standards and tests of competency can be understood best when viewed in light of the basic purpose of competency determinations: to protect the best interests of the alleged incompetent. As noted earlier, the right to self-determination is sacred in U.S. law. The state's authority to restrict that right by declaring a person incompetent stems from its *parens patriae* power. This so-called power is a source of both authority and obligation traceable to the medieval English notion of the king as parent to his subjects.[8] Although the exercises of this power have not always been faithful to its underlying purpose, it is clear that its sole justification is the protection of the disadvantaged.[9] Thus, individuals may be deprived of freedom of choice and personal autonomy on grounds of incompetency only when necessary, and only to the extent necessary, to provide for their protection.

This is not to say that any personal decision that causes harm or risk, or that is otherwise ill-advised, demonstrates a lack of legal competency warranting state intervention. The law permits us to smoke, to drink, and to overeat; it allows us to make foolish purchases and imprudent investments. It has allowed a committed mental patient to refuse hip surgery urged by her physician.[10] It has upheld an "elderly derelict's" choice to risk gangrene rather than lose his leg.[11] And, with few exceptions, it allows mental-health clients to reject medication prescribed by their psychiatrists.

In short, the law does not require that one make wise decisions. It requires only that one's ability to make decisions not be so impaired as to substantially threaten one's safety or welfare. In this light, it should be apparent that competency is a product of one's circumstances as well as of one's innate or inherent abilities. The greater the jeopardy to one's health or welfare, the greater must be the abilities to provide for one's own protection. Thus, in circumstances presenting no extraordinary threat or demands, a lesser level of innate ability will establish competency. A recent court opinion will illustrate the point.

In *Matter of Fabre,* the Supreme Court of Louisiana considered an appeal by a moderately retarded woman challenging a lower court's determination of her general legal incompetency.[12] In reversing the lower court and declaring the woman competent, the state high court noted that "mental infirmities are of infinite degree, and to what extent the mind must be affected to warrant a judgment of [incompetency and the appointment of a guardian] is largely dependent on the facts of each case."[13] Only after reviewing in detail the woman's rather placid, undemanding daily routine and domestic environment did the court decide that she was, under these circumstances, able, ergo competent, to care for herself.

It is because the peculiar circumstances of each case bear so directly on competency that no single test of competency can serve all situations. Still, all tests of competency may be analyzed as entailing three basic stages. The first is a determination of the purposes for which the competency is being tested, as, for example, the purpose of giving consent to experimental psychosurgery in *Kaimowitz* and of deciding the need for general guardianship in *Matter of Fabre*. The second is a consideration of relevant circumstances; in *Kaimowitz*, for instance, this stage involved both an assessment of the cost-benefit ratio to the patient of the proposed surgery and an evaluation of the effects of confinement on the patient's ability to freely choose for or against the surgery. Finally, the third stage is an assessment of the individual's abilitites for the purposes and under the circumstances of the particular case.

Thus it should be clear that one can be incompetent for some purposes or under certain circumstances and still be competent for other purposes. Statutory law, however, has been slow in recognizing this fact. Some state guardianship statutes fail to acknowledge gradations of competency and permit courts to decide only whether one is wholly incompetent or fully competent. These statutes are anachronisms from the days when the most severely disabled were made wards of the state and all others were left to fend for themselves in a world of rugged individualism. Reform of these statutes to reflect the relativity of competency and to tailor protective services to individual needs has been urged by such distinguished groups as the International League of Societies for Persons with Mental Handicap, the President's Commission on Mental Health, the President's Committee on Mental Retardation, and the American Bar Association's Commission on the Mentally Disabled.[14] As explained in chapter 9, persons declared wholly incompetent under such statutes still may retain their rights to self-determination, including the right to make personal decisions, to the full extent of their abilities to exercise those rights.

In summary, legal competency is a relative concept, and the standards and tests of that concept can vary according to circumstances. Courts require at a minimum that persons appreciate the consequences of their decisions in order to be considered legally competent to make them. But even this level of understanding will vary depending on the potential risks of a given decision. What courts do not require to establish competency is that a person make unquestionably correct decisions. Mental-health clients, no less than others, enjoy what one court called "a right to be wrong."[15] A determination of incompetency and the resultant restriction of free choice is permissible only where one's mental incapacity presents a threat to one's best interests that is more serious than the harm of the restriction of free choice. This standard is patently vague, but necessarily so.

Competency to Stand Trial

The standards and tests of competency are perhaps most specific and refined in the area of competency to stand trial. The following is but an overview of a subject that has provoked much controversy and scholarly elucidation.[16]

To preserve the fundamental fairness of criminal proceedings, defendants are accorded a host of constitutionally protected rights, including the right to testify, to present evidence and witnesses, and to confront adverse witnesses. Largely because these essential procedural rights are ineffective if the defendant is incapable of exercising them, the law grants special deference to mentally disabled defendants. A defendant found incompetent to stand trial is typically excused from trial, at first temporarily and perhaps eventually altogether. A finding of incompetence to stand trial generally does not relieve the defendant of responsibility for criminal charges.[17] Those charges, especially if they represent grave allegations, will remain pending possibly indefinitely or until the defendant becomes competent, at which point a trial can proceed. In this and other respects, incompetency to stand trial is quite distinct from the defense of not guilty by reason of insanity, which, if proven, results in acquittal. Another significant distinction is that the issue of incompetency, unlike the defense of insanity, may be raised by the court or the prosecutor as well as by the defendant or the defendant's attorney.[18]

The test of competency to stand trial takes slightly different forms in different states, and indeed it may differ even between courts in the same state. All variations, however, include some version of the following questions: Does the defendant understand the charges? Does the defendant appreciate the nature of the proceedings, the functions of the various persons involved (the judge, prosecutor, defense attorney, and so on), and the potential consequences of the proceedings? Finally, is the defendant able to communicate with, and assist, a defense attorney? If all three questions can be answered in the affirmative, the defendant is competent.

If incompetent, the defendant will likely be required to undergo some form of treatment to restore competency. The once-common practice of subjecting incompetent defendants to automatic civil commitment has been declared unconstitutional by the United States Supreme Court.[19] Still, if the standards applied in regular civil commitment cases are satisfied, the defendant can be committed.

A determination of incompetency to stand trial is of no legal effect outside of the criminal process. In other words, it does not limit the defendant's competency for any other purpose than standing trial.

Consent to Treatment

As a general rule, client consent is necessary before any treatment, psychiatric or medical, can be administered lawfully. An important exception to this rule arises in the case of incompetent clients. Much of the present section, therefore, describes the specific requirements of competency necessary for a client to validly give or withhold consent to treatment. Before delving into the subject of consent, however, a few words of caution are in order.

Securing valid consent prior to initiating a course of treatment is crucially important for the clinician, both to preserve the basic right of clients to self-determination and personal autonomy and to avoid liability for assault and battery, the consequence of administering treatment without consent. This section presents the requirements of valid consent in some detail, but the requirements are unavoidably general. Here, then, it will be especially useful for the clinician to refer to the cases described in the notes for illustrations of how the requirements are applied in specific cases. A brief presentation of historical background should also help to explicate this rather complex doctrine of consent.

The doctrine can be traced back over two hundred years to an English case in which the King's Court opined that medical surgery performed without consent of the patient constituted a tortious assault.[20] Modern decisions continue to impose liability for unconsented medical treatment, even where that treatment is, from an objective view, beneficial to the patient.[21] The requirement of consent has long been considered necessary to protect not just the right of self-determination but also the very inviolability of one's person. Thus, treatment without consent constitutes unlawful assault and battery.

The Essential Elements of Valid Consent to Treatment

The requirement of consent in contemporary law consists of three essential elements. The consent must be preceded by the disclosure of adequate information; it must be voluntarily given; and, finally, the client providing the consent must be competent or, more precisely, must have the requisite capacity to do so. Each of these elements deserves elaboration.

Information. Some thirty years ago, courts began to note that the consent doctrine afforded too little protection, for it failed to ensure that patients be given sufficient information on which to base their decisions. In 1960, two landmark decisions cured this shortcoming by extending the doctrine to require informed consent.[22] These decisions and the many that have followed have established, in addition to the requirement of consent, the duty of health-care providers to disclose information relevant to a patient's decision to give or withhold consent.[23]

Although the duty to disclose is now well settled in the law, there remains some uncertainty as to precisely what information must be disclosed. Of course, some amount of uncertainty is inevitable since different treatments and different patients present different informational needs. Still, the case law provides several general rules and standards.

The basic dimensions of the duty to disclose were announced in the leading case of *Canterbury* v. *Spence*, where it was held that "the test for determining whether a particular peril must be divulged is its materiality to the patient's decision: all risks potentially affecting the decision must be unmasked."[24] The *Canterbury* opinion made clear, and subsequent cases have confirmed, that although providers need not disclose absolutely all risks of proposed therapies, they must disclose all but the most insignificant and highly improbable risks.[25] In addition, the cases require disclosure of potential side effects and of all reasonable alternatives to the treatment proposed, including the alternative of no treatment.[26]

From the case law concerning purely medical procedures, five exceptions to the duty to disclose have evolved. To what extent these exceptions might apply in cases of mental-health treatment is a matter of conjecture, but the exceptions are surely worth considering.[27]

Commonly Known Risks. Physicians are not obligated to disclose risks that are so widely known that any reasonable patient would be aware of them. An example of such a risk is the inescapable danger of infection during surgery. But the reasonable-patient standard applied in medical cases may well translate into an average-client standard in mental-health cases, considerably reducing what assumptions as to prior awareness will be permitted.[28] Moreover, the case law suggests that a physician must disclose even commonly known risks of which he knows or should know that a particular patient is unaware.[29] Hence, this exception will not apply where a client's mental condition indicates a lack of knowledge regarding commonly known risks. Conversely, of course, a provider need not inform a client about risks that the provider knows are already familiar to the client, whether commonly known or not. That is, the clinician need not repeat the full catalog of risks each time a particular treatment is repeated. It cannot lightly be supposed, however, that a client remembers, or ever knew, all the information relevant to a treatment decision. And the fact that a client was previously informed does not preclude a claim for failure to reinform prior to later treatment of the same sort.[30]

Waiver. Another exception obtains when clients state explicitly that they would rather not be told of risks or alternatives. Few cases address this exception, and they shed little light on the requisites of a valid waiver.[31] Court rulings on waivers of other sorts, however, establish that to be valid a waiver must be, like consent to treatment, both voluntary and informed.[32] Accordingly, a waiver of the right to information would seem valid only if the client is first told of the right to choose one's own course of treatment and to receive information bearing on that choice.[33]

Emergencies. Under certain exigent circumstances, neither disclosure nor consent are required. The clearest application of this exception arises in the case of an unconscious patient certain to die or suffer serious, irreversible harm if treatment is not administered. But serious harm must be imminent and consent wholly unobtainable for this exception to apply.[34] A special variation on this exception has developed in cases involving treatment by antipsychotic drugs in state psychiatric institutions. As will be described in further detail in later chapters, this exception permits forcible medication when necessary to prevent serious physical harm. A fortiori, the duty to disclose is excepted under such circumstances.

Total Incompetency. Where it is unmistakably clear that a client is completely incapable of making a treatment decision or intimating a preference between various treatments, disclosure to the client is unnecessary. It must be reemphasized that a judicial declaration of general incompetency does not, without more, obviate the need for disclosure. A legally incompetent client may yet be specifically competent for the purpose of giving or withholding consent to treatment and hence may yet be entitled to information necessary to that choice.[35]

Therapeutic Privilege. The final exception applies when disclosure is certain to do a patient far more harm than good. This exception is the law's recognition of the traditional trust relationship between physician and patient; it permits concealment of information that the physician reasonably believes would seriously jeopardize a patient's health. A provider who takes advantage of this privilege would have a heavy onus to discharge should the undisclosed risk materialize and the patient bring suit.[36] As one court observed, "[t]he privilege does not accept the paternalistic notion that the physician may remain silent simply because divulgence might prompt the patient to forego therapy the physician feels the patient really needs."[37]

In summarizing the duty to disclose, it must be emphasized that the duty is far more than a simple preamble to this bill of exceptions. In the absence of a clear, factually grounded exception, the clinician is duty bound to provide a client with all information material to a treatment decision. At a minimum, this information must include an explanation of the processes involved in a proposed treatment, of the prognosis, of the risks and side effects, and of alternative treatment modalities.

Several commentators have urged that the doctrine requires somewhat more than judicial decisions have established thus far. For instance, one pair of commentators interprets the duty as obligating therapists to keep abreast of all risks and alternatives to prescribed treatments.[38] Although not readily apparent in the case law, this obligation flows logically from the obvious fact that one can disclose only what one knows. Another commentator has argued that the duty requires disclosure of legal and social, as well as physical, risks to proposed treatment.[39] Hence, it might oblige the clinician to warn clients, before admitting them to a program, that admission could affect their prospects for employment, for entry into licensed professions, and for a host of other pursuits. Again, present case law imposes no such obligation, yet there is much in reason and law to commend this argument.

Voluntariness. The second essential element of consent, voluntariness, requires simply that clients be afforded true freedom of choice. The case of *Kaimowitz* v. *Michigan Department of Mental Health* made clear that coercion precludes valid consent.[40] That case held that the very fact of involuntary confinement could so influence a committed patient's choice, so undermine the voluntariness of consent to psychosurgery, as to render it invalid.[41] It requires no explanation that affirmative, intentional coercion will likewise vitiate informed consent.

Capacity. The final requirement of valid consent is that the person supplying the consent be competent to do so.[42] In this regard, the law uses the special term *capacity* to distinguish this concept from that of general competency and to emphasize the particular standards and tests of competency applicable in this context. In short, capacity signifies special competency for a particular purpose, here for the purpose of giving or withholding consent to treatment.

As explained earlier, competency is a measure of both a person's innate abilities and the factors and circumstances relevant to that person's need for protection. So too is capacity. Capacity must be determined by reference to the particular treatment proposed, as well as to the client's mental abilities. As the risks involved in a treatment decision increase, so too does the level of mental ability necessary to establish capacity. For example, a client with markedly impaired mental ability may have sufficient capacity to give valid consent to a relatively innocuous form of therapy (for example, group counselling or nonaversive behavior modification) and still lack the capacity to consent to more dangerous, more intrusive treatment forms (for example, psychosurgery or electroconvulsive therapy). Consequently, the reliance that a clinician can place on a client's consent depends as much on the purpose of that consent as on the client's mental abilities in the abstract.

In regard to the client's abilities, commentators in this area analyze the test of capacity as requiring three distinct abilities: the ability to gather information; the ability to evaluate that information; and the ability to make and express a decision.[43] The test does not require that the client's decision necessarily comport with the clinician's decision. As one court stated in ruling on a committed mental patient's capacity to deny consent to electroshock, "it does not matter whether this court would agree with her judgment; it is enough that she is capable of making a decision, however unfortunate that decision may prove to be."[44]

The requirement of capacity has been criticized as being both unnecessary to, and erosive of, the informed-consent doctrine.[45] It is challenged as unnecessary on the grounds that the more objective requirement that consent be informed is alone sufficient to invalidate the decisions of truly incapacitated persons. And it is denounced as erosive because it requires a highly subjective judgment that permits clinicians too much discretion in overriding client decisions. Thus far, the lawmakers have not accepted these criticisms, and capacity remains an essential element of valid consent.

All the legal doctrines and standards described so far have their roots in the fundamental "right to be let alone." Yet they are also expressions of a competing, and equally fundamental legal and social value: altruism. These standards represent an attempt to guarantee a proper balance between clients' rights to personal autonomy and clients' rights to protection from dangers that they cannot avert without help. The law does not forbid a client that help; quite the contrary, it establishes elaborate protective devices, of which involuntary hospitalization is one obvious example. But the law strives diligently to prevent excesses of paternalism, and so it firmly prohibits interference with a client's freedom of choice except when interference is imperative for the client's protection.

Practical Suggestions

The foregoing rules and principles reveal the importance that the law attaches to the right of self-determination and specifically to the right of clients to participate in determining their own courses of treatment. But what do these rules and principles require in daily practice? And how is the clinician to treat a client who is legally incompetent, lacks the capacity to consent, or is a minor?

Before taking up these questions directly, it must be stressed that informed consent is a means of protecting not just the client's rights but also the clinician's. It is a critically important shield against liability for assault and violation of a client's civil rights. Hence, the clinician must secure consent, ideally in written form, prior to instituting any course of treatment for any client. And in close cases, where the validity of a client's consent is at all questionable, the clinician would be well-advised to discuss the matter with a legal advisor.

The Form of Consent

Clinicians must exercise their own judgment in deciding what form of consent, written or oral, is sufficient in most cases. The law values written consent over oral, for obvious reasons. And for more intrusive and potentially harmful treatments, including treatment by antipsychotic medications, the law appears to insist that consent be written.[46]

The Duration of Consent

Case law in the mental-health field speaks of consent to a *course* of treatment or a *mode* of therapy. Plainly, specific written consent is not required at every stage of such a course; consent need not be obtained each time medication is dispensed, for instance. Yet it is clear from at least one case addressing this issue that an oral refusal at any time subsequent to prior written consent invalidates that consent. Treatment must then cease unless and until a fresh consent is given.[47]

Consent from Minors

As a general but by no means absolute rule, minors are incompetent to give effective consent to treatment. Deviations from this rule are abundant, however, both in statutes and in case law.[48] Courts seem inclined to reject age as the sole criterion of capacity to consent, especially where other factors indicate that a minor is capable of making an informed decision in respect to treatment. Thus, courts look to a minor's maturity and level of education, and to the nature of the particular treatment at issue, its risks, and its benefits.

Every state has enacted statutes that, with varying degrees of specificity, address the competency of minors to consent to medical treatment.[49] Only a few of these refer explicitly to mental-health treatment, but the general principles applicable to medical treatment seem equally applicable to psychiatric treatment.

In all but six states the age of majority is eighteen.[50] Some states provide that marriage automatically ends minority,[51] and many others presume married minors to be competent to give or withhold consent, their age notwithstanding.[52] In addition, a large number of state statutes grant the right to give or withhold consent to "emancipated" minors.[53] The requisites of emancipation are rather unclear; some states consider minors living apart from their parents and managing their own financial affairs to be automatically emancipated, whereas certain others may require court proceedings to establish emancipation.[54] Some states set minimum ages for emancipation, and others consider age to be an important but not determinative factor.[55] A few states consider high-school graduates automatically capable of making valid treatment decisions.[56] Several states permit consent by minors, irrespective of age or other factors, to treatment of special disorders such as drug abuse and venereal disease.[57]

The conclusion to be drawn from these statutes is that the law permits minors to make their own treatment decisions under proper circumstances. The statutes set forth only some of these circumstances. Irrespective of marriage or emancipation, minors should be considered competent to give or withhold consent if they are capable in fact of fully comprehending their choices, of undertaking reasonable analyses of those choices, and of appreciating the consequences of their decisions.[58] But the capabilities of a minor must be manifest to establish competency. Just as the law presumes all adults to be competent, it presumes all minors to be incompetent, with some statutory exceptions. The presumption of juvenile incompetency, unlike the presumption of adult competency, is not a wooden rule, unalterable except by judicial decree. Still, it does require that clinicians scrutinize the treatment decisions of minors with care and caution.

Third-Party Consent

Given a client who lacks the capacity to make a treatment decision, the clinician must seek the decision of a third party. For a minor, the party authorized to make the decision is typically a parent or one standing in loco parentis, for example a relative or custodian of the minor. Yet the clinician must be extremely guarded in relying on the judgment of a party in loco parentis; therefore, it is generally advisable, whenever a parental decision is unobtainable, to seek a judicial decision.[59] The procedures for obtaining judicial action are described in the later chapter on protective services, but it can be noted here that where necessary they can be swift and simple. Hence, the clinician need not be deterred by the fact that securing judicial relief of other sorts so closely resembles waiting for Godot.

For an adult client who lacks the capacity to make treatment decisions, the clinician's options are several. If the client is under guardianship, of course, the guardian is authorized to give or withhold consent on the client's behalf. If the client is not under guardianship, the clinician should consider first whether the client is so incapacitated, so in need of protective assistance, that guardianship proceedings should be instituted. If this rather extreme measure seems unwarranted, the clinician might seek a judicial decision on the narrow question of treatment. In the alternative, the best solution is for the clinician to seek approval of the client's own decision from responsible others. The clinician can present the client's personal treatment decision to those persons who would likely be empowered to act on the client's behalf if the client were adjudicated incompetent; for example, a next of kin or closest competent friend. If those persons object to the client's decision, then court action would seem in order. If they approve, however, then the clinician can more safely rely on the validity of the client's decision and hence can enjoy a greater measure of protection from liability. Of course, this solution raises obvious problems of confidentiality, but client consent to the disclosures would cure those problems. Admittedly, this whole method assumes that the client's capacity to consent is questionable. Recall, however, that capacity is relative; that a client who lacks the capacity to make complex, risk-laden decisions may yet be capable of making decisions involving less complexity and less danger. Thus, a client who is only marginally competent to make a treatment decision may be fully competent to authorize the disclosure of confidential information to a next of kin or closest competent friend. In sum, then, this solution is a workable means of preserving the marginally competent client's autonomy while also shielding the provider from liability for administering treatment without valid consent.[60]

In those situations where a third party must make a treatment decision on a client's behalf, the law offers some guidance as to how that decision should be made. Judicial opinions have drawn a distinction between two forms of third-party decision making: objective, best-interest decisions and substituted judgments. An objective, best-interest decision is one made by a third party based on an objective assessment of what would be best for the incompetent client. Underlying such a decision are professional, psychiatric considerations of the client's needs. A substituted-judgment decision, by contrast, is one based on a subjective assessment of what the incompetent client would choose if capable of making a reasoned choice. Underlying a substituted-judgment decision are considerations of the client's desires as distinct from needs. Recent court rulings indicate a trend toward substituted judgments and away from best-interest decisions,[61] and one court's statement on the matter explains why:

> The court, as surrogate for an incompetent, is to determine as best it can what choice that individual, if competent, would make with respect to medical procedures. We believe this approach is sound, . . . for it is the only way to pay full respect to the individuality and dignity of a person who . . . no longer has the capacity to decide.[62]

The substituted-judgment approach is especially useful where a client has previously expressed a relevant preference. This suggests that clinicians might avert many of the difficulties attendant to incompetency and third-party decision making by discussing future treatment options with clients when they are stable and lucid. Of course, a client cannot be bound later by a prior decision, even if incorporated in the increasingly popular form of a so-called treatment contract.[63] Still, a preference expressed by a client in anticipation of an incapacitating setback will be a valuable reference for a surrogate decision maker.

Conclusion

The law on competency and consent forces clinicians, as well as judges, to confront some utterly perplexing decisions. It requires a delicate balance between the fundamental rights of self-determination and personal autonomy, and the values of altruism and beneficence. But the clinician should be guided in this respect by the law's apparent preference for liberty over even beneficent intervention. As noted earlier, "law starts with the premise of thorough-going self determination."[64] And it holds that premise dear. In the words of the United States Supreme Court: "No right is held more sacred, or is more closely guarded, by the common law, than the right of every individual to the possession and control of his own person, free from all restraint or interference of others, unless by clear and unquestionable authority of law."[65]

Notes

1. Natanson v. Kline, 186 Kan. 393, 406, 350 P.2d 1093, 1104, *reh'g denied*, 187 Kan. 186, 354 P.2d 670 (1960). The court's opinion, one of the very first to enunciate the doctrine of informed consent, continued from the sentence quoted in the text with the following: "It follows that each man is considered master of his own body, and he may, if he be of sound mind, expressly prohibit the performance of life-saving surgery, or other forms of medical treatment." *Id.* at 406-07, 360 P.2d at 1104.

2. Olmstead v. United States, 277 U.S. 438, 478 (1928) (Brandeis, J., dissenting).

3. In a very few states, persons who are civilly committed are automatically deemed incompetent for the duration, but only for the duration, of their commitment. Such a rule is defensible only on the grounds that in these few states competency is adjudicated together with commitability, for it is well settled now that the two issues are distinct and that incompetency does not flow from the mere fact of mental illness. *See, e.g.*, Rennie v. Klein, 653 F.2d 836, 846 (3d Cir. 1981) (absent adjudication of incompetency, committed persons remain legally competent), *vacated and remanded,* 458 U.S. 1119 (1982); Rogers v. Okin, 634 F.2d 650, 658-59 (1st Cir. 1980) (incompetency may not be inferred from fact of commitment), *vacated and remanded sub nom.* Mills v. Rogers, 102 S.Ct. 2442 (1982); Boyd v. Board of Registrars of Belchertown, 368 Mass. 631, 635-36, 334 N.E.2d 629, 634 (1975) ("profound" distinction between commitment and determination of competency; residents of state facility for the retarded presumed competent to vote); Winters v. Miller, 446 F.2d 65 (2d Cir. 1971) (civil commitment does not defeat presumption of competency to give or withhold consent to psychiatric treatment). Given the apparent judicial and legislative trend away from equating commitment with incompetency, we may expect the contrary rule to be abandoned by even those few states that retain it. *See generally,* D. Wexler, Mental Health Law 40, 201 (1981); Comment, *Developments in the Law—Civil Commitment of the Mentally Ill,* 87 Harv. L. Rev. 1190, 1214-15 (1974).

4. One federal-district-court opinion, later effectively vacated on appeal, held that in institutional contexts, competency determinations may be made by administrative rather than judicial proceedings. Rennie v. Klein, 476 F. Supp. 1294, 1310-15 (D.N.J. 1979), *modified and remanded,* 653 F.2d 851 (3d Cir. 1981), *vacated and remanded,* 458 U.S. 1119 (1982). On appeal, the federal circuit court effectively vacated the procedures prescribed by the district court without expressly deciding whether nonjudicial competency procedures were legally permissible. The circuit court did intimate its view, however, when it stated in its decree: "A patient is considered incompetent only if he has been adjudicated incompetent by a court." 653 F.2d at 852. Even if the district court's procedures had been upheld on appeal, they would have marked only a slight derogation from the presumption of competency absent judicial action. In the first place, the lower court's procedures entailed virtually all the same safeguards that characterize judicial procedures, including the right of representation for patients and an independent arbiter. And secondly, nothing in the reasoning of the lower court's opinion suggested that similar nonjudicial proceedings would be permissible outside of state pyschiatric institutions. To the contrary, the justifications presented by the district court were quite peculiar to the institutional context. In a case raising the same right to refuse treatment issues presented in *Rennie,* the Supreme Court of Oklahoma stated in no uncertain terms that "[p]arens patriae arises only when an adult patient has been

judicially determined incompetent." *In re* K.K.B., 609 P.2d 747, 750 (Okla. Sup. Ct. 1980) (emphasis added). The highest court in Massachusetts echoed that ruling in Rogers v. Comm'r of the Dept. of Mental Health, 390 Mass. 489, 458 N.E.2d 308 (1983).

5. *In re* K.K.B., 609 P.2d 747, 752 (Okla. Sup. Ct. 1980). Because this synopsis of the very complex issue of client-treatment decisions is potentially misleading, the reader is urged to consult chapter 5 on the right to refuse treatment.

6. Meisel, Lidz & Roth, *Tests of Competency to Consent to Treatment*, 134 Am. J. Psychiatry 279, 283 (1977).

7. Civ. No. 73-19434-AW (Cir. Ct. of Wayne County, Mich., July 10, 1973), *reprinted in* A. Brooks, Law, Psychiatry and the Mental Health System 902 (1974). For an analysis of *Kaimowitz*, see D. Wexler, Mental Health Law 201-206 (1981).

8. Sir William Blackstone, in his eighteenth-century treatise, *Commentaries on the Laws of England*, bases the *parens patriae* power in the sovereign's role as "general guardian of all infants, idiots, and lunatics." 3 W. Blackstone, Commentaries 47, *quoted in* Rogers v. Okin, 634 F.2d 650, 657 (1st Cir. 1980), *vacated and remanded sub nom.* Mills v. Rogers, 102 S.Ct. 2442 (1982).

9. For critical reviews of the *parens patriae* power in general, and of exercises of the power in the area of psychiatry in particular, see Coleman & Solomon, *Parens Patriae "Treatment": Legal Punishment in Disguise*, 3 Hastings Const. L.Q. 345 (1976); and Curtis, *Checkered Career of Parens Patriae: The State as Parent or Tyrant?* 25 De Paul L. Rev. 895 (1976).

10. Hanes v. Ambrose, 437 N.Y.S. 2d 784 (N.Y. App. Div. 1981).

11. Matter of Roosevelt Hospital (Otis Simmons) (N.Y. Sup. Ct., N.Y. County, Jan. 10, 1977), *reported in* N.Y.L.J., Jan. 13, 1977, at 7, col. 2.

12. 371 So.2d 1322 (La. Sup. Ct. 1979).

13. *Id.* at 1324.

14. *See* International League of Societies for Persons with Mental Handicap, Symposium on Guardianship of the Mentally Retarded (1969); President's Committee on Mental Retardation, Report to the President—Mental Retardation: Century of Decision (1976); President's Commission on Mental Health, Report to the President (1978); Developmental Disabilities State Legislative Project of the A.B.A. Commission on the Mentally Disabled, Guardianship and Conservatorship (1979).

15. Rogers v. Okin, 478 F. Supp. 1342, 1367 (D.Mass. 1979), *aff'd in part, rev'd in part, and vacated and remanded in part*, 634 F.2d 650 (1st. Cir. 1980), *vacated and remanded* 102 S.Ct. 2442 (1982).

16. The seminal study of the law on this subject is A.L. McGarry & W. Curran, Competency to Stand Trial and Mental Illness: Final Report (1972). *See also* W. Curran, A.L. McGarry & C. Petit, Modern Legal Medicine, Psychiatry & Forensic Science (1980). For a critical view of the subject, see Group for the Advancement of Psychiatry, Committee on Psychiatry and

Law, Misuse of Psychiatry in the Criminal Courts: Competency to Stand Trial (1974). And for a critique urging the abolition of this power altogether, see Burt & Morris, *A Proposal for the Abolition of the Incompetency Plea*, 40 U. Chi. L. Rev. 66 (1972).

17. See D. Wexler, Mental Health Law 120-21 (1981), *citing* A. Matthews, Mental Disability and the Criminal Law: A Field Study 214-15 (1970). In many states, statutes prescribe specific periods during which the charges remain pending. In some states the period is a fixed portion of the potential prison term faced by the defendant. In New York, for instance, misdemeanor charges remain pending for ninety days, and felony charges remain for a period equal to two-thirds of the maximum prison sentence allowable for the most serious of the charges. N.Y. Crim. Proc. Law §730.50(1), (3) (McKinney 1980). In several states, a single period is fixed for all charges. For example, in Michigan all charges, misdemeanors and felonies alike, remain pending for eighteen months. Mich. Comp. Laws §767.27(a)(7)(1980).

18. There is support in case law for the proposition that both the prosecutor and the judge are not just permitted but obliged to raise the issue when there is reason to doubt a defendant's competency at time of trial. *See, e.g.,* Lokos v. Capps, 625 F.2d 1258 (5th Cir. 1980).

19. Jackson v. Indiana, 406 U.S. 715 (1972); *cf.* Baxstrom v. Herold, 383 U.S. 107 (1966) (commitment of state prisoner violates constitutional right to equal protection under law when standards of commitment are lower than those applied in regular civil commitment proceedings).

20. Slater v. Baker and Stapleton, 95 Eng. Rep. 960 (K.B. 1767).

21. *See, e.g.*, Bailey v. Belinfante, 135 Ga.App. 574, 218 S.E. 2d 289 (1975) (fact that unconsented tooth extraction was "skillfully done" did not defeat patient's claim against dentist; directed verdict for dentist reversed); Lloyd v. Kull, 329 F.2d 168 (7th Cir. 1964) (doctor liable for removing mole without consent); Mohr v. Williams, 95 Minn. 261, 104 N.W. 12 (1905) (physician liable for assault and battery for operating on both left and right ears with consent only for operating on right ear).

22. Mitchell v. Robinson, 334 S.W. 2d 11 (1960), *reh'g denied*, 360 S.W.2d 673 (Mo. 1962) (insulin-shock treatments); Natanson v. Kline, 186 Kan. 393, 350 P.2d 1093 *reh'g denied*, 187 Kan. 186, 354 P.2d 670 (1960) (cobalt-irradiation therapy).

23. An excellent, comprehensive book detailing the law on consent to medical treatment cites nearly five hundred cases ruling on the issue of patient consent. Approximately four hundred of these were decided in the two decades following the 1960 *Natanson* and *Mitchell* decisions. Few of these cases, however, concern psychiatric treatment. A. Rosoff, Informed Consent: A Guide for Health Care Providers 471-93 (1981).

24. 464 F.2d 772, 788 (D.C. Cir.), *cert. denied*, 409 U.S. 1064 (1972) (failure to disclose risks attendant to laminectomy, an operation on the posterior arch of the vertebra).

25. The following cases illustrate the type of risks that must be disclosed. Note the relationship between severity of risks and likelihood of occurrence: a risk of very serious harm must be disclosed even if highly unlikely. Cases in which failure to disclose was or may have been negligent: Canterbury v. Spence, 464 F.2d 772 (D.C. Cir.), *cert. denied*, 409 U.S. 1064 (1972) (1 percent chance of paralysis); Cobbs v. Grant, 104 Cal. Rptr. 505, 502 P.2d 1 (1972) (any risk whatever of death); Cooper v. Roberts, 220 Pa. Super. 260, 286 A.2d 647 (1971) (0.04 percent chance of stomach puncture); Scott v. Wilson, 396 S.W.2d 532 (Tex. Civ. App. 1965) (1 percent chance of hearing loss). Cases in which risk was not so serious or probable that nondisclosure was negligent: Starnes v. Taylor, 272 N.C. 386, 158 S.E. 2d 339 (1968) (0.4 percent to 0.8 percent chance of esophagus puncture); Yeates v. Harms, 193 Kan. 320, 393 P.2d 982 (1964) (1.5 percent chance of loss of eye); Stottlemire v. Cawood, 213 F.Supp. 897 (D.D.C. 1963) (0.0000125 percent chance of aplastic anemia). At least one commentator has argued that for moral, if not legal, reasons patients should be informed of all possible risks. Murphy, *Therapy and the Problem of Autonomous Consent,* 2 Int'l J. L. & Psychiatry 415, 422 (1979).

26. *See, e.g.,* Rennie v. Klein, 653 F.2d 836, 853 (3rd Cir. 1981), *vacated and remanded,* 458 U.S. 1119 (1982); *In re* K.K.B., 609 P.2d 747, 750 (Okla. 1980).

27. For a complete presentation of these exceptions, see the influential article, Meisel, *The "Exceptions" to the Informed Consent Doctrine: Striking a Balance between Competing Values in Medical Decisionmaking*, 1979 Wis. L. Rev. 413.

28. *See, e.g.*, Canterbury v. Spence, 464 F.2d 772, 786-87 (D.C. Cir.), *cert. denied*, 409 U.S. 1064 (1972); N.Y. Pub. Health Law §2805-d(3) (McKinney 1980).

29. *See* A. Rosoff, Informed Consent 52 (1981).

30. *Cf.* Roberts v. Wood, 206 F.Supp. 579 (S.D. Ala. 1962) (liability of physician for failure to disclose risks of thyroidectomy to patient who had already undergone one such operation; risks of second thyroidectomy generally greater than first).

31. *See, e.g.*, Holt v. Nelson, 11 Wash. App. 230, 523 P.2d 211 (1974); Cobbs v. Grant, 8 Cal. 3d 229, 502 P.2d 1, 104 Cal. Rptr. 505 (1972). *See also*, N.Y. Pub. Health Law §2805-d(4)(b) (McKinney 1980).

32. *See, e.g.*, Miranda v. Arizona, 384 U.S. 436 (1966) (waiver of arrestee of the rights to remain silent and to be represented by counsel). *But cf.* Schneckloth v. Bustamonte, 412 U.S. 218 (1973) (waiver of right to deny police request of permission to search car held valid despite claim that defendant was unaware of the right to deny such a request).

33. See Meisel, *supra* note 27, at 454. In his authoritative article, Meisel analyzes a valid waiver in the field of medical practice as consisting of capacity, voluntariness, and information. The last component is said to place

on physicians the duty to provide the following information: (1) that they bear a duty to disclose; (2) that patients have a legal right to decide on treatment options; (3) that physicians cannot treat without patient consent; and (4) that patients' options include refusal.

34. See A. Rosoff, Informed Consent 14-19 (1981), in which several court decisions denying the emergency exception are summarized.

35. See chapter 9, *infra.*

36. In one case denying the privilege, a physician was held liable for failure to disclose the full extent of risks involved in a certain heart surgery. This, despite the fact that the physician had been treating the patient-plaintiff over the course of fourteen years and considered him so predisposed to anxiety that, in the physician's opinion, full disclosure would have rendered him incapable of an intelligent decision regarding the surgery. The patient, a paraplegic as a result of the operation, was awarded damages of $1 million. Jones v. The Regents of the University of California (Cal. Super. Ct., San Francisco, February 22, 1977), *summarized in* A. Rosoff, Informed Consent 54-55 (1981). In the leading case in which the privilege was allowed as a defense, a physician was held not liable for failure to fully disclose the risks of a certain kidney operation. The case is replete with extraordinary facts that tend to explain the result: the patient himself was a physician; he had suffered for thirty years from a chronic kidney disease; he was "highly apprehensive"; and he suffered recurring chest pains just before the operation. Nishi v. Hartwell, 52 Hawaii 188, 473 P.2d 116 (1970).

37. Canterbury v. Spence, 464 F.2d 772, 789 (D.C. Cir.), *cert. denied,* 409 U.S. 1064 (1972). Another court, ruling on the question in the specific context of treatment by psychotropic drugs, also emphasized the limited availability of the therapeutic privilege: "although disclosure of potential side-effects of medication may be frightening to the mental patient this court is not persuaded that such a prospect, standing alone, justifies a failure to provide a patient with sufficient information to make an informed treatment decision." Rogers v. Okin, 478 F. Supp. 1342, 1389 (D. Mass. 1979), *aff'd in part, rev'd in part, vacated and remanded in part,* 634 F.2d 650 (1st Cir. 1980), *vacated and remanded,* 102 S.Ct. 2442 (1982).

38. Waltz & Scheuneman, *Informed Consent to Therapy,* 64 Nw. U.L. Rev. 628 (1970). Whether a provider could defend against a failure-to-disclose charge by pleading ignorance of undisclosed risks may depend on the general standard of negligence applied by the court. Older cases employed what was called a "locality" standard of negligence, whereby a provider's actions were automatically nonnegligent if they conformed to the customary practice of similar providers in the same locality. The rule served to distinguish between big-city doctors with modern resources at their disposal and country doctors practicing with less advanced equipment and technology. This approach, still adhered to in some jurisdictions, would likely

relieve a therapist from knowing and disclosing any more information than is customarily known and disclosed by local colleagues. *See, e.g.*, Brune v. Belinkoff, 354 Mass. 102, 235 N.E.2d 793 (1968) ("The rationale of the [locality] rule . . . is that a physician in a small or rural community will lack opportunities to keep abreast with the advances in the profession."). The more common standard today measures the propriety of a provider's actions by reference to a fictional reasonable provider. By this rule, a court would determine, taking account of all the advances in the profession, whether an undisclosed risk is one that a reasonable therapist would have known and disclosed. Similarly, modern courts measure the materiality of information for a patient by determining whether a so-called reasonable patient would consider the information significant. *See generally*, A. Rosoff, Informed Consent 34-41 (1981).

39. Noll, *The Psychotherapist and Informed Consent*, 133 Am. J. Psychiatry 1451 (1976).

40. Civ. No. 73-19434-AW (Cir. Ct. of Wayne County, Mich., July 10, 1973), *reprinted in* A. Brooks, Law, Psychiatry and the Mental Health System 902 (1974).

41. In the words of the *Kaimowitz* court: "It is impossible for an involuntarily detained mental patient to be free of ulterior forms of restraint or coercion when his very release from the institution may depend upon his cooperating with the institutional authorities and giving consent to experimental surgery. . . . Involuntarily confined mental patients live in an inherently coercive institutional environment. . . . They are not able to voluntarily give informed consent because of the inherent inequality in their position. [footnote omitted]" *Id.*, Brooks at 914-15. For criticisms of this holding, see Murphy, *Therapy and the Problem of Autonomous Consent*, 2 Int'l. J. L. & Psychiatry 415, 425-26 (1979); D. Wexler, Mental Health Law 205 (1981). Both these critiques argue that the court too readily discounted the ability of committed patients to resist the subtle pressures and inherent coercion of the institution.

42. *See generally*, Restatement (Second) of Torts §892 (1979), where the rule is succinctly stated as follows: "To be effective, consent must be made by one who has the capacity to consent." *Id.* at §892A(2)(a).

43. For an elaboration of this tripartite test of capacity in particular, and a very instructive presentation of the informed-consent doctrine in general, see American Association on Mental Deficiency, Consent Handbook (H.R. Turnbull ed. 1977).

44. New York City Health and Hospital Corp. v. Stein, 70 Misc. 2d 944, 947, 335 N.Y.S.2d 461, 463 (Sup. Ct. N.Y. Co. 1972).

45. *See, e.g.*, Barnhart, Pinkerton & Roth, *Informed Consent to Organic Behavior Control*, 17 Santa Clara L. Rev. 39 (1977).

46. *See, e.g.,* Rennie v. Klein, 476 F. Supp. 1294, 1312 (D.N.J. 1979), *modified and remanded,* 653 F.2d 836 (3d Cir. 1981), *vacated and remanded,* 458 U.S. 1119 (1982) (describing a particular form on which written consent to psychotropic medication must be secured). The U.S. Congress, in the Mental Health Systems Act, goes even further and urges that consent to any "mode or course of treatment" be written. 42 U.S.C. §9501(1)(D) (1980).

47. Rennie v. Klein, 476 F. Supp. at 1311-12.

48. See A. Rosoff, Informed Consent 187-92 (1981), where a host of cases upholding a minor's right to give effective consent are presented.

49. An excellent, concise analysis of the relevant statutes in all fifty states and the District of Columbia is presented in A. Rosoff, Informed Consent 211-31 (1981).

50. The six exceptions are as follows: In Alabama the majority age is nineteen, Ala. Code §26-1-1 (1979). In Kentucky, the majority age is eighteen, except for handicapped persons, who attain majority at age twenty-one, Ky. Rev. Stat. §2.015 (1971). In Mississippi, majority age is 21, Miss. Code Ann. §1-3-27 (1980 Supp.). In Missouri, the age of majority is twenty-one in general but eighteen for purposes of consent, Mo. Rev. Stat. §475.010 (1980 Supp.). And in Nebraska the majority age is nineteen, Neb. Rev. Stat. §38-101 (1978).

51. *E.g.*, Fla. Stat. Ann. §743.01 (1980 West Supp.); Hawaii Rev. Stat. §577-25 (1980 Supp.); Mich. Comp. Laws Ann. §722.4 (1978); Or. Rev. Stat. §109.520 (1976).

52. *E.g.*, Cal. Civ. Code §25.6 (1980 West Supp.); Conn. Gen. Stat. Ann. §19-142a (1977); Del. Code Ann. tit. 13 §707 (1974); N.J. Stat. Ann. §9:12A-1 (1976 West); N.Y. Pub. Health Law §2504 (1977 McKinney); Va. Code §32-137 (1980 Supp.).

53. *E.g.*, Alaska Stat. §09.65.100 (1980 Supp.); Ark. Stat. Ann. §82.363 (1976); Cal. Civ. Code §34.6 (1980 West Supp.); Colo. Rev. Stat. §13-22-103 (1973); Minn. Stat. Ann. §144.341 (1980 West Supp.); Miss. Code Ann. §41-41-3 (1972); Mont. Rev. Codes Ann. §41-1-402 (1978); N.M. Stat. Ann. 24-10-1 (1978); N.C. Gen. Stat. §90-21-5 (1980 Supp.); Okla. Stat. Ann. tit. 63 §2602 (1979 West); Tex. Fam. Code Ann. §11.01 (1975).

54. *E.g.*, Alaska Stat. §09.65.100 (1980 Supp.); Okla. Stat. Ann. tit. 63 §2602 (1979 West); Pa. Stat. Ann. tit. 35 §10101 (1977 Purdon); Tex. Fam. Code Ann. §35.03 (1975).

55. *E.g.*, Cal. Civ. Code §34.6 (1980 West Supp.) (minimum age for emancipation, fifteen years old); Colo. Rev. Stat. §13-22-103 (1973) (minimum age, fifteen); Tex. Fam. Code Ann. §35.03 (1975) (minimum age, sixteen).

56. *E.g.*, Ala. Code §22-8-4 (1979); Mont. Rev. Codes Ann. §41-1-402 (1978); Pa. Stat. Ann. tit. 35 §10101 (1977 Purdon).

57. *See, e.g.*, Ala. Code §22-8-6 (1979); Kan. Stat. Ann. §65-2892 (1973); Minn. Stat. Ann. §144.343 (1980 West Supp.); N.M. Stat. Ann. §26-2-14 (1978); N.C. Gen. Stat. §90-21.5 (1980 Supp.); Ohio Rev. Code Ann. §§3709.24.1, 3709.01.2 (1980 West Supp.); W.Va. Code §60A-5-504 (1977).

58. As with the general tests of competency considered earlier it is impossible to set forth the precise level of ability that is necessary in any given situation to establish the competency of a minor. *See generally*, T. Grisso, Juvenile's Waiver of Rights: Legal and Psychological Competence 132 (1982).

59. See A. Rosoff, Informed Consent 194-95 (1981), describing the case of Moss v. Rishworth, 222 S.W. 225 (Tex. 1920), in which consent by an adult sister for a nonemergency operation on her minor brother was held invalid. The consent was invalid despite the following: the parents had left the boy temporarily in the custody of the sister; the sister was a nurse; and the operation was routine (tonsillectomy-adenoidectomy). The child died while being anesthetized.

60. At least one court has explicitly recognized the propriety of a clinician's consulting with parents and family members of a client with respect to the client's condition and course of treatment. Rogers v. Okin, 478 F. Supp. 1342, 1363 (D.Mass. 1979), *aff'd. in part, rev'd in part, vacated and remanded in part*, 634 F.2d 650 (1st Cir. 1980), *vacated and remanded sub nom.* Mills v. Rogers, 102 S.Ct. 2442 (1982).

61. Several recent cases raising the issue of euthanasia for incompetent persons drew national attention to this subject. In each of the following cases, termination of life-sustaining treatment was authorized on the basis that the incompetent client would choose to die if competent to make that choice. Eichner v. Dillon, 426 N.Y.S.2d 517 (App. Div. 1980), *modified and aff'd*, 438 N.Y.S.2d 266 (Ct. App. 1981); *In re* Spring, 380 Mass. 629, 405 N.E.2d 115 (1980); Superintendent of Belchertown State School v. Saikewicz, 373 Mass. 728, 370 N.E.2d 417 (1977); *In re* Quinlan, 355 A.2d 647 (N.J. Sup. Ct. 1976). *See also, In re* Boyd, 403 A.2d 744 (D.C. 1980) (substituted-judgment approach requires that medication be refused on behalf of incompetent who, while competent, had expressed objection to medication on religious grounds).

62. *In re* Boyd, 403 A.2d 744, 750 (D.C. 1980) (citations omitted).

63. Client-therapist contracts, although they may be clinically valuable, are generally ineffective legally, at least insofar as they purport to bind clients to particular courses of treatment. This is so for several reasons. First, any agreement that claims to vitiate a constitutionally protected right, as is the right to refuse treatment, will meet with strict legal scrutiny. Secondly, co-

ercion or duress will likely be inferred from the unequal relationship between therapist and client. And finally, since psychiatric treatment involves so many variables and must be responsive to changes in both the client's condition and the state of the science, it does not admit of advance planning; in short, it is an unfit subject for contractual obligations. For a more in-depth analysis of these and other legal defects of client-therapist contracts, see Dresser, *Ulysses and the Psychiatrist: A Legal and Policy Analysis of the Voluntary Commitment Contract,* 16 Harv. C.R.-C.L. L. Rev. 777 (1982).

64. Natanson v. Kline, 186 Kan. 393, 406, 350 P.2d 1093, 1104, *reh'g denied*, 187 Kan. 186, 354 P.2d 670 (1960).

65. Union Pacific Railway v. Botsford, 141 U.S. 250, 251 (1891) (ruling on the right to refuse medical examination).

Part II
Rights in the Treatment Process

Right to Treatment

The clinician now faces an array of conflicting pressures. Just as legal mandates for the least restrictive treatment settings are required, tax cuts are reducing the resources for their fulfillment. Yet this situation is hardly unprecedented. In the early 1970s when domestic social programs suffered and taxpayer revolts led to freezes in state budgets and havoc in state mental institutions, court actions helped protect mental patients who were out of the public sight and mind. Commenting on the use of a federal-court order to remedy this situation and hire additional personnel and provide more treatment, Milton Greenblatt, then Massachusetts commissioner of Mental Health, correctly predicted that "the era of use of judicial procedures in behalf of the disenfranchised in our health system has just begun."[1] The taxpayer revolts and Proposition 13s of this decade will not only lead to new petitions to courts but will call for renewed alliances between advocates and mental-health-service providers.

For those who saw a national health insurance that included inpatient mental-health care as the ultimate solution, that object seems more elusive than ever. In the meantime, patients, clinicians, and advocates must turn to the tools at hand that can pry resources to sustain humane laws and clinical promises.

The *Wyatt* Case and the Judicially Enforceable Right

The right to receive treatment in the least restrictive settings is now embedded in American law. That development is as much a product of mental-health practitioners as it is of lawyers and judges. The case of *Wyatt* v. *Stickney* was the first to recognize the constitutional right of mental patients to receive adequate care and treatment. Chief Judge Frank M. Johnson, Jr., an eminent federal jurist, held that the patients of Alabama's Bryce Hospital had a legal remedy for the state's unfulfilled paternalistic responsibility: "To deprive any citizen of his or her liberty upon the altruistic theory that the confinement is for humane therapeutic reasons and then fail to provide adequate treatment violates the very fundamentals of due process."[2]

Behind this truly landmark decision, there lies a tale of human misery and state bureaucratic recalcitrance. Treatment was virtually nonexistent for the five thousand patients at Bryce State Hospital, and a budget cut threatening the jobs of ninety-nine hospital employees foretold further neglect. On 23 October 1970, the patients at Bryce and the soon-to-be-discharged employees filed suit, alleging that conditions at the hospital—even before the budget cuts—were unconstitutional. They complained that the staff reductions would deny patients any prospect of receiving adequate treatment. The court focused on the patients' plights and their rights to treatment. The entry as amici curiae of the American Psychological Association and the American Orthopsychiatric Association also underscored the national significance of the treatment issues involved. Those associations, together with nationally prominent mental-health professionals, played key roles in developing what the court later declared were minimum constitutional standards of treatment.

The vast majority of the *Wyatt* standards were agreed to by the defendants as necessary for safeguarding adequate treatment. The testimony of leading psychiatrists, psychologists, and community-service planners provided the basis for the court's rulings on the remaining standards. Thus, *Wyatt* standards were not some judicial edict conceived in lofty isolation but rather represented a knowledgeable view of the minimum professional standards of realistic treatment.

Throughout many years of litigation, the *Wyatt* court has allowed state administrators every opportunity to improve conditions on their own. Indeed, it initially deferred to the state in the establishment of the standards. The court granted the defendants' request for a six-month period in which state officials would independently determine the necessary standards for adequate treatment. It was only after the state failed in this effort that the court allowed the parties and amici to propose the minimum standards, which later became law.

It is at this stage that the mental-health professions left their most enduring mark on the case. The amici, by then joined by the American Association on Mental Deficiency, the American Civil Liberties Union, and the U.S. Justice Department, were fully involved in these hearings. Some of the nation's leading mental-health professionsals served as expert witnesses, reviewed the professional literature on standards, inspected the facilities, and consulted with staff, patients, and relatives. The result was a court-ordered set of "minimum constitutional standards for adequate treatment of the mentally ill," which included thirty-five specific measures for ensuring the presence of individualized-treatment plans, adequate and qualified staffing, and a humane psychological and physical environment.[3] Those standards served as a blueprint for and a prod to reducing inappropriately held patient populations, upgrading staffs, and curbing neglect.

In the wake of *Wyatt* and its pioneering set of reform standards, other courts and state legislatures have followed. There have been refinements and shifts in emphasis—especially toward more community-centered care.

But the basic pattern remained consistent: courts entered broad affirmative injunctive decrees, with remedies focusing not on the merits of an individual's treatment but on the capacity of a mental-health service to implement standards and provide conditions that offer hospitalized patients a "chance to receive adequate treatment."[4] Although the United States Supreme Court has so far declined to rule on whether mental patients have a constitutional right to treatment,[5] lawsuits challenging treatment inadequacies in mental-health, mental-retardation, juvenile, and other care facilities are now routinely heard by federal and state courts.[6] Most of these suits urge the provision of the least restrictive care, a vital element in the right to treatment (see chapter 6).

Origins and Development of the Right to Treatment

Long before these court cases, many states had statutes and regulatory codes that required that treatment facilities and services be offered to mental patients. As early as 1952, the federal government prepared a model statute stating that "every patient shall be entitled to humane care and treatment."[7] Numerous states have now gone further by enacting laws that promise a right to quality treatment and by adopting specific statutes and regulations for carrying out this broad command. The following language is characteristic: "Each patient in a facility and each person receiving services for mental disability shall receive care and treatment that is suited to his needs, and skillfully, safely, and humanely administered with full respect for his dignity and personal integrity."[8] These provisions reflect society's ethical and legal duty to provide effective services to both voluntary and involuntary mental patients who are accepted for care and treatment in publicly supported facilities.

Unfortunately, the reality of many public institutions is a far cry from this norm. In endorsing the legal right to adequate care and treatment, the American Psychiatric Association acknowledged that mentally disabled persons have suffered neglect and discrimination, "especially in public hospitals, which are usually underfunded and consequently understaffed."[9]

The concept of a legally enforceable right to remedial treatment was first articulated by Dr. Morton Birnbaum, a physician and an attorney.[10] Writing mainly in his role as a medical professional, Dr. Birnbaum maintained that a person involuntarily institutionalized for care and treatment has a right to receive adequate medical care and treatment. He argued that the state, by indefinitely confining the mental patient in custodial facilities without treatment, deprived the patient of liberty in violation of substantive due process. Other advocates and clinicians who followed condemned that policy as bad law and bad medicine: such denials of patient liberty and dignity were unlawful as well as untherapeutic.

Six years later, the U.S. Court of Appeals endorsed this position. The court held that involuntarily committed patients had a judicially enforceable right to adequate treatment.[11] Chief Judge David L. Bazelon wrote that in meeting this requirement the hospital need only show a bona fide effort to cure or alleviate the patient's condition. Although *Rouse* v. *Cameron* was decided on statutory gounds, Judge Bazelon's opinion acknowledged the serious constitutional questions presented by the forced confinement of patients in the name of treatment for whom no treatment is forthcoming.

In line with *Wyatt* and *Rouse,* courts and commentators have recognized the right to treatment under a wide variety of constitutional and other legal theories. The outpouring of scholarship—legal, sociolegal, and philosophical—is overwhelmingly supportive of that right. Appellate courts have ruled that the right to treatment poses a justiciable controversy and that the right itself can be implemented through judicially manageable standards.[12] And those standards have now been erected in many contexts and for many groups: mental patients,[13] residents of mental-retardation facilities,[14] juvenile offenders,[15] dependent juveniles,[16] prisoners, [17] and children placed in public-school classes for the emotionally handicapped.[18]

Nationwide standards implementing the statutory right to treatment for mental patients are also established under the Medicaid program. For example, patients receiving Medicaid-reimbursed care must be provided with a carefully structured program of "active treatment."[19] Accreditation standards and position statements by professional associations offer additional guidance on the specific methods of realizing particular treatment standards.[20] Indeed, professional associations have often entered cases as amicus curiae to lend support to the development and articulation of right-to-treatment principles.

Right-to-Treatment Principles

Although the right-to-treatment litigation began as a technique to remedy the chronic neglect of the mentally ill in state institutions, advocates sought to apply such principles in wider contexts. Although court cases as a matter of priority and precedent were closely tied to involuntary hospitalization, they were followed by a wave of statutory and regulatory reforms aimed at a wider objective: securing treatment opportunities for users of mental-health services without regard to the individual's legal status. Right-to-treatment principles, as already noted, were extended beyond the mental-health field to virtually every form of noncriminal confinement. Out of this mass of reform statutes, regulations, and court decisions, we can sketch certain broad principles that now command widespread clinical, social, and legal support.

Respect for Individual Dignity

Whatever the state of the law or of mental-health budgets, there are some patients' claims to dignity and individuality that cannot be ignored. To voice a grievance or make a recommendation requires no state expenditure. To obtain fair, timely, and impartial review of an alleged infringement of rights demands more diligence than capital. To be protected from experimentation demands only compliance with well-established safeguards. To be listened to and heard takes only patience. To be free of discrimination on the basis of handicap may require only a willingness to discard old stereotypes for new, factually grounded perceptions.

The government has long proclaimed that each recipient of federally funded mental-health services "must be treated with consideration, respect, and full recognition of his or her dignity and individuality."[21] The breadth of those phrases do not make them of lesser importance than those standards setting out the operational details. Indeed, within their compass fall the human concerns that truly matter. And every mental-health professional must gauge whether his or her practices strengthen or strip away the stuff of individual dignity. The reality of dehumanized care is too painful to overlook this essential element in any meaningful right to treatment.

Individualization

At the core of the right to treatment is the notion that treatment and related services must be geared to the needs of each and every individual. For example, Congress has declared that a person admitted to a mental-health-services program has more than a right to some treatment. States have been urged to enact a patients' bill of rights, articulating, among its many other principles, the "right to appropriate treatment and related services in the least restrictive setting and conditions."[22] In accordance with the recommendations of the President's Commission on Mental Health, such statutory revision aims to reconcile treatment needs and liberty interests as well as to avoid the harms of regimented or stereotyped treatment, oppressive treatment, or the lack of even a proffer of treatment. Legislation at the state level is increasingly giving such rights binding effect, both in community and institutional programs.

The right to an individualized, written treatment or service plan is a means toward this end. Under Medicaid regulations, the resident's overall plan of care must set goals to be accomplished, prescribe an integrated program of activities, therapies, and treatments designed to help each resident achieve these goals, and indicate the professional responsible for each service prescribed in the plan.[23] But residents are entitled to more than the creation of a pile of paper; they have the right to treatment based on an individualized plan. Thus, federal case law specifies the elements of such a treatment plan, including intermediate and long-range treatment goals, projected timetables for their attainment, criteria for release to less restrictive treatment conditions, criteria for discharge, and a posthospitalization plan.[24] State legislatures have enacted similar requirements that agencies or institutions providing mental-health services develop and place into effect individualized treatment plans promptly after admitting a person to its services.[25] In recent years, at least fourteen states have adopted comparable statutory bills of rights for the mentally ill, and more legislation along these lines can be expected.

Periodic Revision

The right to periodic review of treatment needs and the right to appropriate revision of treatment plans have also been recognized by a variety of sources. The absence of such review and reassessment can lead to prolonged confinement of a type condemned as constitutionally impermissible by the Supreme Court and other appellate courts.[26] Medicaid and accreditation programs also require a continuous and self-correcting process of updating treatment plans to ensure their relevance to the individual's current needs and to changing resources and treatment results. Indeed, the *Wyatt* standards require that the treatment plan be "continuously reviewed" by the responsible mental-health professional. The findings of periodic reviews should assess the "success and failures of the treatment program" and incorporate in the plan "whatever modifications are necessary."[27] Flexibility in the timing of periodic reviews is implicit in these standards, but statutes require certain types of reviews at stated intervals, in part as a safeguard against the problem of the so-called forgotten patient. In addition to revisions of treatment plans, these reviews may determine a client's suitability and willingness to remain as a voluntary patient, fiscal competency, Medicaid-assistance eligibility, or, if the client is of school age, the need for changes in an individual educational plan. Sometimes these reviews can be jointly scheduled to make the most efficient use of all participants' time.

Participatory Planning

Earlier chapters stressed that the receipt of mental-health services should not lead to a patient's forfeiting his or her right to choose. Clinicians have long encouraged the maximum client participation in the design and carrying out of treatment programs as a therapeutic end in itself. In recognition of these principles, Congress recommended that laws reflect the "right to ongoing participation," in a manner appropriate to the individual's capabilities in the planning of mental-health services.[28] At a minimum, this should include the right to participate in the development and periodic revision of one's own individualized treatment or service plan. For the person who is noncommunicative or nonresponsive, this should require inviting a surrogate, close relative, or other advocate to join the planning process. Progressive state regulations, as well as the federal law on access to special education, already impose a similar obligation.[29] Thus, the law establishes a framework for a planning alliance between advocates and clinicians.

However, participation without adequate information can amount to a hollow gesture. The Medicaid program requires policies and procedures to ensure that all residents are fully informed of their rights, responsibilities, and of all services available in the facility.[30] But the program's intent goes well beyond a paper documentation that facilities have statements of patients' rights and that residents have given written acknowledgment that each has received this information. Instead, each resident must be encouraged and assisted to exercise "his rights as a resident . . . and as a citizen," must be fully informed by a physician of his or her health and medical condition unless this is medically contraindicated, must be given the opportunity to participate in "planning his total care and medical treatment," and must be given the opportunity to refuse treatment.[31] In its recommendations to the states, Congress laid great stress on the mental patient's right to be provided with a reasonable explanation not only of one's general mental and physical condition but also of reasons and options for treatment.[32] In terms appropriate to the person's condition and ability to understand, this explanation should include, but not be limited to, such matters as treatment objectives, possible adverse effects of recommended treatment, and any appropriate and available alternative treatments and services.

Least Restrictive Alternatives

The principle of the least restrictive alternative is emerging as perhaps the central test for accommodating potentially conflicting civil liberties and therapeutic interests. (Indeed, the whole of chapter 6 in this book is devoted to that topic.[33]) The least-restrictive-alternative theory can constitute a constitutional basis for the right to treatment and can offer a legally coherent rationale under which virtually all mental-health patients can demand treatment. According to one commentator, under the standard of review derived from the least-restrictive-alternative principle, "virtually all patients are entitled to superior, individual treatment, irrespective of the purpose of their commitment, unless the state can meet the heavy burden of demonstrating either that treatment would neither hasten release nor enhance freedom within the institution or that confinement with treatment would be less effective" than simple custody in meeting the commitment goals.[34] Given the varieties of treatment, the state would have to sustain a very high evidentiary burden before a patient could be subjected to only a custodial regime.

Protection from Harm

An evolving body of constitutional, administrative, and common law protects the physical and mental integrity of persons living in care facilities. The right to protection from harm, derived from either the constitutional prohibition against "cruel and unusual punishment" or the Fourteenth Amendment requirements of due process, provides an alternative constitutional ground for securing rights to affirmative programming in mental facilities. The court in the *Willowbrook* case was the first to apply this theory to compel remedies and standards to preserve the residents' developmental capacities and ensure therapeutic services to prevent their regression and deterioration. Although those standards sought both to improve institutional conditions and to provide community-based alternatives, the federal court has come to place the highest priority on the creation of community programs as the soundest hope for protecting Willowbrook's residents from abuse and neglect.[35] Similar decisions have been reached in class actions involving the residents of Massachusetts's Northampton State Hospital[36] and Pennsylvania's Pennhurst State School and Hospital.[37] Although the Supreme Court rejected one potential federal statutory basis for that case's deinstitutionalization remedies, a recent Third Circuit opinion has upheld this right to community-living arrangement on the basis of state law.[38]

Mental patients also have legal remedies to ensure their basic safety, health, and security while under residential care. Courts have repeatedly held that patients have rights to be protected from painful behavior-control techniques,[39] corporal punishment,[40] and unsanitary conditions of confinement.[41] Suits by individuals have also sought relief from denial of adequate medical treatment for persons confined to mental-health facilities.[42] The litany of complaints that may lead to judicial or administrative redress are too numerous to list. Serious problems include physical abuse of patients by staff or other patients, overcrowding resulting in lack of privacy, increased aggressive behaviors, health and safety hazards, poor nutrition, inadequate medical and health-related services, and other forms of inhumane care or treatment. Evidence of such patterns and practices may serve as a basis for individual or classwide remedies. Indeed, lawyers may argue that the totality of circumstances, as revealed by these various categories of harm, defeat not only the mental patient's right to treatment but also the right to a minimally wholesome physical and psychological environment.[43]

Humane Treatment Environment

Courts and legislatures have frequently affirmed the right to a humane treatment environment, one that affords reasonable protection from harm and appropriate privacy to a person receiving mental-health services.[44] But of the many specific features that comprise a humane treatment environment, what types of concerns have prompted specific judicial and legislative safeguards? One such area is the right to freedom from unnecessary or excessive restraint or seclusion. Another is the patient's right to protection from unnecessary or excessive medication and to safeguards against drugs as unwarranted chemical restraints. But *Wyatt* and the long line of cases that have followed have added other elements: the rights to wear one's own clothing; to have physical exercise on a regular basis; to go outdoors at frequent intervals; to have interaction with members of the opposite sex; to send sealed mail; and to enjoy visitation and telephone communications with those outside the treatment facilities.[45] Although some of these rights may not be absolute, laws have required that any restrictions imposed by a physician (or other mental-health professional) be only for a specific, limited, and reasonable time, with the reasons for such restriction entered in the patient's medical record. One state, for example, requires that any limitations on visiting must first be discussed with the patient and his or her family. If an agreement is not reached, the treatment team, if it should decide to limit visiting rights, must give reasons and have its decision subject to appeal.[46]

Medicaid and state regulations pose other sources of positive prescription. These include standards designed to ensure a client's health, safety, comfort, and privacy. They may be as specific as requirements that buildings be accessible to and usable by disabled individuals. Or they may emphasize certain liberties such as allowing each resident to participate in "social, religious, and community groups activities" and to use personal possessions and clothing.[47] Clearly, the exact nature of these rights will vary from state to state and according to the nature of the services provided.

Contact with Qualified Professionals

When Kenneth Donaldson's fifteen-year confinement in a state mental hospital was reviewed by the United States Supreme Court, the justices were deeply disturbed by the patterns of inattention it revealed. "For substantial periods, Donaldson was simply kept in a large room that housed 60 patients."[48] The evidence also revealed that his requests for ground privileges, occupational training, and an opportunity to discuss his case with staff members were repeatedly denied. Although the case was decided on the grounds of the deprivation of Donaldson's liberty rather than the denial of his treatment needs, it is clear that the irregularity and superficiality of the treatment staff's contact with Donaldson was a major basis for his judicial victory.

Other cases have required facilities to have a qualified staff in numbers sufficient to administer adequate treatment. Although standards have differed on the required staff complement and staffing ratios, and Medicaid regulations favor a "services for each resident as needed" approach, all would prohibit keeping patients in "cold storage."[49] Without a staff adequate in training, numbers, and compassion, all other rights possessed by the users of mental-health facilities are in jeopardy. Tragically, just as the economic downslide intensifies the demand for mental-health services, government budget cuts threaten the supply of service providers. The gravity of staffing cutbacks is emphasized by the director of one department's office of recipient rights, who observed that:

> The Department of Mental Health can no longer assure, for many recipients in DMH hospitals and centers, the right to a safe environment or the right to treatment suited to condition.
>
> This is not to deny that most people providing direct care to recipients are working hard with the limited resources available, but to acknowledge that these resources are stretched to the point that rights guaranteed by the Mental Health Code cannot help but be violated.[50]

In today's environment of scarcer resources, clients under the umbrella of class-action decrees enjoy greater protection than their peers. So, too, may the personnel who work with them. Where the constitutional rights of class clients are at stake, advocates and clinicians possess legal and political tools to resist the dismantling of treatment programs. For instance, a recent court order prevented the reduction of 408 staff positions at state institutions, reductions inimical to the clients' treatment rights and based not on clinical considerations but on predetermined dollar savings.[51] In the federal judge's words, these massive firings would have resulted in a return to the "medieval custodial practices of a decade ago."[52] One lesson from all this is clear: coalitions between advocates and mental-health-service providers for clients' rights are imperative.

The Impact of the Right

Courts, legislatures, and executive agencies have had nearly a decade of experience in implementing the right to treatment. But the jury is still out on precisely what that experience has meant for the lives of its intended beneficiaries—the consumers of mental-health services. In those cases in which the courts and the parties have maintained a close review of compliance with reform decrees, there are real gains: humane deinstitutionalization, an increase in quality community-care living arrangements, and incremental improvements in treatment and care conditions even in traditional settings. But responses to these decrees have by no means been uniform, and large questions shadow the enterprise of legal reform of mental-health systems. Here are four of the thorniest:

1. Will voluntary patients share in the fruits of the right to treatment? One irony in the declining use of involuntary commitment is its impact on the reach of certain constitutional arguments for the right to treatment. Since the constitutional right stems from the protections against deprivation of liberty, "voluntary" patients who are truly free to leave may be unable to pose an enforceable release-or-treat claim. The pioneering lawsuits on treatment adequacy were brought by persons confined as criminally insane or by institutional residents who were, nominally or in fact, the involuntary subjects of care and treatment. Do the residents of a community-care facility who can actually leave at anytime have the same right? The answers to that dilemma may well be found in statutory rather than constitutional law and in the obligations that a state creates or its vendors assume when they accept a person for care and treatment. Indeed, federal and state statutes increasingly recognize the mentally disabled person's right to active treatment, a right guaranteed without distinction as to the patient's voluntary or involuntary status.[53]

2. Are there any settings in which the right to treatment is either infeasible or counterproductive? Imagine an isolated, large-scale custodial institution. Can it ever attract a sufficient staff of qualified professionals and create conditions conducive to normalized, least restrictive treatment? That concern is at the heart of the *Pennhurst* and *Willowbrook* class actions, legal sagas in which federal judges tenaciously enforce sweeping community-based remedies. Although those cases involve state schools for the mentally retarded, their ultimate outcome will have reverberations for all types of mental-care systems. But the problem of deficient care goes beyond the custodial institution and what nine Supreme Court justices may choose to say, or not to say, in confronting stark and novel legal questions. For example, people with mental disabilities may be isolated in callous board-and-care homes that are insensitive to their social and treatment

needs. Some nursing homes also prove wholly inappropriate and restrictive settings for a mental patient's care and treatment. Securing the right to treatment on a broad basis for many clients will therefore mean adopting multifaceted advocacy strategies to increase the supplies of decent community-based alternatives. Federal class-action litigation is but a harbinger of such strategies and the search for more precisely drawn remedial legislation.

3. The looming question is whether governments at national, state, and local levels will ensure the resources for the right to treatment in effective community settings. Commentators have frequently criticized the perverse subsidies and disincentives that encourage the use of the most costly and restrictive form of assistance—institutionalization. Scholars and practitioners also fear that community care "on the cheap" will damage the credibility of alternatives and create new victims of societal neglect. As the U.S. comptroller general concluded, federal agencies must bear a share of this blame for their failure to develop "a comprehensive and clearly defined national plan" to achieve the long-established national goal of positive deinstitutionalization of the mentally disabled.[54] In a time of budget austerity, these critiques will fuel demands for redirecting the expenditure of public monies away from costly but substandard facilities to expand the continuum of community-based services and residences.

A number of states have begun to require such a redirection of resources. For example, Florida law acknowledges that institutions "are unreasonably costly, are ineffective in bringing the individual client to his or her maximum potential, and are in fact debilitating to the great majority of clients."[55] Like Florida, other states may soon commit themselves to "a redirection in state treatment programs" to give "greatest priority . . . to the development and implementation of community-based residential placements, services and treatment programs."[56]

Litigation challenging deficiencies in the mental-health system may play a part in spurring this reallocation. As a result of the *Wyatt* decision, funds supporting community-based services in that state expanded almost tenfold over a six-year period. But given the primitive condition of those services in prelitigation days, the largest absolute increases in Alabama's mental-health expenditures have gone to upgrading the institutional sector. More recent cases have shunned this direction. Advocates and providers have instead attempted to focus reform energies on bolstering the malnourished community-care sector. Indeed, much of the newer litigation rests on the policy consensus that government has the responsibility to provide treatment in less restrictive settings. The problem comes in overcoming the roadblocks to implementing this policy.

4. Another difficult issue centers on who reviews the adequacy of treatment when the patient raises this objection. The law clearly holds that the

mental patient's complaint on treatment adequacy can present a justiciable question, that is, a dispute within the competence of a judge to decide.[57] Although courts have the ability to formulate judicially manageable standards in determining the right to treatment, and in administering the claim to a remedy, it does not mean that they are the preferred forum for hearing all, or even a majority of, such cases. Many states now offer the patient a chance to be heard by a neutral arbiter without the need to go before a court. Along with patient-advocacy plans, such arrangements give patients an alternative to exhausting their energies in otherwise futile petitions up the bureaucratic chain of command. Individual-service-plan reviews, grievance procedures, human-rights committees, and other innovative devices present alternate ways to interpret broad guidelines, test the adequacy of treatment plans, and fashion a speedy, efficient remedy. The right to treatment is now a legal reality. However, it could become little more than a noble ideal unless coupled at a ground level with the resources, mechanisms, and clinicians' commitments to make it a concrete reality.

Notes

1. Greenblatt, *Class Action and the Right to Treatment,* 25 Hosp. and Community Psychiatry 449, 452 (1974).

2. Wyatt v. Stickney, 325 F. Supp. 781, 785 (M.D. Ala. 1971). The *Wyatt* court adopted comparable standards for the adequate habilitation of mentally retarded persons. *See* S. Herr, The New Clients: Legal Services for Mentally Retarded Citizens (1979).

3. Wyatt v. Stickney, 344 F. Supp. 373, 379-386 (M.D. Ala. 1972).

4. Wyatt v. Aderholt, 503 F.2d 1305, 1315 (5th Cir. 1974).

5. *See* O'Connor v. Donaldson, 422 U.S. 563 (1975). In a recent unanimous decision, the Court has, however, affirmed the right to adequate training to ensure safety and freedom from undue restraint for a profoundly retarded, involuntary resident. Youngberg v. Romeo, 102 S. Ct. 2452 (1982), discussed in chapter 6, *infra.*

6. *See* McRedmond v. Wilson, 533 F.2d 757, 762 (2d Cir. 1976).

7. Federal Security Agency, A Draft Act Governing Hospitalization of the Mentally Ill §19 (Public Health Service Publ. no. 51, Sept. 1952).

8. *See, e.g.,* N.Y. Mental Hyg. Law §33.03(a) (McKinney 1978); Fla. Stat. Ann. §394.459 (1), (2), (4)(a) (West Supp. 1982).

9. American Psychiatric Association, *Position Statement on the Right to Adequate Care and Treatment for the Mentally Ill and Mentally Retarded,* 134 Am. J. Psychiatry 354 (1977).

10. Birnbaum, *The Right to Treatment*, 46 A.B.A. J. 499 (1960).

11. Rouse v. Cameron, 373 F.2d 451 (D.C. Cir. 1966).

12. *E.g.*, Wyatt v. Aderholt, 503 F.2d 1305, 1314 (5th Cir. 1974).

13. *E.g.*, Dixon v. Weinberger, 405 F. Supp. 974 (D.D.C. 1975); Lake v. Cameron, 364 F.2d 657 (D.C. Cir. 1966).

14. *E.g.*, Welsch v. Likins, 373 Supp. 487, *aff'd.* 550 F.2d 1122 (8th Cir. 1977). For a comprehensive analysis, see S. Herr, Rights and Advocacy for Retarded People (1983).

15. *E.g.*, Nelson v. Heyne, 491 F.2d 352 (7th Cir. 1974).

16. *E.g.*, Gary W. v. Louisiana, 437 F. Supp. 1209 (E.D. La. 1976).

17. Newman v. Alabama, 349 F. Supp. 278, *aff'd*, 503 F.2d 1320 (5th Cir. 1974), *cert. denied*, 421 U.S. 948 (1975); Pugh v. Locke, 406 F. Supp. 318, 333 (M.D. Ala. 1976); Klein, *Prisoners' Rights to Physical and Mental Health Care*, 7 Fordham Urb. L.J. 1 (1978).

18. Lora v. N.Y. City Board of Education, 456 F. Supp. 1211 (E.D.N.Y. 1978), *vacated on other grounds*, 623 F.2d 248 (2d Cir. 1980).

19. 42 U.S.C. §1396(d)(2)(1974); 42 C.F.R. §441.154 (1981).

20. Joint Commission on Accreditation of Hospitals, Consolidated Standards Manual for Child Adolescent, and Adult Psychiatric, Alcoholism, and Drug Abuse Facilities (1981 ed.); Accreditation Council for Services for Mentally Retarded and Other Developmentally Disabled Persons, Standards for Services for Developmentally Disabled Persons (1980); Schoenfeld, *Human Rights for the Mentally Retarded: Their Recognition by the Providers of Services*, 4 Human Rights 31 (1974). See *supra*, note 9.

21. 42 C.F.R. §442.311(g)(1) (1981).

22. Mental Health Systems Act, 42 U.S.C. §9501(1)(A) (1981 Pamphlet).

23. 42 C.F.R. §442.319 (1981).

24. Wyatt v. Stickney, 344 F. Supp. 373, 384-5 (M.D. Ala. 1972) (Standards 26-31); Davis v. Watkins, 384 F. Supp. 1196, 1203-06 (N.D. Ohio 1974).

25. *See, e.g.*, N.J. Stat. Ann. §30:6D-10 (West 1981); Cal. Welf. and Inst. Code §5352.6 (West Supp. 1982).

26. O'Connor v. Donaldson, 422 U.S. 563 (1975); U.S. *ex.rel.* Schuster v. Vincent, 524 F.2d 153, 158 (2d Cir. 1975) ("undisputed tendency of prolonged confinement in a mental hospital to exacerbate rather than alleviate any pre-existing condition").

27. Wyatt v. Stickney, 344 F. Supp. 373, 384 (M.D. Ala. 1972)(Standards 29 and 31 g).

28. Mental Health Systems Act, *supra* note 22, §9501(1)(C).

29. N.J. Stat. Ann. §30-4-24.1 (West 1981); Massachusetts Department of Mental Health, *Mental Health Regulations,* Mass. Admin. Code tit. 104 §16.05(2)(c)(1981); 20 U.S.C. §§1414(a)(1)(C)(iii), 1415 (1978).

30. 42 C.F.R. §442.311(a) (1981).

31. *Id.* §§442.311(d)(1), (b)(1)(i)-(iii).

32. 42 U.S.C. §9501 (1)(C)(i)-(vi). *See* President's Commission on Mental Health, 1 Report to the President 43-44, 72 (1978).

33. On the principle of the least restrictive alternative in the field of mental retardation, see S. Herr, Rights and Advocacy for Retarded People (1983).

34. Spece, *Preserving the Right to Treatment: A Critical Assessment and Constructive Development of Constitutional Right to Treatment Theories,* 20 Ariz. L. Rev. 1, 36-38 (1978).

35. New York State Ass'n for Retarded Children v. Carey, 393 F. Supp. 715 (E.D.N.Y. 1975); No. 72 Civ. 356/357 (slip op. of June 10, 1977) (transfers barred to newly constructed, but isolated, 250-bed facility). *See* 466 F. Supp. 479, 485 (E.D.N.Y. 1978), *aff'd* 612 F.2d, 644 (2d Cir. 1979); No. 72 Civ. 356/357 (slip op. of April 28, 1982) (consent-decree limitations on community placements in 10- to 15-bed facilities upheld).

36. Brewster v. Dukakis, No. 76-4423-F (D.Mass. Dec. 6, 1978).

37. Halderman v. Pennhurst State School and Hospital, 446 F. Supp. 1295 (E.D.Pa. 1977), *aff'd in part, remanded in part,* 612 F.2d 84 (3rd Cir. 1979), *rev'd and remanded,* 451 U.S. 1 (1981).

38. Halderman v. Pennhurst State School and Hospital, 673 F.2d 647 (3rd Cir. 1982) (independent state law adequate to support remedial order), *rev'd and remanded,* 104 S.Ct. 900 (1984).

39. *E.g.,* Wyatt v. Stickney, 344 F. Supp. 373 (M.D. Ala. 1972); Gundy v. Pauley, 619 S.W.2d 730 (Ky. App. 1981) (refusal of electroshock therapy).

40. *E.g.,* Wheeler v. Glass, 473 F.2d 983 (7th Cir. 1973) (residents bound and spread-eagled to a bed for 77.5 hours).

41. *E.g.,* Rozecki v. Gaughan, 459 F.2d 6 (1st Cir. 1972); New York State Ass'n for Retarded Children, *supra* note 35, slip op. at 10-13 (E.D.N.Y. April 28, 1982).

42. Scott v. Plante, 641 F.2d 117 (3rd Cir. 1981); Smith v. Wendell, No. 74-2779 (E.D. Pa., Feb. 28, 1975) (denial of medical treatment for patient's known heart ailment in state mental hospital actionable under the Civil Rights Act).

43. *See* Wyatt v. Stickney, 344 F. Supp. 373 (M.D. Ala. 1972); Rone v. Fireman, 473 F. Supp. 92 (N.D. Ohio 1979).

44. *See* 42 U.S.C. §9501(1)(G) (1981 Pamphlet); Herr, *Rights of Disabled Persons: International Principles and American Experiences,* 12 Colum. Human Rights L. Rev. 1, 46-50 (1980).

45. Wyatt v. Stickney, 344 F. Supp. 373, 379 (Standards 4-5, 11-17).

46. New York State Office of Mental Health, Rights of Patients in Psychiatric Centers of the New York State Office of Mental Health 6 (1981).

47. 42 C.F.R. §442.311(j)(k) (1981).

48. O'Connor v. Donaldson, 422 U.S. 563, 569 (1975).

49. *Compare, "Wyatt Standards" Found to Be Widely Observed,* Psychiatric News, Oct. 21, 1977, at 1 *with* 42 C.F.R. §442.342-344 (1981) (nursing care, rehabilitative and social services provided "as needed").

50. Memorandum from Janet Coye, director, Michigan Office of Recipient Rights to Frank M. Ochberg, director, Department of Mental Health (Aug. 25, 1980). Reprinted with permission.

51. Ricci v. Okin, No. 72-469-T (D. Mass. April 21, 1982) Order and slip op.

52. *Id.* at 20. *See also,* Brewster v. Dukakis, No. 81-1688 (1st Cir. March 24, 1982) (state officials legally obligated to use best efforts to ensure compliance with consent decree).

53. *E.g.,* Social Security Act, *supra* note 19; Mental Health Systems Act, 42 U.S.C. §9501 (1981 Pamphlet); Developmental Disabilities Assistance and Bill of Rights Act, 42 U.S.C. §6010 (1977); N.J. Stat. Ann. §§30.4-24.1 (West 1981); Cal. Welf. & Inst. Code §5325.1(a) (West Supp. 1982). On the voluntary patient's constitutional right to treatment, see Seide v. Prevost, 536 F. Supp. 1121, 1136 (S.D.N.Y. 1982).

54. U.S. Comptroller General, Returning the Mentally Disabled to the Community: Government Needs to Do More (1977).

55. Fla. Stat. Ann. §393.062 (Supp. 1982).

56. *Id. See also,* Fla. Stat. Ann. §394.453 (Supp. 1982).

57. O'Connor v. Donaldson, 422 U.S. 563, 574 n. 10 (1975); Wyatt v. Aderholt, 503 F.2d 1305 (5th Cir. 1974).

The Right to Refuse Treatment

The right to refuse treatment is unquestionably the most controversial subject in mental-health law today. There is little room for controversy over the existence of the right, for courts have settled that dispute. Several courts, federal and state, have affirmed that even involuntarily confined mental patients have a qualified constitutional right to refuse treatment. The focus of the controversy is on the nature and extent of the qualifications.

Reduced to its most simple form, the right to refuse treatment is merely a corollary of the legal requirement of informed consent prior to treatment, described in chapter 3. As explained in that chapter, the administration of even beneficial treatment without consent is prohibited as unlawful assault and battery. And that prohibition has been enforced by Anglo-American law for more than two centuries now. Against this historical background, the basic right to refuse treatment appears well established indeed.

What remains unsettled is the application of this time-honored, fundamental right to modern treatment modalities in modern psychiatric institutions. In years past, state psychiatric hospitals, by and large, were excepted from the general rules of consent and refusal; individuals entering the hospitals left their rights to decline treatment at the door. The last decade saw several challenges to this de facto exception in lawsuits brought by state-hospital patients from Massachusetts, New Jersey, Ohio, Oklahoma, and elsewhere. The challenges were successful. Courts extended the general rules to institutional settings, with special qualifications.

Significantly, the general rules have applied since their inception outside of the institutions. No exceptions have been recognized for community mental-health programs, and even today the right of clients in community programs to refuse treatment is in several respects stronger than that of institutionalized patients. Of course, the line between institutions and community programs is not always easy to draw. Some standards for distinguishing between them will be set forth later in this chapter, along with an explanation of how the limitations placed on the right to refuse by recent court decisions might apply in community settings. First, however, an overview of the recent cases will introduce the qualifications and the controversies that surround them.

Recent Case Law

By far, the most important cases raising the right to refuse treatment are *Rennie* v. *Klein*,[1] from New Jersey, and *Rogers* v. *Okin*, from Massachusetts.[2] The facts presented by the two cases are strikingly similar. Both were class actions brought by patients of state hospitals. Both asserted the right to refuse treatment by antipsychotic medication. Both were first decided by federal district courts in 1979. And both were appealed to and decided by federal circuit courts.

The two district and two circuit courts all upheld what one described as "an intuitively obvious proposition: a person has a constitutionally protected interest in being left free by the state to decide for himself whether to submit to the serious and potentially harmful medical treatment that is represented by the administration of antipsychotic drugs."[3] They expressed a variety of opinions, however, on the qualifications to this constitutional right.

The particular limitations announced in the *Rennie* and *Rogers* decisions are not immutable rules binding throughout the mental-health system. Rather, they are guideposts that mark a general course to be followed by psychiatric professionals. This is so largely because the qualifications were tailored for the particular institutions and individuals before the courts. More importantly, courts and legislatures in other jurisdictions can be expected to differ with the *Rennie* and *Rogers* courts on both the fine points and the balances struck. Finally, it must be noted that the *Rennie* and *Rogers* decisions are no longer binding, even in the jurisdictions where they were rendered, because both have been vacated by the United States Supreme Court. The Supreme Court vacated *Rogers* because, while an appeal of that case was pending before the Court, the highest court in Massachusetts ruled in an unrelated action that state law grants mental patients a right to refuse treatment.[4] The Supreme Court suggested that the newly announced state ruling might provide a more thorough remedy than the federal constitutional minima announced in the *Rogers* decision. Thus, the justices vacated the *Rogers* decision and remanded the case for consideration in accordance with the intervening state court decision. Similarly, the Supreme Court vacated *Rennie,* while an appeal of that case was pending, because the Supreme Court issued its own decision in an unrelated but analogous case, *Youngberg* v. *Romeo,* described in chapter 6. In the *Youngberg* case, the Supreme Court ruled on issues of treatment in institutions for developmentally disabled persons. It remanded the *Rennie* case for further consideration in accordance with its *Youngberg* opinion. The Supreme Court's actions transform the *Rogers* and *Rennie* decisions from binding case law to nonbinding judicial opinions. The opinions remain valuable as guideposts, but only as guideposts.

In framing the scope of the right to refuse, the courts have articulated two important limitations, described in turn in the following subsections.

Treatment in Emergencies

Relevant court decisions all recognize that forced medication must be permitted in certain emergencies, at least in institutions. But the decisions present diverse opinions on the question of what constitutes an emergency. The lower court in *Rogers*, for one, held that nothing short of a "substantial likelihood of physical harm" could justify emergency medication.[5] The *Rogers* appellate court rejected this narrow definition of emergency, ruling that psychiatrists must be allowed wider latitude in deciding when antipsychotic drugs are necessary to prevent harm. Still, the appellate court stressed that emergency medication is permissible only to avert physical violence and only when no less intrusive action would suffice.[6] Thus, it joined with the lower court in rejecting a broader definition proffered by the defendants and the American Psychiatric Association as amicus curiae. That definition would have allowed forced medication during "psychiatric emergencies," meaning circumstances that threaten a client's mental condition but not his physical well-being.

In general then, clinicians in institutional settings are accorded considerable discretion in deciding when drugs are necessary to prevent violence. But that discretion is bounded by a set of unyielding rules. The decision to medicate must be made by a qualified physician. Less restrictive alternatives to medication must be insufficient. And the primary purpose of the medication must be to mitigate a physical emergency, not merely to treat.[7]

A further limitation might be implied from the case law: the emergency exception might apply only in institutional settings. The courts have not been called on to decide whether the exception applies in community-based programs, but there are indications that it does not. The rulings upholding the exception in institutions emphasize the extraordinary levels of tension and danger that characterize many institutional wards. In the words of the First Circuit Court of Appeals, "we deal with an institution to which many individuals are involuntarily committed because of a demonstrated proclivity for committing acts of violence. . . . The volatility of a large concentration of such individuals adds substance and immediacy to the state's concern in preventing violence."[8]

Insofar as the legal authority to prevent violence by forced medication is based on these special concerns, that power may be limited to institutions. Whether courts will so limit it is a question for the future. For the present, clinicians in noninstitutional programs should devise procedures for averting violence that employ the wide variety of techniques, well documented in professional literature, short of forced medication.[9]

Treatment of Incompetent Clients in Institutions

Litigation in the *Rennie* and *Rogers* cases focused heavily on the issue of whether clients with seriously impaired judgment can decline treatment. From this heated aspect of the litigation emerged one clear rule on which all four courts agreed: all persons are presumed competent and remain so unless found legally incompetent by judicial proceedings; and all presumptively competent voluntary patients may refuse medication, subject only to the emergency exception.

The courts diverged somewhat in regard to incompetent patients. The lower court in *Rogers* held that incompetent patients, like others, cannot be medicated without consent except in emergencies, and furthermore, only a patient's legal guardian can supply the necessary consent. The appellate courts in both *Rogers* and *Rennie* prescribed procedures giving greater leeway to attending clinicians. The *Rennie* court, for example, would permit teams of clinicians, acting according to specified procedures, to override ill-advised decisions of guardians, or to make independent treatment decisions when it is impracticable to secure guardian consent.

Thus, an exception to the right to refuse was established, permitting nonconsensual medication of incompetent clients. But the exception arises only in respect to clients judicially declared incompetent. And the courts stated in no uncertain terms that a judicial finding of mental illness and involuntary commitment does not amount to a declaration of incompetence.

Still, involuntary commitment may provide the basis for a third exception to the right to refuse. The appeals court in *Rennie* ruled that a committed patient may be medicated against his will if "without [medication], the patient is incapable of participating in any treatment plan that will give him a realistic opportunity to improve his condition, or if it will shorten the required commitment time."[10]

It is uncertain whether other jurisdictions will recognize a similar exception for involuntary patients. The *Rogers* court expressly rejected such an exception, as did a federal court in Ohio,[11] and the Supreme Court of Oklahoma.[12] Those courts reasoned that, absent an emergency, the sole justification for medication is to help the recipient patient; and, absent a finding of incompetence, all persons, including those involuntarily confined, have a right to decide whether and how they wish to be helped. The controversy over this issue, evinced by the inconsistent court rulings on the matter, promises to figure prominently on court dockets and legislative schedules for some time to come.

Origins of the Right to Refuse

Before considering the right to refuse in the context of community-based programs, it should help to understand the legal origins of the right. As noted earlier, the right can be traced back to English common law that predates our own constitution. Indeed, one recent federal decision traces the right to refuse to the year 1215, to what most authorities agree was the world's first constitution, the Magna Carta.[13] These early sources of law established a right of personal security, of freedom from unauthorized invasions of bodily integrity. That nonconsensual medical treatment constitutes such an invasion was recognized by U.S. courts over a hundred years ago.[14]

More recently, courts have rested the right to refuse on various constitutional bases. The constitutional provision forming the strongest basis is the due process clause of the Fourteenth Amendment. That clause incorporates the common-law guarantees of privacy, bodily integrity, and personal security.[15] Among other constitutional guarantees cited as supporting the right to refuse are the First Amendment rights to free belief, free speech, and the included freedom to generate ideas,[16] and the Eighth Amendment right to be free from harm or cruel and unusual punishment.[17]

Although these constitutional bases form the foundation for the right to refuse, recognition of the right in recent years has been spurred largely by nonlegal concerns. It is no coincidence that the right has emerged during a period of growing awareness, in the community at large as well as in legal and psychiatric circles, of the competence, the capabilities, and the human dignity of people deemed mentally ill. At the same time, skepticism of the psychiatric profession has risen. In calling for increased client participation in treatment decisions, proponents of the right to refuse point to a host of shortcomings in both the profession and the state of the science. No doubt, the reader has heard or engaged in debates over some of these asserted shortcomings: the fallability of diagnoses and treatment choices; the dangers, side effects, and questionable benefit of psychotropic drugs; the intrusiveness of forced treatment of any sort; the ineffectiveness of one-sided therapy, where the client is but a passive recipient; the double-agent function of psychiatry, policing and treating at once; and the many, if isolated, incidents of mistreatment and abuse of authority that taint the system.[18]

These are among the nonlegal origins of the right to refuse. Together with the constitutional and common-law bases for the right, they determine the applications and set the boundaries of the right in noninstitutional contexts.

The Right to Refuse in Community Programs

The foregoing discussion has focused on the institutional context for the basic reason that case law on the right to refuse has concerned institutions exclusively.[19] Moreover, the case law, like the discussion thus far, has focused exclusively on one mode of treatment, antipsychotic medication.

The singular focus of the case law can be explained by two observations. First, medication is rarely, if ever, forcibly administered in noninstitutional programs. Insofar as it may be forcibly administered, it is done so unlawfully, for the law is well settled on this score: "An individual who has not been committed to a mental institution has a right to refuse medication sought to be administered against his will."[20] Second, nonconsensual treatment less intrusive than psychotropic medication has not been brought to the attention of the courts. Simply put, a client forced to accept counselling or group therapy, for instance, has no wish "to make a federal case out of it," in either the colloquial or the literal sense. That is not to say that the client has no right to refuse such mild treatment but only that enforcing the right by litigation is too troublesome and expensive. Moreover, clients generally can avail themselves of faster and more accessible grievance procedures.

In any event, the result is an absence of case law concerning the right to refuse in community programs. The absence leaves open two important questions: first, can antipsychotic medication be forced on a client in a community program under emergency circumstances? Second, what right has a community-based client to refuse treatment other than antipsychotic medication?

Before answering, it is necessary to define a community program, as distinct from an institution. The distinction is somewhat muted. In general, a facility to which persons may be involuntarily committed is considered to be institutional. For the purpose of applying the right to refuse, that is the chief distinction. To the extent that the law permits emergency medication against a client's will, it does so largely in response to the security and management problems that beset facilities to which dangerous clients are committed. Moreover, the only nonemergency exception announced in the case law—and only in one jurisdiction, at that—pertains to involuntary clients. Thus, the right to refuse antipsychotic medication seems to be unqualified in facilities that do not confine involuntary patients. These we may call community programs.

Still, many facilities that do accept involuntary clients are nonetheless noninstitutional, either because they are relatively small or because they provide only nonresidential services. Examples include group homes, sheltered workshops, and day-treatment centers. Although individuals may be involuntarily committed to programs of this sort, the programs are best categorized as community, not institutional, facilities for present purposes. The reason is that they do not suffer the management and security problems that typify the large state institutions. Consequently, they cannot claim the same need for forcible medication that justifies the emergency exception in the large, residential, and often volatile state institutions.

In sum, the precedents suggest that the emergency exception will be permitted only in large, residential facilities to which patients are involuntarily confined.

The question remains whether, and under what circumstances, treatment other than by antipsychotic medication might be administered over a client's objection. It should go without saying that certain types of extraordinarily intrusive forms of treatment cannot be involuntarily administered under any circumstances without a special court order. Although there are statutory variations, the direction is toward prohibition of nonconsensual psychosurgery, sterilization, and electroconvulsive therapy.[21] The real grey area concerns the less intrusive treatment modes: group counselling; instruction in activities of daily living; nonaversive behavior modification; occupational therapy, and the like.

The legal origins of the right to refuse suggest that a distinction might be drawn along lines of intrusiveness. Indeed, at least one state court has done as much.[22] It is clear from all the cases that a client's right to refuse becomes stronger as the treatment proffered becomes more invasive, more dangerous, and more likely to produce painful side effects. Conversely, it may be that the right weakens as the treatment in controversy becomes less intrusive and dangerous. In other words, the foundational interests that support the right to refuse—the interests of personal security, bodily integrity, freedom from harm, and freedom of thought and belief—are threatened less by group therapy, for instance, than by a shot in the buttocks of phenothiazine. The question, then, is whether the client interests threatened by group therapy and similarly nonintrusive treatments are strong enough, and the threat itself severe enough, to warrant an absolute right to refuse.

For involuntary clients, the answer seems to be no. Commitment to a treatment program, institutional or community, does not deprive one of a limited right to refuse psychotropic medication, but it does constitute an order to accept less intrusive forms of treatment. In this regard, it probably matters not whether the program is community-based or institutional, large or small.

For voluntary clients, the answer would be quite the opposite. By definition, a voluntary client in any program retains an unqualified right to refuse any mode of treatment. This unyielding rule begs yet another question: how is a program to respond to a voluntary client who declines a particular form of treatment? Must the program provide what the client desires and only what the client desires? Or must the client accept what is offered on threat of expulsion?

The question was addressed squarely in the *Rogers* case, and the district and circuit courts reached opposite conclusions. The lower court held that voluntary patients in the institution could refuse medication with impunity; the hospital was forbidden from discharging them upon refusal, for fear that threats of discharge would be used to coerce consent to medication.[23] The appellate court reversed on this point, ruling that voluntary patients have no constitutional right "to dictate to the hospital staff the treatment that they are given."[24]

The appellate court was undoubtedly correct. Still, clients do have a constitutionally based right to treatment, as the preceding chapter on that subject explains. And their right to refuse treatment cannot be extinguished by coercive threats of expulsion. There is no short answer to the knotty dilemma. Plainly enough, clients are not entitled to prescribe their own courses of treatment. They are entitled, however, to options, to choices from among available treatment modes. The clinician's obligation is merely to make appropriate treatment available, not to demand that it be accepted. On the other hand, clients who refuse the full gamut of appropriate therapies cannot assert a right to more; they cannot force clinicians to provide the inappropriate. Nor, however, can clinicians force clients to choose between a single form of treatment and no treatment at all. A balance must be struck between the client's interests in free choice and the clinician's interest in maintaining professional standards of quality in treatment.

Perhaps the best indication of the law's direction on this issue is the federal Mental Health Systems Act. That act expressly does not "prevent" programs from discharging clients when "the provision of appropriate treatment . . . has become impossible as a result of such person's refusal to consent to such treatment." The act does not actually authorize discharge, and it may even be read as prohibiting it where the client is willing to accept some form of appropriate treatment. But it does suggest that programs are free to expel clients who refuse all "appropriate treatment, consistent with the professional judgment of the person primarily responsible for such person's treatment."[25]

Incompetent Clients, Community Programs, and the Right to Refuse

It has already been noted that incompetency forms a sort of exception to the right to refuse. One who is legally incompetent may be forced to accept treatment if consent to the treatment is furnished by that person's legally appointed guardian. Still, as the chapters on competency and guardianship explain, incompetent clients should be permitted to make decisions within their capabilities. Thus, if a person under guardianship can rationally choose between treatment modes, that choice warrants respect by both the guardian and the clinician.

As previously mentioned, the courts have shown a willingness to permit psychiatrists in institutions to prescribe medication for incompetent patients in extenuating circumstances without first securing guardian consent. Nothing in these court decisions, however, suggests that similar latitude will be accorded to clinicians in community programs. Like the emergency exception, this deviation from the general rule of law requiring guardian consent rests on the exigencies of institutional conditions. In institutions, budgetary constraints and staff shortages combine with extraordinarily high rates of incompetency among severely disturbed patients, making the requirement of substituted consent largely impracticable.[26] Because community programs are not so constrained, they will not likely be exempt from the guardian-consent requirement. Even in institutional settings, however, the courts may insist on administrative procedures by which independent third parties make treatment decisions for incompetent clients in the stead of guardians.[27] Thus, some form of substituted consent is always required for the treatment of incompetent clients.

In sum, then, the incompetency exception to the right to refuse permits forcible treatment only of persons judicially declared incompetent and only when substituted consent is provided. And it must be emphasized that legally competent clients, however irrational or functionally incapacitated, enjoy the same right to refuse as the most sane and solid among us. The courts have been unequivocal on this point.

> The very foundation of the doctrine of [informed consent] is every man's right to forego treatment or even cure if it entails what *for him* are intolerable consequences or risks, however warped or perverted his sense of values may be in the eyes of the medical profession, or even of the community, so long as any distortion falls short of what the law regards as incompetency. Individual freedom here is guaranteed only if people are given the right to make choices which would generally be regarded as foolish.[28]

Conclusion

The law has yet to specify the exact dimensions of the right to refuse. Nevertheless, the law has pronounced some settled principles, and these will surely guide future efforts to resolve the many questions and conflicts that remain. Increasingly, these principles are being incorporated into state statutes and regulations. At present, most state laws on the right to refuse concern only the more intrusive forms of treatment: psychosurgery, electroshock, and drug experimentation.[29] If, as Congress and the President's Commission on Mental Health have recommended, states add the right to refuse to their statutory lists of patients' rights, then legislatures will play active roles in resolving the remaining questions and in further refining the governing principles.[30]

For now, much is left to the clinician's discretion. In exercising that discretion, the clinician would do well to bear in mind that it is the client, above all others, who will bear the consequences of a treatment decision; who will suffer the side effects; who will feel better or worse, improve or decompensate. Only the right to be let alone, to be unwise, allows the client to bear those consequences with dignity.

Notes

1. 462 F. Supp. 1131 (D.N.J. 1978) (on motion for preliminary injunction), 476 F. Supp. 1294 (D.N.J. 1979) (classwide preliminary injunction issued), *aff'd in part, modified in part, and remanded,* 653 F.2d 836 (3d Cir. 1981), *vacated and remanded,* 458 U.S. 1119 (1982).

2. 478 F. Supp. 1342 (D.Mass. 1979), *aff'd in part, rev'd in part, vacated in part and remanded,* 634 F.2d 650 (1st cir. 1980), *vacated and remanded sub nom.* Mills v. Rogers, 102 S.Ct. 2442 (1982).

3. Rogers v. Okin, 634 F.2d at 653.

4. In the Matter of Guardianship of Richard Roe, III, 1981 Mass. Adv. Sh. 981, 421 N.E. 2d 40 (1981). Since the first printing of this book, the Massachusetts Supreme Judicial Court (SJC) has ruled on the many controversial issues raised in the *Rogers* case. After the U.S. Supreme Court vacated the prior federal-court decisions in *Rogers,* the federal appeals court submitted to the SJC a list of questions to determine Massachusetts law on the right to refuse. In response, the SJC rendered a detailed opinion that reflects not only its own in-depth analysis, but also the positions of a host of organizations that pled their views before the SJC. Rogers v. Comm'r of the Dept. of Mental Health, 390 Mass. 489, 458 N.E.2d 308 (1983). In short, the SJC held that all competent persons, including involuntarily committed patients, enjoy the right to refuse antipsychotic drugs except in emergencies.

5. Rogers v. Okin, 478 F. Supp. at 1365.

6. *Id.,* 634 F.2d at 656. *But see,* Rogers v. Comm'r of the Dept. of Mental Health, 390 Mass. at 503, 458 N.E.2d at 322 (under Massachusetts law, an institutionalized patient who seems incompetent, but has not been so found by a court, may be forcibly medicated pending adjudication of competency "in rare circumstances . . . to prevent the 'immediate, substantial, and irreversible deterioration of a serious mental illness' ").

7. *See, e.g.,* Rennie v. Klein, 653 F.2d at 846-48; Rogers v. Okin, 634 F.2d at 656; Davis v. Hubbard, 506 F. Supp. 915, 934-35 (N.D. Ohio 1980).

8. Rogers v. Okin, 634 F.2d at 656.

9. See, for example, Crain & Jordan, *The Psychiatric Intensive Care Unit: An In-Hospital Treatment of Violent Adult Patients*, 7 Bull. Am. Acad. of Psychiatry & L. 190 (1979).

10. Rennie v. Klein, 653 F.2d at 848.

11. Davis v. Hubbard, 506 F. Supp. at 935-37.

12. *In re* K.K.B., 609 P.2d 747, 750 (Okla. 1980).

13. Davis v. Hubbard, 506 F. Supp. at 931.

14. Munn v. Illinois, 94 U.S. 113, 142 (1876) (Field, J., dissenting). *See also,* Union Pacific Railway Co. v. Botsford, 141 U.S. 250, 251 (1891).

15. Rennie v. Klein, 653 F.2d at 843-44; Rogers v. Okin, 634 F.2d at 653; Davis v. Hubbard, 506 F. Supp. at 931-33.

16. *See, e.g.,* Mackey v. Procunier, 477 F.2d 877,878 (9th Cir. 1973); Winters v. Miller, 446 F.2d 65 (2d Cir.), *cert. denied,* 404 U.S. 985 (1971). *See generally,* Barnhart, Pinkerton & Roth, *Informed Consent to Organic Behavior Control,* 17 Santa Clara Law. 39 (1977); Lafferty, Lawrence, & Lusvardi, *A Mental Patient's Right to Refuse Antipsychotic Drugs: A Constitutional Right Needing Protection,* 57 Notre Dame Law. 406 (1981).

17. *See, e.g.,* Scott v. Plante, 532 F.2d 939,947 (3rd Cir. 1976); Souder v. McGuire, 423 F. Supp. 830, 832 (M.D. Pa. 1976); Knecht v. Gillman, 488 F.2d 1136, 1140 (8th Cir. 1973); Nelson v. Heyne, 355 F. Supp. 451, 455 (N.D. Ind. 1972). *But see,* Rennie v. Klein, 462 F. Supp. at 1143; 653 F.2d at 844 (Eighth Amendment inapplicable). *See generally,* Symonds, *Mental Patients' Rights to Refuse Drugs: Involuntary Medication as Cruel and Unusual Punishment,* 7 Hastings Const. L.Q. 701 (1980).

18. An excellent presentation and analysis of the nonlegal origins of the right to refuse can be found in Brooks, *The Constitutional Right to Refuse Anti-Psychotic Medications,* 8 Bull. Am. Acad. Psychiatry & L. 179, 182-92 (1980). For presentations of opposite sides of the controversy, *compare* Appelbaum & Gutheil, *"Rotting with Their Rights On": Constitutional Theory and Clinical Reality in Drug Refusal by Psychiatric Patients,* 7 Bull. Am. Acad. Psychiatry & L. 306 (1979) *with* Plotkin, *Limiting the Therapeutic Orgy,* 72 Nw. U.L. Rev. 461 (1977). *See also,* DuBose, *Of the Parens Patriae Commitment Power and Drug Treatment of Schizophrenia: Do the Benefits to the Patient Justify Involuntary Treatment?,* 60 Minn. L. Rev. 1149 (1976); Note, *Madness and Medicine: The Forcible Administration of Psychotropic Drugs,* 1980 Wis. L. Rev. 497.

19. One case, decided by the Supreme Court of Colorado, affirmed the right of a client in a county mental-health center to refuse medication. However, the client was an involuntarily committed inpatient at that center, and so, at least so far as that client and the court were concerned, the center was a total institution. Goedecke v. State, 603 P.2d 123 (Colo. 1979). 1979).

20. Rennie v. Klein, 653 F.2d at 843.

21. *E.g.,* Cal. Welf. & Inst. Code, §5325(f)(West Supp. 1982); N.J. Rev. Stat. §30:4-24.2(d)(2)(1981). *See generally,* National Commission for the Protection of Human Subjects of Biomedical and Behavioral Research, Report and Recommendations: Psychosurgery (1977); Note, *Regulation of Electroconvulsive Therapy,* 75 Mich. L. Rev. 363 (1976).

22. Price v. Sheppard, 307 Minn. 250, 239 N.W.2d 905 (1976).

23. Rogers v. Okin, 478 F. Supp. at 1368.

24. *Id.,* 634 F.2d at 661.

25. Mental Health Systems Act, 42 U.S.C. §9501(3)(B)(ii) (Supp. 1981).

26. *See generally,* Gutheil, Shapiro & St. Clair, *Legal Guardianship in Drug Refusal: An Illusory Solution,* 137 Am. J. Psychiatry 347 (1980).

27. Rennie v. Klein, 653 F.2d at 853; Rogers v. Okin, 634 F.2d at 660-61.

28. Davis v. Hubbard, 506 F. Supp. at 932, *quoting* 2 F. Harper & F. James, Jr., The Law of Torts 61 (1968 Supp.) (emphasis in original).

29. A 1977 survey of state statutes on the right to refuse reported that fully forty-two states statutorily conferred on mental patients some form of the right to refuse electroconvulsive therapy and/or psychosurgery. Plotkin, *Limiting the Therapeutic Orgy: Mental Patients' Right to Refuse Treatment,* 72 Nw. U.L. Rev. 461, 504-25 (1977).

30. Mental Health Systems Act, *supra* note 25, at §9501; President's Commission on Mental Health, Report to the President 44 (1978).

The Principle of the Least Restrictive Alternative

We have referred to it in previous chapters. We call it a principle, others call it a doctrine, a maxim, a rule. It is the least-restrictive-alternative principle, a concept that applies throughout the field of mental-health law. Indeed, as the following pages will reveal, it applies to many, widely diverse legal areas. In mental-health law the principle operates primarily as a legal catalyst in the process of deinstitutionalization, and it is in this capacity that it can best be introduced.

Before proceeding, however, a note on terminology: to avoid tiresome repetitions of "least restrictive alternative," it will be shortened to *LRA*.

The *Brewster* Case and Community Care

The case of *Brewster* v. *Dukakis,* a federal lawsuit in Massachusetts, is a prime example of the LRA principle in action.[1] Its history dates back to 1966, when the Massachusetts legislature enacted a statute that empowered the state Department of Mental Health to create community-based residential programs as alternatives to its system of large institutions.[2] The statute was a legislative stamp of approval on the community mental-health movement. Over the following ten years the Department of Mental Health significantly reduced its state-hospital populations, but it made very little progress in creating community alternatives. In western Massachusetts, where the *Brewster* case originated, there were but two community residences as of 1976, and these together accommodated fewer than twenty of the more than two thousand mental-health clients in that region who were, on any given day, either in an institution or at risk of being admitted.[3]

It was at this point, a full decade after the state had proclaimed its goal of community-based care, that the LRA principle was asserted. The *Brewster* suit was brought as a class action seeking to compel the state to develop a comprehensive system of community programs, both residential and nonresidential. The plaintiff class included, among others, all residents of the single state hospital in western Massachusetts. For them, the suit represented not only a way out of the institution but also an avenue to better, more normalized care. Even the most impaired among them, the suit alleged, could benefit by community placement. Their potential for obtaining quality treatment, individualized programming, education, training, and experience in the mundane tasks of everyday living was likely to increase in community settings. Moreover, their ability to exercise the fundamental right to personal freedom and their enjoyment of a list of other basic rights, including the constitutional right of association, of travel, and of privacy, would likely increase as well.

The *Brewster* claim did not stop here, however. It went on to assert the LRA principle on behalf of noninstitutionalized persons as well. In the years before *Brewster* was filed, Massachusetts had significantly reduced its state-hospital populations, but the reduction was accomplished largely by so-called dumping, by discharging patients en masse with little or no aftercare. Northampton State Hospital, the focus of this class action, had seen its population plummet from over 2,000 in 1971 to 576 by late 1976 when *Brewster* was filed. The suit claimed that the state was obligated, under the LRA principle, to create suitable programs for former inpatients, many of whom had become "revolving-door" admissions to the state hospital.[4] For these plaintiffs, *Brewster* asserted a right to less restrictive, community-based alternatives not only to hospitalization but also to the marginal community existence in which institutionalization is for some an omnipresent threat and for others an avoidable reality.

The case sought community programs that would provide individually tailored services for clients with vastly divergent needs. It asked that the federal court order the state to develop a comprehensive system, a full spectrum of community programs.

The legal showdown was ultimately averted as the *Brewster* litigation was settled two years after it was filed. The state acquiesced in 1978 to nearly all the plaintiffs' demands. It agreed to implement a remarkably detailed plan for a comprehensive community-based mental-health system. It agreed to do what it had set out to do twelve years earlier.

The state entered into a consent decree, a binding contract sanctioned by the court obligating it to establish "appropriate, less restrictive treatment, training, and support services for each member of the plaintiff class." According to the decree, all or very nearly all the clients in western Massachusetts are to be served in a decentralized system, a dynamic system in which they can move at their own pace along a continuum of individualized services ranging from long-term, highly supervised group homes to independent living with a wide variety of support services.

The consent decree, the actual document prepared by the parties and enforceable by the court, is impressive for both its detail and its breadth. It represents the collaborative efforts of reform-oriented attorneys and mental-health professionals (including some of this country's preeminent authorities on community mental-health systems) and is nothing short of a master plan for a complete systemic transition from institutional to community care. The decree illustrates several salient features of the LRA principle. Above all, it illustrates that the principle has broad applications, for it served to guide the formation of treatment programs and residential settings for five thousand plaintiffs with widely divergent needs. Moreover, it illustrates that a client need not be actually institutionalized to assert a right to be placed in a community residential program. In this light, it is clear that the principle is both remedial and prophylactic; it can prevent, as well as remedy, unnecessary restrictions of liberty such as those that result from hospitalization. Additionally, *Brewster* illustrated that the LRA principle can entitle a client to more than simple freedom; it can secure as well the services necessary to make that freedom meaningful and lasting. Furthermore, the case shows that the principle applies not just in individual cases, where the placement of a single client is at issue, but also in class actions, in administrative procedures where policy is set, and in all manners of decision making that affect the availability or quality of mental-health care.

Finally, the *Brewster* decree illustrates more than divergence in the principle's applicability; it also demonstrates convergence between law and psychiatry. It illustrates the fact that the LRA principle, perhaps more than any other principle of mental-health law, is endorsed by the mental-health profession. Indeed, *Brewster* is an outstanding example of cooperation between lawyers and clinicians in the pursuit of a common objective: community-based care. Of course, the principle is not without doubters in either the mental-health or the legal professions,[5] but the words of Dr. Robert Okin, former commissioner of the Massachusetts Department of Mental Health and a defendant in *Brewster,* are telling: "I see the [*Brewster*] consent decree as a model for the state in terms of principles and program designs."[6]

Origins of the LRA Principle

An explanation of the constitutional and other legal roots of the LRA principle should help to explain the result of the *Brewster* case and the additional examples of the principle in action that are to follow. As the *Brewster* defendants agreed, the principle seems worthy of support as it applies to mental-health care, but that it is endorseable for the clinician does not make it enforceable for the judge.

The LRA principle evolved from a series of judicial decisions articulating it as a constitutionally rooted safeguard of fundamental rights. Here, it must be stressed that, although the LRA principle is constitutionally rooted, it is not itself an independent constitutional right.[7] It is, rather, a safeguard on the exercise of constitutional rights, and only of the most basic rights: those which fall under the legal rubric of fundamental rights. It safeguards these rights—most importantly, the right to liberty—by requiring that where a constitutional interest can be legitimately restricted, it be restricted only to the extent necessary to carry out a valid purpose. A quick overview of the landmark cases will illustrate when and how the principle operates.[8]

The most significant of the cases, *Shelton* v. *Tucker,* was decided by the United States Supreme Court in 1960.[9] The case was a product of a time of zealous anticommunism. The state of Arkansas, in an effort to guard its school children from influences believed insidious, enacted a statute requiring all teachers in state-supported schools to file annual lists of all organizations to which they belonged or contributed over the preceding five years. Shelton was one among many teachers who considered that law an excessive infringement on the rights of privacy and of association, both fundamental rights. The Supreme Court agreed. The Court agreed not because the state's purpose was objectionable but because its method was unnecessarily intrusive, for it required teachers to publicize private information of no valid interest to the public, and it chilled their freedom to join or support even noncommunist organizations. In the Court's words:

> [E]ven though the governmental purpose be legitimate and substantial, that purpose cannot be achieved by means that broadly stifle personal liberties when the end can be more narrowly achieved. The breadth of legislative abridgement must be viewed in light of less drastic means of achieving the same basic purpose.[10]

The rule announced in *Shelton* applies to all forms of state action that curtail fundamental rights, whether that action be legislative, judicial, or administrative. One such form of state action is the civil commitment of the mentally ill, and in 1972 a federal court applied the *Shelton* rule to the commitment process. The case was *Lessard* v. *Schmidt,* a class action brought on behalf of all civilly committed adults in Wisconsin, challenging the constitutionality of the state's commitment laws.[11] The *Lessard* decision first addressed the legitimacy of the state's goals in confining mentally ill persons: the protection and treatment of the committed person and, in certain cases, the protection of the community at large. The decision then set forth the judicial-commitment procedures by which the state pursued these goals, and finally it detailed the standard of commitment: mental illness and dangerousness to self or others. Beyond these standards, it added to the statutory scheme the further requirement drawn from *Shelton* v. *Tucker:* "Even if the standards for an adjudication of mental illness and potential dangerousness are satisfied, a court should order full-time involuntary hospitalization only as a last resort."[12]

The court suggested a number of potential alternatives to commitment, including day treatment, night treatment, and home health care, and ruled that no person may be committed unless all available less restrictive alternatives have been explored and deemed unsuitable. The Wisconsin procedure, it declared, was "constitutionally defective insofar as it fails . . . to require those seeking commitment to consider less restrictive alternatives to commitment."[13]

Since the 1972 *Lessard* case, the principle of the LRA has been reaffirmed by several cases concerning the involuntary confinement of the developmentally disabled as well as the mentally ill.[14] More importantly, it has been explicitly incorporated into many state commitment statutes.[15]

This trend to state legislative revision continues to gather momentum. It recently received support from the U.S. Congress through the new Mental Health Systems Act. That act urges states to review and revise their mental-health statutes to incorporate the bill of rights proposed by both the Congress and the President's Commission on Mental Health. The very first in the act's list of rights is the right to treatment and services under conditions which: "(i) are the most supportive of . . . personal liberty; and (ii) restrict such liberty only to the extent necessary consistent with . . . treatment needs, applicable requirements of law, and applicable judicial orders."[16] Consequently, even those states that have not specifically incorporated the LRA principle into their statutory schemes may soon do so, spurred by the federal legislative lead.

In summary, the LRA principle now carries judicial, and in many states, legislative, as well as constitutional force.

The Principle at Work in Mental-Health Law

Although its impact in the mental-health field is most evident in the context of placement decisions, the LRA principle prevails throughout mental-health law. Returning to the three exemplary cases, *Shelton* v. *Tucker, Lessard* v. *Schmidt,* and *Brewster* v. *Dukakis,* a common thread can be identified: in each case some form of state action imposed restrictions on fundamental rights. In *Shelton,* it was legislative action in the form of a statute; in *Lessard,* it was judicial action through civil commitment; and in *Brewster,* the action was primarily administrative in the form of systemic design, program development, and staff policy. All three cases involved various interrelated fundamental rights, including the rights of liberty, privacy, and association. As these diverse cases demonstrate, the LRA principle is triggered whenever fundamental rights or liberties are curtailed by some form of governmental action, irrespective of the government's motive or purpose. In the mental-health field, state action affecting fundamental rights occurs, and so the LRA principle applies, in four general areas: civil commitment and placement decisions, involuntary treatment, confidentiality, and protective services. Although the principle does apply, to various degrees and in various ways, in all these areas, a few words of caution are in order.

The question of exactly where, when, and how the principle operates in the context of mental-health services is much debated. The uncertainty stems from two distinct problems, which the following discussion attempts only to illuminate, not to resolve.

The first source of uncertainty concerns the legal preconditions to the application of the principle: the presence of state action and the curtailment of fundamental rights. A very substantial body of law has developed on the topic of what constitutes state action. Here, it should be sufficient to note that official governmental action, whether legislative, judicial, or administrative, is state action. Moreover, individual acts or omissions may also constitute state action if compelled or authorized by a government body or agent. Thus, it has been held that emergency commitment effected by a private psychiatrist in accordance with state law is state action.[17]

The second precondition, the curtailment of fundamental rights, is obviously satisfied in cases of civil commitment, where there can be no doubt of the fundamental nature of the rights at stake, including the rights of liberty, privacy, association, and travel. These are all constitutionally guaranteed rights that are unquestionably restrained by institutional confinement. The issue is troublesome, however, in regard to placement decisions not made through court-ordered commitment and in instances where physical freedom is not so directly curtailed. Of course, a statutory provision expressly requiring consideration of less restrictive alternatives will render these constitutional preconditions unnecessary. But in the absence of such a statute, the LRA principle can be enforced by a court only to preserve fundamental rights from state action. Because both preconditions are somewhat nebulous, there are obvious grounds for argument as to whether the LRA principle can be enforced in certain cases.

The second major difficulty in applying the principle concerns the appropriateness of legal intervention. The proper realm of intervention is circumscribed not only by the rules of law—here, the limitations of the constitution itself—but also by the practical limits of the law's competence in psychiatry. Where the LRA principle applies, it requires only the use of the least restrictive appropriate alternative. It does not, for instance, outlaw civil commitment on the grounds that discharge is always a less restrictive alternative, for, even as a matter of law, discharge is not always an appropriate alternative. Plainly, the determination of appropriateness involves clinical considerations often of a very complex nature. Although judges and lawyers may join with mental-health professionals in outlining the requirements of the principle through regulations and case law, the law rarely ventures beyond the formulation of general rules. It defers in no small measure to the judgment of mental-health professionals. There is disagreement, however, among and between jurists and clinicians as to where the limits of the law's intervention should be drawn and where legal concern for clients' rights should yield to psychiatric concern for clients' treatment.

In summary, it can be said that the LRA principle is but a fulcrum on which legal rights and clinical concerns are balanced. The remainder of this chapter describes how the principle operates in the four major areas: commitment and placement, nonconsensual treatment, confidentiality, and guardianship.

Commitment and Placement Decisions

Civil commitment entails greater deprivations of freedom than any other form of state action in the mental-health area. It is not surprising, therefore, that the principle has been most frequently and strictly applied by courts and legislatures alike in respect to commitment. The case of *Lessard* v. *Schmidt* represents what is now settled law across the country: civil commitment is constitutionally permissible only if no appropriate, less restrictive alternative is available. In other words, one may be forcibly confined in an institutional setting only if no appropriate community placement is available.[18] But what of placement decisions made outside of the courtroom: does the principle apply even after commitment when clinicians contemplate placement or transfer of an involuntary client? And what of voluntary clients, have they a right to live and be treated in the LRA?

In general, any decision that determines where and under what conditions a client will live must reflect consideration of the LRA principle. It matters not whether the decision is made by a judge, an administrator, or a clinician. Nor does it matter whether the decision contemplates placement to, from, or even within an institution. Thus, in a case that actually predates the *Lessard* decision, it was held that the same right to the LRA that attaches in civil commitment hearings also applies to administrative, intrahospital-transfer decisions that could result in further losses of freedom.[19]

Overall, systemic planning or policy decisions by mental-health officials can determine the liberty afforded clients just as fatefully as do specific commitment or transfer decisions. If a system offers few or no alternatives to institutionalization, then clients in need of treatment will be forced, in effect, to accept institutional care and all the attendant sociolegal deprivations. Under such circumstances, even nominally voluntary patients are deprived of liberty by state action, in the form of design or planning decisions, which leaves them without option. The lack of meaningful choice confines them just as surely as a commitment order confines the involuntary client. Recognition of this fact has led several courts to conclude that the LRA principle applies to policy decisions as well as to individual placement decisions and that the right to live and be treated in the least restrictive setting can be asserted by voluntary as well as involuntary clients.[20]

Courts thus far have struggled primarily with cases involving placement to or within institutional settings. They have not yet expressly settled the question of the principle's applicability to placement to or within community systems. However, there appears to be no basis in case law for a categorical distinction between institutional and community systems that would limit the principle to institutional clients. Rather, as suggested by statutes and consent decrees, the LRA principle should apply wherever substantial liberty interests are at stake. Thus, a client in a strictly supervised or unduly isolated residential program might invoke the principle to secure placement in a less restrictive program. Nothing in law or logic suggests that the liberty interests of community clients should be less well protected than those of institutionalized persons.

Treatment without Client Consent

The legal deprivations that may result from forced or coerced treatment were described in detail in chapter 5. There it was noted that a host of legal rights support the client's right to refuse treatment: the right to liberty, to privacy, to self-determination, to freedom of thought and expression, and, in instances of especially intrusive treatment, the right to be free from harm. These all fall within the legal category of fundamental rights. Therefore, since forced treatment infringes on these rights, it is governed, when it is permissible at all, by the LRA principle.

Although the law is still in flux, case law and commentary concerning the use of psychotropic medication suggest that this form of treatment may be forcibly administered only in cases of emergency (that is, where there exists a present threat of serious physical harm) or of client incompetency.[21] In these instances, the LRA principle combines with prudent professional judgment in defining the extent and type of allowable forced treatment.

It is important to stress that the clinician is not stripped of discretion in these cases. The LRA principle requires only that choices between available, comparably effective treatment modes—choices defined primarily by clinical judgments—be made in favor of that treatment that least offends the client's liberty, privacy, and freedom of choice.

But how far should courts go in securing this right for individual clients? Here again arises the complex problem of finding an accommodation between legal and psychiatric judgments. A federal appellate court recently issued an opinion that wrestled with this question in a somewhat different context, the treatment of developmentally disabled persons in state institutions. In *Romeo* v. *Youngberg,* the Third Circuit decided that an initial choice between major treatment approaches requires a mixed legal-psychiatric decision and so may be subjected to judicial scrutiny.[22] In the court's words: "appropriate deference to medical expertise does not diminish the judicial duty to safeguard liberty interests implicated in treatment decisions." But here, at the point of the initial choice between treatment modes, the court drew the limit on the applicability of the LRA principle. Again, quoting from the court's majority opinion:

> Once the least intrusive regime has been selected . . . the application of a constitutional standard of "least intrusive alternative" to continuing treatment programs, which often involve qualitative medical determinations subject to daily, possibly hourly changes, would prove unworkable. The judiciary is not in a particularly advantageous position to determine which of two medications is less intrusive, nor especially competent in assessing present therapeutic benefits versus long-term consequences and side effects for each administration of a drug.[23]

The court's assessment of judicial competence is surely accurate, but the limitations it draws around the LRA principle on the basis of that assessment does not dispose of the applicability problem. Other courts have started with the same premise and reached very different conclusions. Although the Supreme Court upheld the circuit court's ruling in *Romeo* on the constitutional right to "minimally adequate training," including "reasonably non-restrictive confinement conditions," it emphasized the presumptive validity of the balances and determinations reached by qualified clinical professionals.[24] By doing so, the Court limited the scope of the constitutional liability for damages of those administrators and clinicians who must make a myriad of treatment decisions on a daily basis, often under pressing institutional conditions.

Disclosures of Confidential Information

The law regarding client records and other forms of confidential information is presented in chapter 7. Suffice it to say at this point that although confidentiality is the general and strict rule, there are numerous exceptions. When an exception obtains and the clinician is allowed or required to divulge information concerning a client to a third party, the client plainly suffers some loss of privacy. That privacy is a fundamental right protected by the LRA principle.

Here the principle can be reduced to a short and simple rule: when confidential information may or must be disclosed, only so much information should be disclosed to only so many persons as is minimally necessary to satisfy the valid purpose of the disclosure.

Guardianships, Conservatorships, and Other Protective Services

Clearly the involuntary imposition of protective services warrants safeguards and individually tailored limitations. Since chapter 9 places special emphasis on less drastic interventions, only a preliminary comment is needed at this stage.

Guardianships and conservatorships are judicial methods of securing one's person or property from the dangers resulting from incompetence. By either of these methods, the individual's personal or financial affairs may be placed under the control of an appointee charged by a court with a duty to act in the incompetent's best interest. The purpose of these protective services is benevolent, but they obviously entail deprivations of fundamental personal liberties. Hence, they are subject to the LRA principle.

In this area the principle requires first and foremost that incompetent persons be subjected only to that form of protective service that least restricts their personal autonomy, yet at the same time satisfies their need for protection. Thus, every effort should be made to assist seemingly incompetent clients in managing their affairs through voluntary measures before resorting to involuntary means. And when involuntary means are necessary a court should vest an appointed surrogate with only the powers needed under the existing circumstances.

Conclusion

The LRA principle is a pervasive rule of general application. It governs all instances in which fundamental rights are infringed by state action. It should be obvious by now that no individual right is wholly absolute; under proper circumstances and through proper procedures, any right may be circumscribed. In essence, the LRA principle demands that basic rights not be curtailed more than is necessary to achieve the purpose that justifies the curtailment in the first place. As courts and legislatures continue to apply the principle, greater specificity as to its bounds and mechanics can be anticipated. Compared to the slow march of common law, the principle is still in an early stage of doctrinal development, but it is developing rapidly and surely.

This chapter has focused on the legally mandated application of the principle as a rule of constitutional law. But the principle is of great value and utility even where not legally compelled. In many respects, it resembles the philosophical principle of mental-health care termed normalization. And like normalization, it can serve as a source of guidance in many spheres of psychiatric decision making. The very simplicity of the principle, and the breadth of its utility, was captured by a noted authority writing for the President's Committee on Mental Retardation: "The right to the least restrictive alternative is little more than a requirement that common sense and respect for the humanity and individuality of every person be the touchstone of the law."[25]

Notes

1. Brewster v. Dukakis, No. 76-4423-F (D. Mass., Dec. 6, 1978) (final consent decree).
2. Mass. Gen. Laws Ann. ch. 19 §17 (Supp. 1981).
3. Brewster v. Dukakis, *supra* note 1, at 8-9.
4. According to data submitted by the Massachusetts Department of Mental Health to the *Brewster* court, more than 63 percent of the patients admitted to the Northampton State Hospital during a six-month sample period had been admitted previously.
5. Perr, *The Most Beneficial Alternative: A Counterpoint to the Least Restrictive Alternative,* 6 Bull. Am. Acad. Psychiatry & L. 4 (1978); Hansen, *The Thorny Problems with LRA Cases,* 3 Mental Health L. Project Summary 1 (1977). Organizations of mental patients also have been critical, arguing that courts reluctant to commit persons to institutions will more readily commit to less restrictive alternatives, thus increasing the number of persons labelled mentally ill and involuntarily confined. *See generally,* A. Scull, Decarceration: Community Treatment and the Deviant—A Radical View (1977).
6. *Treat Them Right,* The Valley Advocate, June 4, 1980 at 10, col. 1.
7. On the LRA principle and its impact, see N. Coleman & L. Gilbert, Stalking the Least Restrictive Alternative: Litigative and Non-Litigative Strategies for the Indigent Mentally Disabled (1979); Hoffman & Foust, *Least Restrictive Treatment of the Mentally Ill: A Doctrine in Search of Its Senses,* 14 San Diego L. Rev. 1100 (1977); Chambers, *Alternatives to Civil Commitment of the Mentally Ill: Practical Guides and Constitutional Imperatives,* 70 Mich. L. Rev. 1107 (1972). For more technical analyses, see L. Tribe, American Constitutional Law §§12-24, 12-28, 12-30 (1978); Note, *Less Drastic Means and the First Amendment,* 78 Yale L.J. 464 (1969).
8. The following United States Supreme Court decisions reveal the diverse applications of the LRA principle: Talley v. California, 362 U.S. 60 (1970) (state statute forbidding distribution of anonymous handbills declared unconstitutional—fraud and libel could be checked by less drastic means); United States v. Robel, 389 U.S. 285 (1967) (federal prohibition on hiring of Communist Party members for all positions in all defense facilities declared unconstitutional—less restrictive measures would suffice in maintaining security); Martin v. City of Struthers, 319 U.S. 141 (1941) (city or-

dinance banning all door-to-door solicitations declared unconstitutional—less restrictive consumer-protection laws could curb intrusions on householders and fraudulent sales).

9. 364 U.S. 479 (1960).

10. *Id.* at 488.

11. 349 F. Supp. 1078 (E.D. Wis. 1972).

12. *Id.* at 1095.

13. *Id.* at 1103.

14. *See, e.g.,* Wyatt v. Stickney, 344 F. Supp. 373, 379, 396 (M.D. Ala. 1972); New York State Ass'n for Retarded Children v. Rockefeller, 357 F. Supp. 752 (E.D.N.Y. 1973); Halderman v. Pennhurst State School and Hospital, 446 F. Supp. 1295, 1315-20 (E.D. Pa. 1977), *aff'd on other grounds*, 612 F.2d 84 (3rd Cir. 1979), *rev'd on other grounds and remanded,* 451 U.S. 1 (1981).

15. *See, e.g.,* Hawaii Rev. Stat. §334-60 (Supp. 1980); Mass. Gen. Laws Ann. ch. 123 §4 (West Supp. 1981); Minn. Stat. Ann. §253 A.02 (West Supp. 1980); Neb. Rev. Stat. §83-1036 (Supp. 1980); N.M. Stat. Ann. §34-2A-10 (Supp. 1980); Ohio Rev. Code Ann. §1522.15 (B)(3) (Page Supp. 1980); Tenn. Code Ann. §33-604(d) (Supp. 1980); Utah Code Ann. §64-7-36(6) (Supp. 1980); Va. Code §37.1-67-3 (Supp. 1980).

16. 42 U.S.C. §9501(1)(A) (Supp. 1981).

17. Leonard v. Fry, No. B-76-338 (D. Conn. Sept. 28, 1980).

18. There is some support in case law for the proposition that states are under a legal duty to create less restrictive alternatives, not only in response to class-action litigation such as Brewster v. Dukakis but also in the context of commitment hearings. At present, the law seems to require only that available alternatives be explored prior to commitment, and it allows commitment where alternative placement is indicated but unavailable. *See,* Johnson v. Solomon, 484 F. Supp. 278, 305 (D. Md. 1979) (no juvenile can be civilly committed except on showing that no less restrictive alternative is available).

19. Covington v. Harris, 419 F.2d 617 (D.C. Cir. 1969).

20. Wyatt v. Stickney, 344 F. Supp. at 390 n.5; Halderman v. Pennhurst, 446 F. Supp. at 1318.

21. The present state of the law on this point is discussed fully in chapter 5, *supra.*

22. 644 F.2d 147 (3d Cir. 1980), *vacated and remanded on other grounds,* 102 S. Ct. 2452 (1982).

23. *Id.* at 166-167.

24. Youngberg v. Romeo, 102 S. Ct. at 2461-63. The Court did not reach the issue of treatment providing the LRA outside the institution because the plaintiff, a profoundly retarded adult, did not make that claim in this case.

25. Kindred, *Guardianship and Limitations upon Capacity,* in The Mentally Retarded Citizen and the Law 62, 66 (M. Kindred, J. Cohen, D. Penrod, and T. Shaffer eds. 1976).

7 Privacy, Confidentiality, and Access to Records

Mental-health professionals universally agree that information from and about clients is confidential and must be guarded staunchly; but what about information that could prevent serious harm? Should it be disclosed? To police? To a potential victim? And who should have access to a client's records? Should attorneys? Should researchers or students or insurers?

The Right to Privacy

Questions of confidentiality are inescapably perplexing. The law's search for answers begins with the right to privacy. As stated by the United States Supreme Court, privacy is a right rooted in our federal constitution:

> The Constitution does not explicitly mention any right of privacy. In a line of decisions, however, going back perhaps as far as Union Pacific Railway Co. v. Botsford [where, in 1891, the Supreme Court ruled that a litigant has a qualified right to refuse medical examination] . . . the Court has recognized that a right of personal privacy, or a guarantee of certain areas or zones of privacy, does exist under the constitution.[1]

The Supreme Court has yet to define fully and clearly the dimensions of this right, although at least two state supreme courts, those of California and Pennsylvania, have decided that confidential exchanges between clients and therapists fall within such a constitutionally protected zone of privacy.[2]

Whether or not the privacy of client-therapist communications is to be accorded constitutional protection, that privacy is certainly a legal right of the client. It is a right protected by statute in almost every state, and reinforced by judicial decisions, administrative regulations, and professional canons.[3] But again, the right to privacy is only a starting point in the law of confidentiality. From this basic premise that individuals, including, and perhaps especially, mental-health clients, are entitled to privacy, a host of exceptions has been carved. The major exceptions are addressed to two distinct categories of confidential information: client records and therapist-client communications. Client records and personal communications are subject to somewhat different rules of law and therefore are treated separately in the sections that follow.

Client Records and Third-Party Access

To expound on the value and necessity of record keeping for an audience of clinicians would be like listing the properties of coal for the folks in Newcastle. Maintaining records of client progress and treatment, detailing highly personal information, is a crucial aspect of providing mental-health services, especially in this age of complex service-delivery systems.[4] And no one knows this better than the clinician. Suffice it to say, then, that maintaining records in community mental-health centers is necessary; state statutes, judicial decisions, federal regulations, insurance rules, intra-agency policies, and sound clinical practice all demand it.[5]

On a larger scale, massive banks of personal data have been compiled by the consumer investigative industry (estimated at some 200 million credit and investigative files on individuals)[6] and by government agencies (federal executive agencies alone maintain over 850 data banks containing more than 1.25 billion records on individuals).[7] The compilation of these banks has generated a flood of lawsuits, legislative proposals, and legal writings seeking to secure the privacy of personal records. Still, confidential information not only leaks but often flows steadily from those who should guard it to those who should not have it.

In regard to these psychiatric records, the law is unambiguous and firm: records must be kept confidential unless disclosure is ordered by a court or authorized by the informed consent of the client or the client's parent or guardian. This rule is not without necessary exceptions, however, and perhaps most obvious among them is that which allows disclosure of records that do not identify individual clients. Whether in the form of mass data or case studies, records that cannot be readily associated with specific clients may be disclosed for legitimate purposes: for example, for government audits, for service-needs assessments, and for clinical instruction.

What triggers this exception, of course, is the anonymity of the records and not the mere fact that disclosure is for a beneficial purpose. Hence, records that do identify individual clients may not be disclosed without proper consent or a court order, even if disclosure appears to be in a client's best interests. For example, the release of records to such agencies as the Social Security Administration or the local welfare office, or to providers of generic services, is usually innocuous enough and may be a prerequisite to a client's obtaining due benefits. In such cases, clients will rarely object to the disclosure, and, in the interest of expediency, the clinician may be tempted to forgo the formality of consent. But the requirement of consent is more than a formality, it is an indispensable safeguard for the rare client who will object to disclosure, who will rather foresake services than compromise privacy. The choice between privacy and even the most beneficial services is a value judgment reserved for the client, the client's guardian, or, in exceptional cases, a court.

It should be noted that even a court order can be successfully challenged when disclosure appears unwarranted and damaging to the client. In a Pennsylvania case where placement of a juvenile was at issue, a noted psychiatrist willfully violated a court order when he refused to disclose records of the juvenile's mother, arguing that the records were irrelevant to the case at bar. He was cited for contempt and fined. On appeal to the state supreme court, the orders of disclosure and contempt were both reversed and the psychiatrist's claim of confidentiality on the mother's behalf was upheld.[8]

A second major exception to the rule of nondisclosure allows the transfer of records within an agency or between related agencies. Differences in the structure and divisions of service systems makes a concise formulation of this exception impossible, however. In general, clinicians employed by the same agency may freely exchange client records, but any disclosure outside of the agency is subject to the rule requiring consent or court order. This exception is based in part on the view that client records are a special form of property, in the legal sense of that term, and as such belong to the agency that keeps them. This view is neither entirely accurate nor widely supported, but it does help to define the scope of this exception. For this purpose, clinicians in a given agency may be thought of as the collective owners of client records kept by that agency and therefore are free to consult those records without prior client consent. It is also helpful in this regard to consider that a client's reasonable expectations of confidentiality are contractual in nature, are thus legally enforceable, and to a large extent determine the application of the rule of nondisclosure. In other words, whether disclosure to a certain person would be lawful may depend on whether the client should reasonably expect that person to have access to personal records.

The boundaries of this exception are blurry. Neither the records-as-property formula nor the reasonable-expectations test is conclusive. And the boundaries are further blurred by the intricacy of relationships within and between agencies. Unsalaried consultants, private vendors, student interns, and the like all make a categorical formulation of this exception impossible. When in this ill-defined area, the clinician would be well advised to seek consent, if not as a personal precaution then as an act of deference to the client. It cannot hurt legally and may help clinically.

A subject on which the law is entirely unclear is that of parental access to a minor's records. State statutes on confidentiality make no special mention of this subject but rather seem to grant minors the same right of privacy as that accorded to adults. As against unrelated third parties, the minor's right to confidentiality is undoubtedly as strong as that of an adult, but as against one's parents, the question is open. The question probably seldom arises, because it is the rare child who asserts a right of privacy against his parents. But should the question arise, the clinician will have to answer according to professional judgment, for there is no legal rule on point. In fashioning an answer, the clinician should bear in mind that no matter how old the client is or how concerned the parents may be, the client is the ultimate object of the clinician's allegiance. That being so, the clinician should take guidance from one of the profession's basic ethics: first, do no harm. Ultimately, the answer must simply reflect what is best for the minor client. The clinician will be better able to decide that than a slew of judges and jurors.

Finally, we turn to an area that, contrary to misconceptions based on common practice, does not constitute an exception: disclosure to insurers. In short, insurers do not have legal access to records without consent or court order.

Typically, one who purchases insurance is required to sign a blanket-consent form, giving the insurance company access to all information concerning one's treatment under the policy. The same is true of those whose employers purchase their insurance. Consequently, insurance companies and/or their centralized information collectors (one large collector, the Medical Information Bureau, boasts a list of subscribers of over seven hundred insurance companies) usually satisfy the requirements of the letter, if not the spirit, of confidentiality laws. Convincing arguments have been put forth as to why insurers should be denied much of the information they routinely acquire, and the most forceful of the arguments is also the most simple: they do not need it all.[9] Clinicians filing insurance claims for clients may want to take note of this argument and furnish only so much confidential information as is necessary to justify claims. Protecting privacy in this way is especially important for clients insured under employers' group policies, for it is not uncommon for confidential records to pass from insurer to policyholder. And any information so passed may lead an employer to oust the client, if only to reduce insurance premiums.

Although some large steps have been taken recently to protect clients from having to trade their privacy for their policies, insurers still pose serious but avoidable threats to confidentiality.[10] One simple way for clinicians to aid clients in avoiding the threats is to inform them of the type of information that must accompany insurance claims and then to advise them of their option to pay for some or all treatment out of pocket. Some may consider the privacy to be worth the price.

Client Access to Records

A comprehensive study of state laws relating to medical records, published in 1973, revealed only nine state statutes that explicitly address the issue of client access. Of these, several are inapplicable to records kept by mental-health facilities; several limit the right of access to individuals who require records to pursue legal claims or defenses; and several others grant the right only indirectly, allowing access by a client representative but not the actual client.[11] The same report uncovered only one legal commentary and two judicial decisions on the issue.[12] Although years have passed since this study was completed, the general state of statutory law on client access does not seem to have changed significantly. The question of access remains for the most part open for state agencies or individual programs to decide. It is significant, however, that the few recent legal pronouncements in this area, including judicial decisions and federal legislation, all serve to expand the client's right of access.

One recent and major advance came with the passage of the Mental Health Systems Act in 1980.[13] That act sets forth a bill of rights developed by Congress to serve as a blueprint for the revision of state mental-health laws. Included in the bill is a broad right of access to one's records. It would allow full client access with only two exceptions. First, information that has been "provided by a third party under assurance that such information shall remain confidential" may be deleted prior to a client's review of the record. Second, a "health professional" may determine in writing that access to specific material would be "detrimental to the health" of a client, in which case the client may select a "similarly licensed health professional" to review the material and to determine independently whether to allow access "or otherwise disclose the information" to the client.[14] The bill of rights thus expresses the view of Congress that clients are entitled to know, in most cases fully and precisely, the contents of their psychiatric records.

Congress had expressed substantially the same view six years earlier when it amended the Freedom of Information Act with the Privacy Act of 1974.[15] The Privacy Act aims to ensure the confidentiality of personal information of all sorts amassed by the many record-keeping branches of the federal government. It does so by several means, including strict reporting requirements for data holders and civil and criminal sanctions for certain violations. Yet the primary mode of protection established by the Privacy Act is its guarantee of individual access to personal records. The act relies on the right of access both to curb improper disclosures and to correct or delete inaccurate, misleading, or privileged information. The act grants individuals not only the right of access but also the right to contest or amend personal records and the right to challenge the purposes for which they are used.[16] Not surprisingly, these rights are qualified; access may be denied, for instance, in the interest of national security or to guard ongoing criminal investigations. But the qualifications are few, and mental-health records are not excepted. Department of Health and Human Services regulations promulgated under the Privacy Act do allow for denial of client access to "medical and psychological" records where access would have an "adverse effect" on the client's condition. But even then, by procedures comparable to those found in the Mental Health Systems Act, clients are entitled to indirect access. In the exceptional case where direct access is denied, a client may designate any "responsible individual" to first review the records and then, in that individual's sole discretion, to disclose all or any portion to the client.[17]

Congressional support for the right of client access has been shared by most of if not all the courts that have ruled on the issue in recent years. And the courts have found several distinct bases for their rulings in favor of client access, each adding to the strength of the client's entitlement. In 1975, a federal appeals court held that former mental patients had no constitutional right of access to records that had been expressly declared by state statute to be hospital property. Yet despite that statute, the court decided that the ex-patients did have certain legally enforceable interests in the information contained in the records.[18]

The Supreme Court of Michigan has decided that the rule of confidentiality that bars disclosure of records is established solely for the benefit of the client. That being so, the client's guardian (and, presumably, a competent client) can waive the rule and thereby gain direct access to records.[19]

Finally, a Florida court held that a state statute that, consistent with the general rule across the country, allows disclosure to third parties with client consent, necessarily requires that clients be allowed direct access. The court reasoned that access is essential for clients to exercise properly and intelligently their statutory right to give or withhold consent to disclosure.[20]

Several legal commentaries also have included recommendations and proposed legislation for securing the mental-health client's right of access.[21] These proposals are grounded on clinical as well as legal bases. A denial of access can cause serious injury to the client-therapist relationship, eroding trust and fostering suspicion; it can instill or compound in the client a sense of incapacity; it can hinder the client's attempts to participate knowledgeably in treatment; and it can force the client to resort to frivolous malpractice claims to subpoena the records.

Of course, there are also well-reasoned arguments against the release of psychiatric records to clients. Records may contain references to third persons who might be harmed by disclosure; they frequently include information supplied by others with an expectation of confidentiality; disclosure may work harm on individual clients and undermine their treatment; and to the extent that records are unintelligible to the layperson, the benefits of disclosure are dubious. These arguments are all answered, however, by qualifications on the right of access such as those prescribed in the Mental Health Systems Act and in the Privacy Act. The qualifications enable record holders to prevent potential harms while still preserving the legal and therapeutic benefits of client access.

In summary, few state statutes now expressly grant the right of client access, although the number is likely to increase as legislatures revise their statutes in response to the Mental Health Systems Act and its bill of rights. Growing interest in client's rights and heightened awareness of privacy invasions should add to the push for statutory reform. In those states where clients currently have no statutory right of access, mental-health programs nevertheless may be required by state or agency regulations to allow client access. In the main, however, programs enjoy discretion in establishing their own policies. If these policies are to follow the trend in case law and commentary, they will accord clients a general, but not absolute, right to review their own records.

Client-Therapist Communications

Like client records, communications between client and therapist are confidential. And like the privacy of records, the privacy of communications has many foundations; state statutes governing treatment programs and professional licensing, judicial decisions, expressed or implied contracts, professional canons, and the basic right of privacy are all sources of the rule that the therapist-client relationship is confidential. In addition, privacy of communications is required, or at least protected, by the so-called psychotherapist-patient privilege.

What is commonly termed a testimonial or evidentiary "privilege" is perhaps better understood as a right.[22] It is yet another manifestation of the right to privacy. In general, an evidentiary privilege is that which allows persons called on to render testimony in legal proceedings to withhold evidence that the law would customarily demand. It reflects society's interest in protecting certain relationships from damage. Many state statutes now include the psychotherapist-client relationship among those that have traditionally been accorded a privilege: the priest-penitent, wife-husband, attorney-client, and physician-patient relationships.[23] In recognition of the special necessity for privacy in pscyhotherapy—both to protect the client from stigma and to encourage the candor that is essential to effective treatment—the statutes in some states grant a more protective privilege to therapist-client communications than to those between physician and patient.[24] In fact, several states that do not recognize a physician-patient privilege do grant a privilege to therapist-client relationships.[25]

To the extent that the privilege merely excludes certain evidence from the reach of courts, it is just an added layer of insulation to an already confidential relationship. But the therapist-client privilege is more than that. It has been held to prohibit disclosures out of court as well as in, and so can be said to require, not just protect, confidentiality.[26] Furthermore, the privilege is decidedly for the benefit of the client alone, and no one else can waive it.[27] Thus it appears not to be a privilege shared by the therapist but rather a right held by the client.

Whether by right or by privilege, the confidentiality of the client-therapist relationship is secured even against intrusion by courts. As with so many other rules of law, however, the rule of confidentiality is not absolute. Several qualifications to the psychotherapist-client privilege are worth noting. First, the privilege is limited to relationships between clients and certain licensed professionals.[28] Second, it generally does not apply in malpractice suits brought by the client against the therapist nor in cases where the client voluntarily raises his mental condition as a claim or defense (for example, in criminal proceedings where the client pleads not guilty by reason of mental illness). In such cases the client is said to have waived the privilege. Finally, some courts have held that the privilege does not apply in civil commitment hearings. These decisions have been based largely on one of two rationales: one is the notion that commitment hearings operate to serve the client's best interests; the other is that the danger posed by the client warrants suspension of the privilege.[29] The first rationale assumes that the client, by opposing commitment, has failed to recognize his or her own best interests; the second assumes that the client is dangerous. Both prejudge the client, assuming the existence of the very facts at issue in the hearing. The better view, adopted by several courts, holds that the constitutional right against self-incrimination and the evidentiary privilege together require that statements made in confidence not be used, in whole or in part, as the basis for commitment.[30] This rule does not unduly obstruct the commitment process, since it does not prevent therapists from testifying altogether. It simply requires that the therapist, after determining that a client should or will be subjected to commitment proceedings, warn the client that their communications are no longer confidential and may be used in the commitment hearings. Any information gathered after such a warning would then be unprivileged and hence admissible.

In the absence of an exception, the therapist is bound to respect the confidentiality of clients both in court and out. A disclosure of communications or records, or possibly even of the fact that a client is in therapy, can give rise to civil liability in several forms.[31] The aggrieved client may bring an action for breach of contract, based on an expressed or implied term of confidentiality; for defamation, if the disclosure was untrue and harmful; or for invasion of privacy.[32] In at least the last action, the client can prevail and recover damages even without having to prove any actual harm from the disclosure.[33] In any of these actions it is possible that therapists could be held liable for disclosures made by others under the therapists' supervision. Moreover, the therapist could incur penalties under state licensing statutes.

Our review of the law of confidentiality thus far can be summed up in a very simple rule, entirely consistent with the mental-health profession's self-imposed norms: "mum's the word." The only significant exceptions arise when the client consents to disclosure or when a court, within the confines of the therapist-client privilege, orders it. Still, one final exception remains to be considered, and that is the category of required warnings.

Confidentiality and the Dangerous Client

Most states statutorily require that physicians report to specified authorities certain cases of grave public concern, typically including cases of venereal disease, tuberculosis, and child abuse.[34] These reports are themselves confidential. The reporting requirements imposed on physicians would seem to obligate psychiatrists, although there is room for contrary interpretation. Some states also impose modified reporting requirements on other health professionals and social-service workers, especially in regard to cases of child abuse. Given the disparity among states as to what must be reported, by whom, and to whom, clinicians should consult local authorities to determine their reporting obligations.

Lastly, there is an emerging, but still controversial, duty of the therapist to warn of imminent danger posed by a client. This duty was announced by the Supreme Court of California in *Tarasoff* v. *The Regents of the University of California*, a case on which the justices deliberated for some three years before finally deciding the case by a mere four to three majority in 1976.[35] The case was brought by the parents of a young woman who was shot and stabbed to death by a client of the principal defendants, a clinical psychologist and a psychiatrist employed by a university health service. The client had told his therapist, the defendant psychologist, of his intention to kill the decedent when she returned from a trip abroad. The psychologist alerted the campus police by phone and letter and asked that they assist him in having the client committed for evaluation. After briefly detaining him, the police released the client, convinced that he was rational and satisfied by his promise to keep away from the decedent. Subsequently, the psychologist's superior, the defendant psychiatrist, directed that the letter to the police and all similar notes kept by the psychologist be destroyed and that no action be taken toward commitment. Shortly later, the client carried out his threat.[36]

As to the *Tarasoff* case itself, the court's decision meant only that the plaintiffs could amend their complaint to state a cause of action, a valid legal claim, against the therapists for failure to protect the decedent. The court remanded the case for trial. To reach that conclusion, however, the court first had to determine that the therapist owed some duty to protect the decedent. Here lies the crux of the court's decision.

In our ruggedly individualistic society, one is generally under no duty to protect or control the conduct of others.[37] A duty to protect or control others is found only where there exists what the law refers to as a special relationship. Thus, parents have a duty both to protect and control their children; and authorities in mental hospitals have a duty to protect and control their patients.[38] The crux of the *Tarasoff* decision is its holding that such a special relationship exists between a therapist and client. The court further ruled that this relationship gives rise to a duty of care owed by the therapist not only to clients but also to third parties.

The *Tarasoff* court noted that the specific obligation of the therapist under this duty can only be determined on the facts of each individual case. It went on to say that:

> In our view, however, once a therapist does in fact determine, or under applicable professional standards reasonably should have determined, that a patient poses a serious danger of violence to others, he bears a duty to exercise *reasonable care* to protect the *foreseeable* victim of that danger.[39]

Subsequent cases have clarified the nature of this duty. A recent California appellate-court decision stressed that the duty applies only where the threat presented by the patient is one of serious and "imminent" danger to a "readily identifiable victim," one who can be identified "with a moment's reflection."[40] Another appellate decision in California held that *Tarasoff* imposes no liability for failure to protect a client from self-inflicted harm.[41] An appellate decision in the state of Washington distinguished *Tarasoff* as applying the duty only when information regarding the client's dangerousness is provided directly by the client rather than a third party and when the identifiable victim is personally unaware of that information.[42] Finally, a federal court in Pennsylvania interpreted *Tarasoff* as applying only where potential danger to a third person would result directly from conduct of the therapist's client; thus, therapists whose clients alert them to danger presented by other persons or causes are under no duty to avert it.[43]

The *Tarasoff* decision suggested that the appropriate steps for the defendant-therapists would have been to warn the decedent or others who could have averted the danger. The court issued no ruling on whether the duty might require therapists to actually restrain or seek the commitment of imminently dangerous clients, since the defendants in that case were statutorily immune from liability for any failure to do so. It is worth noting that, after thorough research, a leading authority on forensic psychiatry reported that he could find no U.S. case in which a therapist was held liable for a failure to commit.[44] It may be surmised, then, that the most the duty requires is that the therapist issue a warning reasonably calculated to inform an identified victim.

The basis of the *Tarasoff* decision is questionable. It first assumes that therapists can predict dangerousness with some accuracy, an assumption that has been contested by legal and mental-health professionals alike.[45] Moreover, it imposes the duty to warn at the expense of confidentiality. By doing so, it may have the effect of deterring clients from seeking treatment, of making them less than honest with their therapists, or even of deterring therapists from accepting potentially violent clients.

Whatever the soundness of the *Tarasoff* rule, it is nevertheless the rule—at least in California. Our research has uncovered only one case outside of California, a lower-court decision, in which the rule has been applied against a therapist.[46] Like *Tarasoff*, this case arose from the murder of a young woman by a client of the defendant, here a private psychiatrist. And like *Tarasoff*, this decision held only that the plaintiff, the decedent's mother, had stated a cause of action. Although the law is yet unsettled, it may comfort the reader to note one clear ruling on the matter: the Supreme Court of Nevada has decided that the *Tarasoff* rule did not subject a massage parlor to liability for failure to warn a cab driver that one of its patrons was dangerous.[47]

Notes

1. Roe v. Wade, 410 U.S. 113, 153 (1973) (state statutes prohibiting abortion struck down as violative of the constitutional right of personal privacy).

2. *In re* B., Appeal of Dr. Loren Roth, 482 Pa. 471, 394 A.2d 419 (1978); *In re* Lifschutz, 2 Cal. 3d 415, 85 Cal. Rptr. 829, 467 P.2d 557 (1970).

3. Helfman, Harrett, Lutzker, Schneider & Stein, *Access to Medical Records*, U.S. Department of Health, Education and Welfare, Report of the Secretary's Commission on Medical Malpractice, 177-178 app. (1973) [hereinafter cited as HEW Report]. This study reported that clients in only seven states were without explicit statutory protection of their right to privacy in psychotherapeutic settings.

4. *See generally*, Slovenko, *On the Need for Record Keeping in the Practice of Psychiatry*, 7 J. Psychiatry & L. 399 (1979); and Hayes, *Patient's Right of Access to His Hospital and Medical Records*, 1978 Med. Trial Tech. Q. 295. The authors explain that as the range of parties involved in service delivery increases, the utility of records and the need for safeguards of privacy increase as well.

5. *See, e.g.*, Wyatt v. Stickney, 334 F. Supp. 373, 385 (M.D. Ala. 1972). Accreditation standards also impose record-keeping requirements.

6. Hayden, *How Much Does the Boss Need to Know?* 3 Civ. Lib. Rev. 23, 25 (1976). These files include information regarding one's financial and employment history, character, reputation, and life-style, and are used primarily by private entities in making decisions on loan, charge-account, insurance, and employment applications.

7. Senate Constitutional Rights Subcommittee, 93d Cong., 2d Sess., *Privacy: The Collection, Use and Computerization of Personal Data—Fact Sheet* (1974); *Joint Hearings before the Ad Hoc Subcommittee on Privacy and Information Systems*, 93d Cong., 2d Sess. 2252 (June 18-20, 1974) (Comm. Print 1974).

8. *In re* B., Appeal of Dr. Loren Roth, 482 Pa. 471, 394 A.2d 419 (1978).

9. For an excellent examination of this subject, see Slovenko, *Psychotherapy and Confidentiality,* 24 Clev. St. L. Rev. 375, 377-82 (1975).

10. *See generally* Task Force on Confidentiality as It Relates to Third Parties, American Psychiatric Association, Summary Report (1974). On the right to expunge all records of unlawful commitment, and thereby to avert third-party disclosures, see *In re* S.C., 421 A.2d 853 (Pa. Super. Ct. 1980).

11. HEW Report, *supra* note 3, at 181, 186-212.

12. *Id.* at 184.

13. 42 U.S.C. §9401 *et seq.* (Supp. 1981).

14. *Id.* at §9501(1) (I).

15. 5 U.S.C. §552a (Supp. 1981).

16. *Id.* at §§552a (d), (g)(1). The actual procedures for gaining access and for correcting, amending, or challenging the use of records, are established separately by the agencies that hold records, and are codified in the Code of Federal Regulations. The procedures of the Social Security Administration, for instance, are found at 20 C.F.R. §442.428 (1981).

17. 45 C.F.R. §5b.6(b)(1)(2) (1981).

18. Gotkin v. Miller, 514 F.2d 125 (2d Cir. 1975), *aff'g* 379 F. Supp. 859 (E.D.N.Y. 1974).

19. Gaertner v. State, 385 Mich. 49, 187 N.W.2d 429 (1971).

20. Sullivan v. State, 352 So.2d 1212 (Fla. Ct. App. 1977). On the legal doctrine of informed consent and the importance of information to the legal validity of consent, see chapter 3, *supra.*

21. *See, e.g.*, Kaiser, *Patients' Right of Access to Their Own Medical Records: The Need for New Law*, 24 Buffalo L. Rev. 317 (1975); Comment, *Access to Medical and Psychiatric Records: Proposed Legislation*, 40 Albany L. Rev. 580 (1976). *Accord*, Contract Research Corporation, Model State Code: Privacy Act for the Developmentally Disabled (prepared for U.S. Developmental Disabilities Office, Sept. 16, 1977).

22. *See* 97 Corpus Juris Secondum §293, at 827 (Supp. 1981).

23. *See* HEW Report, *supra* note 3, at 186-212.

24. For recent reforms eliminating such disparities, see Ark. Stat. Ann. §28-1001 R. 503 (1979).

25. *See* HEW Report, *supra* note 3, at 179.

26. *See, e.g.,* Schaffer v. Spicer, 88 S.D. 36, 215 N.W.2d 134 (1974).

27. *See, e.g., In re* Lifschutz, 2 Cal. 3d 415, 85 Cal. Rptr. 829, 467 P.2d 557 (1970).

28. Most state statutes extend the privilege only to psychiatrists and psychologists. *See, e.g.,* Conn. Gen. Stat. §52-146c & d (Supp. 1981); Del. Uniform Rules of Evid. R503(a) (Supp. 1980); Fla. Stat. Ann. §90.503(1) (West Supp. 1981). California, for one, extends the privilege to state-licensed clinical social workers, marriage, family, and child counsellors as well. Cal. Evid. Code §1010 (West Supp. 1981). For a forceful argument urging extension of the privilege to cover relationships with all qualified psychotherapists, see Note, *The Psychotherapist-Patient Privilege: Are Some Patients More Privileged Than Others?* 10 Pac. L.J. 801 (1979).

29. *See, e.g.,* People v. Lakey, 102 Cal. App. 3d Supp. 962, 162 Cal. Rptr. 653 (1980); Commonwealth *ex rel.* Platt v. Platt, 404 A.2d 410 (Pa. Super. Ct. 1979).

30. *See, e.g.,* Lessard v. Schmidt, 349 F. Supp. 1078, 1100-02 (E.D. Wis. 1972); Matter of Rizer, 87 Ill. App. 3d 795, 409 N.E.2d 383 (1980); Commonwealth v. Lamb, 365 Mass. 265, 311 N.E.2d 47 (1974).

31. Since disclosure of the mere fact of therapy could cause actual harm to a client, for example, loss of a job, it is conceivable that a court would hold that so slight a disclosure is a tort. The court might reason by analogy to statutes that make disclosure of the fact of psychiatric hospitalization unlawful. *See, e.g.,* Wash. Rev. Code Ann. §71.05.390 (Supp. 1981).

32. *See generally* Roedershimer, *Action for Breach of Medical Secrecy outside the Courtroom,* 36 U. Cin. L. Rev. 103 (1966).

33. W. Prosser, The Law of Torts §117, at 815 (4th ed. 1971).

34. *See, e.g.,* Mich. Comp. Laws Ann. §§333.5203, .5213, .5236, .5251, .5261 (venereal and other hazardous communicable diseases) §§722.623-627, .633 (child abuse or neglect) (1980). Reports of occupational diseases and drug addictions may also be required, Conn. Gen. Stat. §31-40a (1980), as well as injuries due to violence, Cal. Penal Code §§11160-61 (West Supp. 1980).

35. 17 Cal. 3d 425, 551 P.2d 334, 131 Cal. Rptr. 14, 83 A.L.R. 3d 1166 (1976).

36. The criminal prosecution of the client is reported in People v. Poddar, 10 Cal. 3d 750, 518 P.2d 342, 111 Cal. Rptr. 910 (1974).

37. Restatement (Second) of Torts §314, Comment c (1965).

38. *Id.* §§314A, 316, 319. Regarding liability for harm resulting from premature release of institutionalized mental patients, see Annot., 38 A.L.R. 3d 699 (1981).

39. 17 Cal. 3d at 440, 131 Cal. Rptr. at 25 (emphasis added).

40. Mavroudis v. Superior Court, 102 Cal.3d 594, 600-01, 162 Cal. Rptr. 724, 729-30 (1980) (no recovery against psychiatrist for failure to warn plaintiff-mother whose son assaulted her, since plaintiff could not establish that psychiatrist was under a duty to warn). *See also,* Thompson v. County of Alameda, 27 Cal.3d 741, 614 P.2d 728, 167 Cal. Rptr. 70 (1980) (generalized homicidal threat created no duty to provide general warning).

41. Bellah v. Greenson, 81 Cal. App. 3d Supp. 614, 146 Cal. Rptr. 614, 579 P.2d 505 (1978) (psychiatrist not liable for failure to restrain suicidal client or to warn client's parents).

42. Hawkins v. King County, 24 Wash. App. 338, 602 P.2d 631 (1979) (court-appointed defense attorney was under no duty to warn of client's dangerousness at bail hearing).

43. Soto v. Franklin Hospital, 478 F. Supp. 1134 (E.D. Pa. 1979) (doctor not liable for failure to warn of possible carbon-monoxide poisoning).

44. Statement of Professor Halleck, Annual Judicial Conference, Second Judicial Circuit of the United States, 82 F.R.D. 22, 292 (1978).

45. *See, e.g.,* Gurevitz, *Tarasoff: Protective Privilege versus Public Peril,* 134 Am. J. Psychiatry 289, 291 (1977); Stone, *The Criteria for Compulsory Commitment and Treatment,* Presentation at Annual Judicial Conference, *supra* note 44 at 249 ("Psychiatrists are incompetent to tell you who is dangerous. Don't ask us to do something we cannot do, and then blame us for not doing it."); Cocozza & Steadman, *The Failure of Psychiatric Predictions of Dangerousness: Clear and Convincing Evidence,* 29 Rutgers L. Rev. 1084 (1976); Ennis & Litwack, *Psychiatry and the Presumption of Expertise: Flipping Coins in the Courtroom,* 62 Cal. L. Rev. 693 (1974).

46. McIntosh v. Milano, 168 N.J. Super. 466, 403 A.2d 500 (1979).

47. Manageris v. Gordon, 580 P.2d 481 (Nev. 1978) (dismissal of complaint against massage parlor charging its management with liability in death of cab driver at hands of a patron allegedly known to be dangerous).

Part III
Rights to Community Services

The Special Problems and Special Rights of Children

Perhaps no problem presents more of a legal, social, and therapeutic thicket than the relationship of children to the mental-health system. Minors, at least preadolescents, clearly have a lesser capacity for rational decision making, and the question of who shall act on their behalf is ever present. The greater vulnerability and dependence of children evoke the protective instincts of society; but these instincts encounter a welter of social ambiguities about the nature of childhood and the definition of a child's best interests. The family is widely presumed to have the obligation and the duty to guide and even control the lives of children, yet the reality of schools, street life, and adult attitudes is that families increasingly surrender to other institutions their responsibilities to their children. Mental-health professionals have become trapped in these societal ambivalences about the role of children and families; and the law rarely helps resolve matters.

The legal maze into which any clinician working with children steps typically consists of three competing interests: (1) the interests of parents in preserving family autonomy from state interference, in providing for the best interests of their children, and in preserving the particular personal and cultural values of their family; (2) the interest of the state in protecting the child, preventing or controlling unwanted behavior, and in providing a system of mental-health care; and (3) the interest of the child in being cared for, loved, and helped to become an autonomous individual with the rights and privileges of an adult. This chapter deals with three areas in which these interests are brought to bear on the work of clinicians and mental-health advocates: the admission of minors to inpatient mental-health facilities at parental request, the problem of consent to treatment of minors, and the provision of special education and psychological services to handicapped children. In each of these areas there is a substantial opportunity and even a need for clinicians and advocates to work together to make sense of extremely vague but emotionally and politically charged problems.

Parental Commitment of Children as Voluntary Mental-Health Inpatients

More than thirty states provide statutory permission for parents or guardians of minors to admit their minor children to mental institutions as so-called voluntary inpatients.[1] The procedure typically requires only the agreement of an admitting physician that the child is mentally ill and could benefit from hospital treatment. This situation is, of course, completely contrary to that which applies to competent adults, who may be involuntarily committed only after a judicial hearing and full due-process safeguards.[2] The ease with which children can be committed to state hospitals, the conditions for treating children in most mental institutions, and the inexact nature of clinical diagnosis all contribute to serious questions about whether children ought not to be entitled to the same constitutional rights as adults when deprivation of liberty is concerned. One commentator put the problem this way: "there is serious cause to be alarmed that voluntary admissions are being abused with regard to minors. . . . At least some evidence [exists] that parents may indeed have resorted to placing their children in mental hospitals in lieu of abandonment."[3] And as Supreme Court Justice William Brennan has observed, "numerous studies reveal that parental decisions to institutionalize their children often are the results of dislocation in the family unrelated to the children's mental conditions."[4]

The statutory schemes of thirty states providing for parental admission of minors have, however, been upheld by the U.S. Supreme Court in a significant decision that affects children's rights in general and the mental-health system in particular.[5] In 1979 the Court handed down *Parham* v. *J.R.*[6] in which it upheld a Georgia statute that permitted a state-hospital physician to admit a minor under eighteen on application of a parent or guardian if the physician found the child "to show evidence of mental illness and to be suitable for treatment."[7] The Court rejected arguments, which had been accepted by a lower federal court, that a minor is entitled to a judicial hearing complete with notice, legal representation, the right to present evidence, and a transcript. In effect, the Supreme Court's ruling leaves the matter of committing a child, even against the child's will, as a decision to be made jointly by parent or guardian and a state-employed physician.

The Court did recognize that errors can be made in determining the suitability of hospitalizing children in mental-health care: "We conclude that the risk of error inherent in the parental decision to have a child institutionalized for mental health care is sufficiently great that some kind of inquiry should be made by a 'neutral factfinder' to determine whether the statutory requirements for admission are satisfied."[8] But the Court went on to declare that the neutral factfinder need not be law trained or a judicial or administrative officer, that the hearing need not be formal or include any representation for the child, and that in making the decision "a staff physician will suffice, so long as he or she is free to evaluate independently the child's mental and emotional condition and need for treatment."[9]

The decision in *Parham* is at odds with a string of other Supreme Court rulings that support the rights and independence of minors when their interests clash with those of the state or their parents.[10] Because *Parham* recasts some of the legal thinking about children, families, and the state, and because the decision contains numerous unresolved issues of potential importance to mental-health clinicians, it is appropriate to discuss the case in some detail.

The law regards the commitment of an adult to a mental hospital as a "massive curtailment of liberty," which invokes the full constitutional protection of due process to prevent unjustifiable commitments.[11] *Parham* indicates, however, that children committed without their own consent are not entitled to the same protections that the law affords adults whose liberty is at stake. The Court's reasoning, however, raises the possibility that it may yet discover some rights that extend to minors in the mental-health system. Therefore, as broadly as *Parham* seems to sweep, further litigation may curtail its application. Moreover, although the Supreme Court has ruled that the Constitution does not require state legislatures to provide complete due process where parental commitment of minors is concerned, it has not ruled that enlightened legislatures are forbidden from applying due-process guarantees to such commitments or that mental-health professionals are prevented from setting up due-process-type inquiries where the lives of children are at stake.

The Nature of Hospitalization for Mental Illness

The *Parham* decision is laced with assumptions about mental health and institutionalization of children that, if rebutted in a future case, could yield an entirely different result. Unlike the situation in which a committed adult has been found "mentally ill and possibly dangerous,"[12] the majority opinion views the commitment of a child by his or her parents as a situation in which the "state through its voluntary commitment procedures does not 'label' the child; it provides a diagnosis and treatment that medical specialists conclude the child requires." The public reaction to the stigmatizing effect of being labelled mentally ill is supposed to be avoided because the parents are viewed as providing an element of voluntarism in their request for the commitment of their child. The reputed benevolence of institutionalizing children for mental treatment is subjected to no close analysis by the Court, in part because the *Parham* case is a class action without massive statistical evidence of inappropriate treatment. The Court did not probe further, even though the lower court ruled in favor of the plaintiff children and discussed a Georgia study that found that over half the children institutionalized in that state "would not need hospitalization if other forms of care were available in the community."[13]

The Supreme Court's assumption of benevolent hospital care for children also disregards the finding in the lower court that after long periods of institutionalization children learn and internalize institutional behavior that becomes an "additional handicap" inhibiting a return to the normal world.[14] In fact the Supreme Court opines that "a person needing but not receiving appropriate medical care may well face even greater social ostracism resulting from the observable symptoms of an untreated disorder."[15] Although the Court concludes that a child has a "protectible interest . . . in being free of unnecessary bodily restraints . . . [and] in not being labelled erroneously by . . . an improper decision by the state hospital superintendent," the Court's assumptions about treatment in hospitals reflect a peculiar view of mental-health treatment and diagnosis.[16] In the Court's view, therefore, a parental decision that is "not agreeable to the child" or "involves risks" poses no greater threat and commands no greater judicial protection than a parental decision to secure "a tonsillectomy, appendectomy, or other medical procedure."[17] Since "most children, even adolescents, simply are not able to make sound judgments concerning many decisions, including their need for medical care or treatment, parents can and must make those judgments."[18] The Court's refusal to examine the nature of mental-health care as compared to tonsillectomies is at odds with its views on parental consent for abortions.[19] If a more sophisticated understanding of the effect and uncertainty of mental-health diagnosis in coercive settings takes hold in the lower courts, the Court may move away from the position that children deserve less due-process protection in matters of commitment than do adults.

The Role of Families in Society

The Court is untroubled about the risks of parental commitment of children to mental institutions in part because of the Court's view of the family. "Our jurisprudence historically has reflected Western Civilization concepts of the family as a unit with broad parental authority over minor children."[20] The Court reasserts that the "child is not the mere creature of the state,"[21] bases its defense of the family on the "presumption that parents possess what a child lacks in maturity, experience, and capacity for judgment,"[22] and labels as "statist" the notion that due process should be required to check the appropriateness of parental decisions to commit children just because "some parents abuse and neglect children."[23] The majority of the Court is thus simultaneously affirming the autonomy of the family from state control and reinforcing the traditional notions of hierarchical authority within the family. This position, while appealing to those who have had enough of government control of their private lives, is not entirely consistent with the Court's historical position. It glosses over three substantial areas in which the Court has had a major role in shaping the relationship of family to state and the relationship among family members. For instance, in the area of education the Court makes much of cases that appear to secure the parental right to control a child's education against competing values of the state; yet the reality of education law is that the balance of power over the schooling of the children of nonwealthy families lies not with the family but with the state.[24] Second, the Court ignores its role in expanding the rights of children to free speech, procreation decisions, and due-process rights in spite of any objections their parents might have to the exercise of these rights.[25] Finally, there is no recognition that the traditional patterns of family authority frequently have not been upheld by the Court where the rights of young women are concerned.

The Court vastly understates the complexity of the problem of voluntary parental commitment of children by assuming that it can be reduced to a question of conflict between family and state and by using this ideology to subsume the interests of children within those of the parents. Apparently the Court is willing to protect the autonomy of the family in some circumstances and not in others; but it has given little guidance as to how much autonomy can be assumed to exist in mental-health decisions. As a result it simply allows parents to substitute their judgment for their children's on the commitment question. The limitations of such an assumption are pointed out in the *Parham* dissent, in which Justice Brennan observes that:

> the parent-child dispute at issue here cannot be characterized as involving only a routine child-rearing decision made within the context of an ongoing family relationship. Indeed, . . . here a break in family autonomy has actually resulted in the parents' decision to surrender custody of their child to a state mental institution. In my view, a child who has been ousted from his family has even greater need for an independent advocate.[26]

Perhaps the part of the *Parham* opinion that points out most clearly the Court's disingenuousness in refusing to require due-process scrutiny into the intimacy and privacy of the parent-child relationship, is its ruling on the commitment of wards of the state. The Court sees no more need for judicial scrutiny of the state's decision to commit a minor ward than of a parent's decision because "we cannot assume that when the State of Georgia has custody of a child it acts so differently from a natural parent in seeking medical assistance for the child."[27] The Court's view of bureaucratic decision making, like its view of mental illness and family dynamics, seems at odds with contemporary reality.

Concerning both the commitment of wards of the state (on which there is a vigorous dissent in *Parham*) and the balancing of parental and children's interests within the family, the *Parham* ruling may be open to future revision, limitation, and attack. Advocates and clinicians alike may expect to become involved in future attempts to bring a more sensitive and realistic understanding of these complex issues to the attention of legislative and judicial authorities. Perhaps one of the earliest contests of this sort will involve the Supreme Court's failure to address the differences in decision-making ability, autonomy, and due-process rights between a child who is seventeen years old and one who is six. The age and meaning of emancipation varies from state to state and may ultimately affect the judgment of child status in mental-health questions.

The Neutrality of the State in Matters of Mental Health

The Court devotes considerable energy to the claim that denying full due-process rights to children protects the family from intrusion by the apparatus of state. In making this claim, significant weight is placed by the Court on the neutrality and good faith of those state officials charged with approving parental commitment decisions. In part, of course, this is simply judicial deference to presumed medical expertise. But the result is to subsume questions of liberty under questions of medicine. When the Court rules that the protectible interest of children in being free of unwarranted deprivations of liberty and stigmatization requires only a nonlegal "neutral factfinder" to remain secure, it views the problem as "essentially medical in character."[28] The Court is, therefore, "satisfied that an independent medical decision-making process . . . will protect children who should not be admitted."[29] Of course this is not a form of trust that the courts have been willing to adopt where the commitment of adults is concerned. Not only is the state-employed physician trusted to detect any abuse of parental power, but the entire bureaucracy is credited with being interested in confining the use "of costly mental health facilities to cases of genuine need."[30] This assumption is made in spite of the Georgia study showing that over half the institutionalized children would be better off in less restrictive settings. The Court argues that no adversary proceeding is needed to check on the necessity of institutionalizing children. Because state mental-health personnel are assumed to be people of good will, and because the medical bureaucracy is believed to have no significant interests or pressures that would prevent it from acting as "neutral" decision maker, no one outside the process need inquire into its fairness. No doubt the attributes of good faith are widespread even if freedom from political or economic pressure within mental-health bureaucracies is not. But in matters of liberty, evidence of the good faith of agents of the state has never before been held sufficient to remove the need for neutral judicial scrutiny. In his dissent arguing for prior hearings for wards of the state subject to commitment, Justice Brennan put the matter succinctly:

> The Court dismisses a challenge to this practice on the grounds that state social workers are obliged by statute to act in the children's best interest. . . . I find this reasoning particularly unpersuasive. With equal logic it could be argued that criminal trials are unnecessary since prosecutors are not supposed to prosecute innocent persons.[31]

The majority of the Court thus seems reluctant to intrude judicial standards on two of society's major institutions, the family and the medical profession. In the former case, as has already been suggested, the reluctance is somewhat disingenuous and serves ideological purposes only. In the second case the Court seems as mystified by medicine and mental illness as most people are mystified by law and legal doctrine. It will be very unfortunate for both professions and for the public if the *Parham* decision imposes a requirement that to secure a minimum of due-process protection for the liberty of children an advocate must attack the good faith of clinicians and the mental-health system.

Although the decision does set out the parameters of a constitutional procedure for dealing with the hospitalization of children, it is the beginning rather than the end of this effort.[32] *Parham* is open to revision based on the differences in the age of children, the nature of mental illness and family therapy, the principle of the least restrictive alternative, and the rights of wards of the state as opposed to children of natural parents. In addition, in the past, the Court has reversed itself on several matters of individual rights based on the experience of the states, as for example in matters of right to counsel and search and seizure. This may also be a possibility in habeas corpus proceedings in which the abuse of parental power to commit or the misapplication of statutory standards in the medical decision-making process is alleged.

The area most open for revision concerns periodic review of institutionalization. The Court ruled that no judicial hearing or due-process requirements (other than the neutral fact-finder staff physician) applies on initial commitment. But it required a periodic review of the adequacy of continued commitment "to reduce the risk of error in the initial admission."[33] In spite of the vigorous protests of the dissenters, the Court did not elaborate on what standards of due process must accompany such periodic review. And in fact the dissent was able to argue that there is significant reason to use more stringent due-process protections once the parent-child bond has been strained or severed by the commitment decision. It may be, therefore, that the periodic review will be the focus of the continuing struggle to protect the rights of children. The argument may be made that the Constitution requires a review of commitment with attendant due-process protections very soon after admission.

Consent to the Treatment of Minors

Chapter 3 makes it clear that the requirement of client consent to medical treatment is an accepted part of both law and medicine. The three elements of a valid consent have been described as voluntariness, information, and competency (or capacity). If the mental status of adults can call into question the element of competency to consent, the social presumptions about childhood clearly suggest that children may not consent or refuse to consent to medical or mental-health treatment and that substituted or surrogate consent is required instead. Certainly the *Parham* decision on voluntary parental commitment of children, even with its ambiguities and flawed reasoning, reinforces the presumption that parents may secure treatment for their children regardless of the child's opinion or preferences. Fortunately, the matter is not so simple.

The presumption that children lack the capacity to consent to treatment or to refuse treatment does have exceptions.[34] But the lack of clarity of these exceptions suggests that clinicians should err on the side of protecting the child's interest where it diverges from that of the parent or guardian.[35] The courts have had little opportunity to examine problems of differing interests among parents and children, and where they have addressed them they have sought to minimize the problems.[36] The result is that children lack protection from inappropriate parental decisions. There are some areas in which independence from parental decisions about health care are beginning to take shape.

In some cases parents may not consent to treatment for their children. In other cases children can consent to treatment over the objection or without the knowledge of parents, and in still others children can be admitted as inpatients without parental consent. Courts have carved out certain areas in which parental wishes (or consent) are regarded as legally insufficient to justify a clinician in proceeding with treatment. In these cases a judicial determination that the child's interests are in fact being considered is typically required. Examples of such requirements are abortion and sterilization.[37] The basis of exceptions of this sort lies in the intrusiveness, severity, or irreversibility of the treatments at issue. Under such a criterion, procedures such as electroshock therapy or psychosurgery would also be beyond the reach of parental consent and would require court-supervised examination of the child's interest through due-process hearings. An additional and closely related basis for these exceptions is whether the treatment in question is a proven therapeutic tool and whether the treatment is in fact beneficial treatment or simply a means of controlling unruly behavior.[38] The courts will also consider the magnitude of the constitutional interest at stake for the child. For example, if the child's liberty, freedom of consciousness, or right to make procreative decisions are at stake, the courts will be more likely to require that the child's interest be represented separately from that of the parents.

In a second set of exceptions to the presumption of minor incapacity to consent, courts and legislatures of various states have insisted that children of certain ages be permitted to secure treatment without parental consent or in spite of parental objection. Examples include emergency medical treatment, abortion,[39] birth-control information,[40] and treatment for venereal disease and drug-abuse problems.[41] Certain states, for example, Maryland[42] and Colorado,[43] permit adolescents of prescribed ages to secure outpatient mental-health treatment without parental consent or knowledge. Finally, the courts of some states hold that emancipated minors or so-called mature minors may consent to treatments of certain types where they are clearly beneficial to the child.[44]

All these exceptions to a minor's lack of capacity to consent seem to depend on (1) the maturity of judgment and intellect of the minor (a question of individual development), (2) the seriousness of the condition that is being treated, and (3) the likelihood of a child seeking help if parents are informed of the problem. The reluctance of parents to consent to treatment is viewed as a much more significant problem than the possibility that the parent will consent to treatment that is not really in the child's best interest. John Wilson and his associates discuss the sources of parental resistance to mental health treatment as follows:

> [Parents] may feel that society attaches a stigma to individuals who require mental health treatment, and may believe that the entire family will suffer social disapproval. They may also feel that they are responsible for the child's illness and may fear that acknowledging the illness will be an admission of their failure as parents. . . . Parents may also fear that, during the course of therapy the child will reveal family secrets.[45]

All these possibilities suggest that clinicians should become familiar with the law in their states. This law will define whether the clinician should seek parental consent, treat on the basis of the consent of the child, or pursue judicial determination of the permissibility of the treatment in question. If the child has or can secure an advocate there will be good reason for clinician and advocate to discuss openly the best course of action from the legal point of view.

The final category of exceptions to the incapacity of children concerns voluntary admission to a mental hospital as an inpatient. Although the general rule is that children may not admit themselves as inpatients without parental consent,[46] some states have enacted legislation specifically allowing minors above a certain age to admit themselves as voluntary patients.[47] Of course, it should be noted that in these circumstances children, like adults, are not automatically presumed incompetent to consent or refuse treatment or to have waived their right to refuse by virtue of their voluntary admission.[48]

The area of consent to mental-health treatment by minors or their parents or guardians is developing very slowly as are all areas of law in which intrafamilial disagreements form the crux of the problem of individual rights. Clearly, however, there are certain issues that the courts have taken into account and that clinicians should consider in choosing a course of action. They are: the maturity and age of the child, the severity or intrusiveness of the treatment proposed, the importance of the personal right or interest of the child affected by the treatment, the likelihood that parents can dissociate their own interests from those of their child, and the specific rulings of courts and legislatures concerning the treatment or age of the child at issue.

Education and Psychological Services for Handicapped Children

In 1975 the Congress passed the Education of All Handicapped Children Act in response to the need for adequate education and related services for children with physical or emotional disabilities.[49] The act creates a set of obligations in each participating state to meet the needs of these children. The process by which families participate in determining the appropriateness of these services for children provides a major opportunity for clinicians and advocates to work together for their common clients. The federal legislation establishes a set of requirements that may be augmented by each state. A general understanding of the law on special education can be provided by discussing the act itself, leaving clinicians and advocates to discover the additional rights and problems of their particular jurisdiction.

The act provides partial funding for the required children's services to those states that adopt special-education legislation that complies with the requirements of federal law. The act requires the states to provide a "free appropriate public education" to all children between the ages of three and twenty-one.[50] If the public-education agency cannot provide an adequate education for the child within public facilities, then a private agency that meets the standards that apply to the public agency may be utilized at no expense to the parents.[51] Private-school children with handicaps are entitled to the same public services provided public-school children.[52]

The definition of handicapped children includes the mentally retarded, learning disabled, physically handicapped, and emotionally disturbed.[53] "Special education and related services" to which these children are entitled include classroom instruction, home instruction, physical education, transportation, psychological services, physical and occupational therapy, counseling, diagnostic and evaluative medical services, and others.[54] The particular services to which the child is entitled are determined under the act through a procedure by which the child's needs are evaluated and an individualized education program (IEP) is formulated for that child. Institutional and hospital instruction must be provided where appropriate.[55] The IEP is a written statement that must be developed with the participation of the local education agency, the child's parents or guardians, and, where appropriate, the child.[56] The IEP must include an evaluation of the child's needs and present level of educational performance as well as the goals, specific services needed, and future evaluation planned.

In the process of evaluating the child's needs, the act proscribes racially or culturally biased tests or evaluation procedures, requires that tests be in the child's native language, and insists that no one test or criterion be used alone to determine the placement of the child.[57] The law also requires that the child be placed in the "least restrictive environment"[58] consistent with the child's needs.[59] Although the school officials have a duty under the act to locate and evaluate children who may be handicapped, no child may be evaluated or tested without parental consent.[60] Parents also have the right of access to all records related to placement,[61] the right to notice of any proposed change in placement, and the right to obtain an independent evaluation of the child.[62] An annual review of the child's progress and IEP is also required.

The heart of this act is not only the involvement of educational and clinical personnel in establishing an individual plan for the handicapped child's education and related services but also the right of the parents to disagree with the conclusions of the evaluation, the proposed placement, or any action affecting the child's entitlement to special education.[63] In some states, few parents take advantage of the detailed procedures established by the act for considering these disagreements. Nevertheless, the appeal procedure provides an avenue for those persons most concerned about the child's special needs—the parents, clinicians, and advocate—to ensure that these needs are in fact met. Thus far it is the unfortunate history of the act and the various state laws related to it that there is insufficient funding to provide the necessary amount and variety of service, so that those families who do not insist on their entitlements are not likely to be given them.

On filing a complaint relating to evaluation, identification, placement, or the provision of appropriate services, the parents are entitled to an impartial hearing before a hearing examiner not employed by the agency providing the education service and, if necessary, to take an appeal to the state agency. At these hearings the parties have extensive rights to counsel and the assistance of persons with special training in dealing with handicapped children, to present evidence including that of independent experts, to cross-examine witnesses and compel attendance of witnesses, and to a record of the proceedings and a written finding of facts as well as decisions.[64] If these administrative reviews fail to resolve the problem satisfactorily, any party may bring an action in state or federal court.[65] In all these proceedings the advocate is in fact representing the interests of the handicapped child. As a result, in those instances in which a division appears between the parental view of their child's best interest and the child's own view, the advocate may be expected to maintain a loyalty to the child even at the expense of requiring that the parents seek separate assistance. In most instances, however, such a split will not occur.

It is beyond the scope of this chapter to discuss the individual state laws that add substantive and procedural rights for families and participation for advocates and clinicians or to examine in detail the practical problems of making the Education of All Handicapped Children Act work in reality.[66] It is possible, however, to identify briefly problem areas in which the clinician and advocate may expect to work together to advance the child's needs.[67]

Most problems encountered under the act and its state counterparts involve the paucity of funds available to provide special education and related services to children. As a result of underfunding many handicapped children are treated substantially more poorly than so-called normal children. Support services such as psychological counseling for child and family may be missing, and the range of available placements or even the judgment of what is appropriate may be skewed by the knowledge that the money to do what is required is not available. In some instances the education agency may attempt to deny its responsibilities under the act altogether in an attempt to shift the burden of services to a mental-health institution or some other state agency. All these pressures and tactics can result in restricting the clinician's judgment about the child's needs, especially if such restrictions are not resisted with a firm knowledge of what the federal and state legislation require.

A second set of problems concerns the adequacy of evaluations of the child in question. Bias or negligence may result in a superficial, inaccurate, or incomplete evaluation of the child's needs. The appeal mechanism provides the opportunity to challenge such evaluations so that children are not misplaced or deprived of services they require. Clinicians may expect parents or advocates to request independent evaluations or advocates to request help in analyzing the adequacy of other evaluations as part of an administrative hearing or court litigation. Clinicians who become aware of sloppy or biased past evaluation of their clients may wish to suggest that the parent or child gain the assistance of an advocate to vindicate the right to appropriate assessment.

Perhaps the most hotly debated problem under the act is that of "mainstreaming"—the placement of a child in the least restrictive setting compatible with individual needs. The issue is a dilemma, since handicapped children can be denied their right to education either by placement in an all-handicapped setting that stigmatizes them or by integration with other children in a setting in which special services are not available. Naturally the fears and misunderstandings of parents of other children are evoked along with considerations of bureaucratic ease and financial austerity from the education agency. The policy of the act is clear on mainstreaming, but the state of research on the actual effects of mixing and separation are not clear.

Considerable difficulty has also been encountered in defining what is appropriate education and service. Some wish to expand the definition of learning disabled and appropriate education so that virtually all children are entitled to individually suitable education programs.[68] Some believe that cultural and religious beliefs of the family should be considered in defining appropriate education. But in terms of the statutory guarantee of a "free appropriate public education," the U.S. Supreme Court would insist that states provide "personalized instruction with sufficient support services to permit the child to benefit educationally from that instruction." In their recent decision in *Hendrick Hudson District Board of Education* v. *Rowley*, the justices have declined to adopt any single test for determining the adequacy of those educational benefits.[69] In the majority's view, the act mandates "a basic floor of opportunity" and a process for supplying "specialized instruction and related services" designed to meet the unique needs of each handicapped child. In making this determination, educators and courts must ensure adherence to the definitional checklist set out under the act, a list with both procedural and substantive elements.[70] Given the breadth of this list and the range of children's needs covered under the act, advocacy and parental involvement will continue to be a decisive factor in securing rights and services for the child with handicaps.

Difficulties have also been encountered in matters relating to the parents' right to have access to their child's records, to amend or comment on those records, and to protect the privacy of the same records from persons outside the family and the agency providing assistance. On this problem the act has substantial provisions that reinforce the more general provisions of the Family Educational Rights and Privacy Act of 1974.[71] Because the provision of special-education services can be used to stigmatize families as well as to aid them, the issues of access and privacy can be very emotional.

Finally, many jurisdictions have attempted to ignore their responsibilities to handicapped children by claiming, in effect, that children with emotional or mental illness are not covered by the act and should be hospitalized. As a result of this attitude and the accompanying fragmentation of service, a child may be shuttled back and forth between school and hospital until parents and child give up in frustration and disgust. The problem is even more acute for those children who have guardians or are wards of the state. Some of these children may lose forever the possibility of a normal life. The act is quite clear in its inclusion of children whose handicaps are mental, emotional, or developmental.[72] The well-informed clinician and advocate may play an important role in preventing these children and their families from becoming the unchampioned victims of official neglect and abuse.

Notes

1. *See* Ellis, *Volunteering Children: Commitment of Minors to Mental Institutions*, 62 Cal. L. Rev. 840 n.1 (1974); J. Wilson, Rights of Adolescents in the Mental Health System 302-308 app. B (1978).

2. *See* Addington v. Texas, 441 U.S. 418 (1979); B. Ennis and R. Emery, The Rights of Mental Patients 57-89 (1978).

3. Note, *Children, Commitment and Consent: A Constitutional Crisis*, 10 Fam. L. Q. 295, 305 (1976).

4. Parham v. J.R., *99 S. Ct. 2493, 2519 (1979)* (dissent), *citing* Vogel and Bell, *The Emotionally Disturbed Child as the Family Scapegoat, in* Modern Introduction to the Family 412 (Bell & Vogel, eds. 1968).

5. *See* Parham v. J.R., 99 S. Ct. at 2509 n.20.

6. *Id.*

7. Ga. Code Ann. §88-503.1(1978).

8. Parham v. J.R., 99 S. Ct. at 2506.

9. *Id.* at 2507.

10. *See, e.g.,* Planned Parenthood of Missouri v. Danforth, 428 U.S. 52 (1976) (unconstitutional for parents to have an absolute veto over minor daughter's abortion decision); Goss v. Lopez, 419 U.S. 565 (1975) (due-process rights apply to children at risk of school suspension); Tinker v. Des Moines, 393 U.S. 503 (1969) (children may not be disciplined for exercise of free-speech rights within school absent material disruption of academic order); *In re* Gault, 387 U.S. 1 (1967) (minors at risk of being sentenced by juvenile court to deprivation of liberty entitled to full due-process hearings); *In re* Smith, 295 A.2d 238 (Md. Ct. Spec. App. 1972) (parents may not compel sixteen year old to have an abortion). *But see* Ginsberg v. New York, 390 U.S. 629 (1968) (certain materials may be restricted in distribution to children that would be freely available to adults under free-speech rights); *see also* Wisconsin v. Yoder, note 36, *infra.*

11. Humphrey v. Cady, 405 U.S. 504, 509 (1972).

12. Parham v. J.R., 99 S. Ct. at 2503.
13. J.L. v. Parham, 412 F. Supp. 111, 117 (M.D. Ga. 1976).
14. *Id.*
15. Parham v. J.R., 99 S. Ct. at 2503.
16. *Id.* at 2504.
17. *Id.* at 2505.
18. *Id.*
19. *See* Planned Parenthood of Missouri v. Danforth, 428 U.S. 52 (1976).
20. Parham v. J.R., 99 S. Ct. at 2504.
21. *See* Pierce v. Society of Sisters, 268 U.S. 510, 535 (1925).
22. Parham v. J.R., 99 S. Ct. at 2504.
23. *Id.*
24. *See, e.g.,* Pierce v. Society of Sisters, 268 U.S. 510 (1925).
25. See note 10, *supra.*
26. Parham v. J.R., 99 S. Ct. at 2519 (dissent).
27. *Id.* at 2512.
28. Parham v. J.R., 99 S. Ct. at 2507.
29. *Id.* at 2509.
30. *Id.* at 2505.
31. *Id.* at 2522.
32. For a model act providing such a sensible procedure, see J. Wilson, The Rights of Adolescents in the Mental Health System 127–28 (1978).
33. Parham v. J.R., 99 S. Ct. at 2511.
34. *See, e.g.*, Gauvey, Leviton, Shuger & Sykes, *Informed and Substitute Consent to Health Care Procedures,* 15 Harv. J. Legis. 431 (1978).
35. Note, *Mental Hospitalization of Children and the Limits of Parental Power*, 88 Yale L.J. 186 (1978).
36. See, for example, Wisconsin v. Yoder, 406 U.S. 205, 243 (1972) (dissent), in which Justice Douglas upbraids the majority for failing to insist that the views of adolescent Amish school children be taken into account in determining whether their parents can withdraw them from high school before the end of their mandatory school year.
37. *In re* Smith, 295 A.2d 238 (Md. Ct. Spec. App. 1972) (parent may not compel child to have an abortion); Ruby v. Massey, 452 F. Supp. 361 (D. Conn. 1978) (parents lack power to consent to sterilization of mentally retarded daughter). On limits to restraint and seclusion, see D. Ferleger, Children in a Bind: the Law and Physical Restraint of Young People in Inpatient Facilities (1979) (unpublished paper).
38. Wyatt v. Stickney, 344 F. Supp. 387, 400 (M.D. Ala. 1972); *Legal Issues in State Mental Health Care: Proposals for Change*, 2 Mental Disability L. Rep. 153 (1977) (model statute on hazardous treatment, §40).
39. *See* Planned Parenthood of Missouri v. Danforth, 428 U.S. 52

(1976) in which the court eliminates any absolute veto by parents of a minor daughter's decision to secure an abortion.

40. Carey v. Population Services International, 431 U.S. 678 (1977).

41. *See generally*, J. Wilson, The Rights of Adolescents in the Mental Health System 127-28 (1978).

42. Md. Health-General Code Ann. §20-104 (1982).

43. Colo. Rev. Stat. §27-10-103(2) (Cum. Supp. 1978).

44. Wilson, *supra* note 41, at 125-26.

45. *Id.* at 124 (notes omitted).

46. *See* Ellis, *Volunteering Children: Parental Commitment of Minors to Mental Institutions*, 62 Cal. L. Rev. 840, 847 (1974).

47. *See, e.g.,* Mass. Gen. Laws Ann. ch. 123 §10(a) (1981); Colo. Rev. Stat. §27-10-103(2) (Cum. Supp. 1978).

48. *See* Rogers v. Okin, 478 F. Supp. 1342 (D. Mass. 1979) (for the subsequent history of this case, see pages 66 and 74 nn. 2,4, supra); N.Y. Mental Hyg. Law §33.01 (McKinney 1978).

49. 20 U.S.C. §§1411-20 (1976).

50. 20 U.S.C. §1412.

51. 45 C.F.R. §§84.33 (c)(3), (4) (1981).

52. 34 C.F.R. §300.403(a) (1981). Although the Department of Education has recently proposed regulations that would dilute many of the handicapped child's placement safeguards, the strong protests of consumer and advocacy groups may lead to congressional disapproval of such amendments.

53. 20 U.S.C. §1401 (1).

54. *Id.* at §1401 (17).

55. *Id.* at §1401 (16).

56. *Id.* at §1401 (19). Some states also require evaluation by a physician, a psychologist, and a nurse or social worker. *E.g.*, Mass. Gen. Laws Ann. ch. 71B §3 (1978).

57. 20 U.S.C. §1412 (5)(C).

58. *Id.* at §1412.

59. For standards of judicial review of individually appropriate education, see Rowley v. Board of Education of Hendrick Hudson Central School District, 483 F. Supp. 528 (S.D.N.Y. 1980), *aff'd*, 632 F.2d 945 (2d Cir. 1980), *rev'd and remanded*, 102 S.Ct. 3034 (1982) (IEP must be "reasonably calculated to enable the child to receive educational benefits").

60. 20 U.S.C. §1414 (a)(1)(c).

61. *See* Shepherd, *Lawyer's Guide to the Educational Rights of Handicapped Children*, 13 U. Richmond L. Rev. 783, 796 (1979).

62. Only some states pay the expense of such evaluations, and then only in limited circumstances. *See, e.g.,* Mass. Gen. Laws Ann. ch. 71B §3 (1978).

63. 20 U.S.C. §1415 (b)(1)(E).

64. *Id.* at §1415 (d).

65. *Id.* at §1414 (e).

66. *See* Children's Defense Fund, Report of Education Advocacy Coalition (1980).

67. *See generally*, Shepherd, *supra* note 61, at 796-825; J. Gleidman and W. Roth, The Unexpected Minority: Handicapped Children in America 173-237 (1980).

68. On measuring the handicapped child's educational opportunity, see Haggerty & Sacks, *Education of the Handicapped: Towards a Definition of an Appropriate Education*, 50 Temp. L.Q. 961 (1977).

69. 102 S. Ct. 3034 (1982). In reversing the lower-court orders on the provision of a sign-language interpreter to a deaf child in a mainstreaming regular class, the Supreme Court held that the act's requirements had been satisfied by the extensive package of special-education services that permitted Amy Rowley to succeed academically. The Court relied on the district court's finding that the child was receiving an "adequate" education.

70. This checklist includes a public education that is free, personalized, supported by sufficient related services, of benefit to the handicapped child, meets the state's educational standards, satisfies the extensive procedural protections under the act, and complies with the child's IEP.

71. 20 U.S.C. §1232g (1976); 45 C.F.R. §99.1-67 (1978).

72. 20 U.S.C. §1401 (1).

Guardianship and Other Protective Services

There are a growing number of service models by which persons with poor judgment, from the totally incompetent to the slightly unwise, can receive assistance in personal decision making. Grouped under the generic heading of protective services, these models can be as varied as the diverse individuals they are designed to serve. Guardianship, for instance, is a coercive or involuntary form of assistance that, in its extreme form, deprives an incompetent person of the right to make any significant decisions while vesting decision-making authority in a court-appointed surrogate, a guardian. By contrast, other protective services are purely voluntary and provide only so much assistance as the recipient of the service desires.

The number and variety of protective services are increasing largely in response to the needs of the many mental-health clients who are now rejoining their communities and facing personal decisions that were beyond their concern while institutionalized, including where to live, how to budget an income, what program to join, and what job to take. As the service models grow, so do the rules that govern them. Applicable laws are becoming clearer, stronger, and more sharply aimed at the dual goal of meeting the protective needs of the disabled while safeguarding their legal rights of personal autonomy and self-determination. In short, the protective-service system is undergoing significant changes, and both providers and consumers of mental-health care are prominent among the reformers. Still, another distinct group deserves much of the credit for recent and current advances in the protective-services system—the elderly. They as much as the mentally disabled have been the victims of what may kindly be called excessive altruism. Both classes, the disabled and the elderly, have long been required to surrender their liberty in exchange for protective service in the form of guardianship.

Historically, guardianship was the primary, and almost exclusive, legal method by which persons were protected from their own imprudence. Guardianship laws were rigid and categorical, causing all persons in need of protective service to be declared legally incompetent, irrespective of the extent of their disability, and subjecting all incompetents to the nearly absolute control of court-appointed surrogates. As noted in chapter 3, the legal system is now coming to recognize and accommodate the unique protective needs of individuals; it is revamping the laws of guardianship to provide needed assistance to incompetent persons without wholly usurping their individual autonomy. Moreover, less restrictive alternatives are being developed, so that persons who formerly might have been subjected to guardianship may instead elect voluntary protective services that are more properly suited to their individual strengths and weaknesses.

This chapter describes a number of these less restrictive alternatives as well as what is still the staple in the protective-services system: guardianship. Before proceeding with the descriptions, however, a general note of caution is in order.

Protective services, and especially guardianship, are double-edged swords. Although they guard disabled persons from the dangers of their own poor judgment, they also cut away at the fundamental rights of liberty, personal autonomy, and self-determination. Moreover, protective services have the potential for fostering client dependence, inhibiting the process of normalization, and offending a client's sense of personal dignity and self-esteem. These considerable psychological hazards, along with the legal deprivations that protective services entail, suggest a need for circumspection.

Guardianship

Guardianship is the legal method by which a court protects a legally incompetent person by appointing another as a surrogate decision maker. Depending on the extent and nature of the needs of the incompetent person, called a "ward," the court may vest the surrogate with authority of various degrees and types. It may appoint a *guardian* (one with the authority to make decisions regarding the ward's person, including where the ward is to live or work, what treatment to accept, and whom to marry), or a *conservator* (one with authority over the financial affairs of the ward), or a *plenary guardian* (one with authority over both the person and property of the ward), or a *guardian ad litem* (one with authority only to make decisions regarding a lawsuit to which the ward is a party). The terms adopted here—guardian, conservator, plenary guardian, and guardian *ad litem*—are the most common descriptions of the various appointments, but they are not universal in our states. In some states, conservators are referred to as guardians of the estate; in others guardians are called conservators of the person; and in still others, completely different terms are used.

Within any of the four categories of guardianship, a court may specially limit the guardian's or surrogate's authority. In addition, certain limitations of authority may be categorically imposed by statute. For instance, several states have recently enacted legislation that prohibits guardians from admitting wards to public psychiatric institutions without their consent.[1] And a recently proposed model statute would limit the power of guardians to choose any residential placement for elderly wards without their consent.[2]

Certain rights have been held to be so personal that they cannot be abridged by a guardian absent express judicial authority. For example, a guardian's attempt to surrender his ward's parental rights by consenting on the ward's behalf to adoption of the ward's child was declared null and void by the Oklahoma Supreme Court. That court reasoned that the guardian's sole duty was to protect the interests of his ward, and abrogating so personal and important a right was outside that duty and therefore was beyond the guardian's authority.[3] Similarly, a Wisconsin appellate court held that a guardian has no power to consent to sterilization of his ward, the ultimate abrogation of parental rights. In that case, the guardian had received express authority from a lower court to permit the sterilization, and the appellate court ruled even that insufficient, since the state legislature had not specifically empowered the courts to authorize such intrusions on incompetent women.[4]

State laws vary as to which rights, if any, may be retained by a ward. Yet the constitutional principle of the least restrictive alternative (LRA) would seem to require that all states permit persons under guardianship to exercise all rights and make ali personal decisions within their capabilities. Thus, it has been held that a ward is not presumptively incompetent for the specific purpose of entering contracts, or even of making a will, despite the ward's general legal incompetency.[5] The LRA principle has also been construed as requiring that courts impose only limited guardianships, that they specifically restrict the guardian's powers to those necessary to satisfy the ward's needs, in cases where total guardianship is unwarranted.[6]

Too often, courts make only general determinations of incompetency, imposing guardianships without precisely assessing the unique capabilities of each ward and limiting the authority of guardians accordingly. And in the absence of court-ordered or statutory limitations, the powers of a guardian or conservator are vast indeed. Plenary guardians have essentially the same authority over their wards as parents have over their minor children. On the appointment of a guardian, a ward typically loses the right to make any significant personal decision. The right to decide such matters as residence, work, and medical treatment is constructively transferred to the guardian. Other rights, however—the right to vote, to hold a driver's license, and to practice a licensed profession, for instance—are not transferrable. Rather, they are simply lost.[7]

Along with the extensive powers of a guardian go certain duties and obligations to the ward. Most state guardianship statutes include some express mandates directed at guardians, but many require no more than that a guardian act in the ward's best interest. In nearly one-half of the states, however, guardians are explicitly required to secure habilitation for their wards where appropriate, by acquiring for the ward educational, vocational, psychiatric, and medical services. Within these broad mandates, the guardian's discretion is nearly absolute. Still, the performance of the guardian is subject to court review in every state by proceedings described later in this chapter, and the clinician should feel encouraged—nay, compelled—to seek review whenever there is reason to suspect that a client's guardian has abused his or her discretion.

Conservators, like guardians, have vast discretionary powers over their wards, also called "conservatees." Although a conservator's authority is technically limited to matters concerning the ward's estate, it should be obvious that control over a ward's finances is tantamount to control over the ward's person as well. That control can be checked by the same procedures for review that apply to guardians, and again it would seem incumbent on the clinician to do so in cases of apparent abuse. Perhaps because the use of property is more easily monitored than the control of a person, conservators are subject to closer court scrutiny than guardians. In every state but Michigan, conservators are statutorily required to post a bond as insurance against their misappropriating their ward's property. Many states also require that conservators submit periodic (usually annual) accountings of transactions conducted on the ward's behalf.

The selection of a person to serve as either a guardian or conservator is largely a matter of court discretion. Even where a statute specifies those who can be appointed, it will specify several possibilities, and the court is left with a choice. Without exception, relatives of the ward are listed among potential appointees, and in general, courts prefer to appoint family members when a willing and capable one can be found.

Judicial Guardianship Proceedings

Every state has an established statutory process by which a person may be declared incompetent and subjected to some form of guardianship.[8] In every state, jurisdiction over the process rests in the probate court or its equivalent. And in every state but one, the determination is made by a judge.[9]

Because guardianship proceedings present potentially great deprivations to fundamental rights, especially to the right to liberty, they must be conducted in accordance with the due-process requirements of the Constitution. The Due Process Clause, as defined and interpreted by judicial decisions, establishes the basic framework of guardianship proceedings, but it does not precisely dictate all the features of the adjudicatory process. Due process is a flexible concept, and the procedural requirements it demands may be greater or lesser depending on the severity of potential deprivations. In criminal cases, for example, due process has been defined as granting the right to trial by jury to defendants facing "serious" charges but not to those facing "petty" charges.[10] Similarly, on the notion that the loss of control over one's property amounts to a lesser deprivation than the loss of control over one's person, some states allow conservators to be appointed by proceedings that involve fewer due-process safeguards than guardianship proceedings.[11] In most states, however, incompetency is adjudicated by the same procedure regardless of what type of court-ordered protection is sought.

The procedures are uniform in the different states only to the extent of the most minimal guarantees of due process. Beyond a few and slight safeguards, however, there is considerable variance among states as to the procedural rights of allegedly incompetent persons.

This is in contrast to the area of criminal law, where the requirements of due process have been defined in comparatively great detail and where the rights of the accused are all well settled. Among the rights deemed constitutionally necessary to ensure the fairness of criminal proceedings and to prevent erroneous convictions are the right to appointed counsel, to confront adverse witnesses, to suppress illegally obtained evidence, and to compel testimony. In guardianship proceedings the requirements of due process are relaxed, since the purported purpose of these proceedings is to protect rather than punish, to serve the subject of the proceedings rather than to exact retribution.

Still, the Due Process Clause does require that alleged incompetents be accorded certain basic procedural rights. To varying degrees, state statutes expand on these rights. And two recently drafted model guardianship statutes may signal even further expansion of procedural rights by state legislatures. The following overview of guardianship proceedings includes references to these model statutes, one of which was prepared by the Developmental Disabilities State Legislative Project of the American Bar Association's (ABA) Commission on the Mentally Disabled[12] and the other by the staff of the U.S. Senate Special Committee on Aging.[13]

Petition and Notice

Proceedings are initiated in every state by the filing of a legal form, the petition, usually with the court having jurisdiction. Although many states require that the petitioner be related to or professionally involved with the alleged incompetent, most allow any interested person to file the petition.

On receipt of the petition, the court schedules a hearing and furnishes the alleged incompetent with some form of notice, stating the date and purpose of the court hearing. The notice may also mention the form of guardianship sought, the evidence presented in the petition, and the person's procedural rights. The requirement of notice in advance of any significant deprivation of liberty or property is among the most basic and important elements of due process, for without notice one can have no opportunity to contest the proposed deprivation, no right to be heard. Yet, several states still fail to guarantee the right to prior notice to persons made subject to guardianship proceedings.[14] The absence of this elementary requirement of notice in some states exemplifies the critical need for reform in this area of law.

Procedural fairness is best served when notice to an alleged incompetent describes the nature of the guardianship proceedings, their rights in those proceedings, the evidence that will be presented in support of the petition, and the potential consequences of the court process. At present, several state statutes require such detailed notice, and similar requirements are prominent in the model statutes proposed by the ABA Commission on the Mentally Disabled[15] and the staff of the Senate Special Committee on Aging.[16] Most states, however, do not mandate this crucial information and thus allow alleged incompetents to be left in the dark, unable to decide knowingly whether to contest or accede to guardianship petitions and unaware of how to do either. The clinician can provide an important service to clients faced with guardianship proceedings by filling in the wide gaps of court notices. By informing clients of the nature and purpose of the proceedings and by referring them to legal counsel for specific information regarding their rights, the clinician can improve the fairness of the entire process.

Prehearing Examination

Almost every state allows its courts to order examinations of alleged incompetents prior to court hearings, and in many states such examinations are actually required. These statutes usually specify who must or may conduct the examinations, and the specified examiners range from a team of a physician and a psychologist in New York, Connecticut, and Kentucky[17] to "qualified persons" in Illinois.[18]

The Right to Counsel

Although it is highly unlikely that any court would affirmatively deny an alleged incompetent the right to be represented by a private attorney in guardianship proceedings, it is significant that nearly one-half of all state guardianship statutes fail to guarantee this right. In the stead of an attorney, most of these states provide that a guardian *ad litem* may represent the interests of the alleged incompetent, as distinct from representing the person. This distinction rests in the fact that guardians *ad litem*—often, but not necessarily, lawyers by profession—are empowered to make decisions for their clients with respect to the proceedings, whereas an attorney typically can act only on a client's direction.

More significantly, only a small minority of states currently grant the right to counsel in guardianship cases to persons who cannot afford private counsel. Although there is strong support for the proposition that indigent persons have a constitutional right to have an attorney appointed for them in guardianship proceedings, that right has not yet been declared in case law.[19] Nevertheless, the right to appointed counsel has been incorporated in the model statutes of both the ABA Commission on the Mentally Disabled[20] and the Senate Special Committee on Aging.[21]

It is important to note that the absence of a statutory right to counsel does not necessarily leave indigent subjects of guardianship petitions without access to legal services. In many states, judges have the discretionary authority to appoint public defenders or funds to retain private attorneys to represent indigent parties to civil matters such as guardianship. Moreover, attorneys from legal-aid programs or the private bar may be available for this purpose. In any event, securing counsel in those states where representation is not guaranteed will take some effort, if only in the form of a request to the right resource, and that effort is sure to be more availing if the clinician supplies some help.

The Hearing

During the period between the filing of the petition and the scheduled hearing, a period generally ranging from three to twenty days, every effort should be made to secure some form of protective assistance less restrictive than guardianship or conservatorship and hence to avoid the need for court proceedings. Only in those cases where less restrictive services would be inadequate or where the alleged incompetent chooses not to accept them should the petition result in a full court hearing.

Illustrative of the relaxation of due-process requirements in guardianship cases is the willingness of several states to allow guardianship hearings to be conducted ex parte; that is, in the absence of the alleged incompetent.[22] It seems probable that statutory provisions allowing ex parte hearings would fall under constitutional attack, for they stand in direct contradiction to the central guarantee of due process, the right to be heard. Until repealed or stricken, however, these laws pose threats to fundamental liberties reminiscent of the chilling fiction of Franz Kafka and Aldous Huxley. In those states where ex parte hearings are still permitted, the clinician should advise clients subject to proceedings that they are nevertheless entitled to attend, or at least to try. No state statute actually demands ex parte hearings, and it is unlikely that a court would actively bar the presence of the person whose rights are at stake. Still, a court could well proceed without the alleged incompetent if he or she makes no effort to attend. And if the client's presence is dispensable, the court notice may fail to apprise the client of even the conditional right to be present. Fairness demands that clients be informed, lest they lose the right without ever knowing they had it, and it would behoove clinicians to inform their clients.

How the actual hearing is conducted is largely a matter of diverse state laws and court rules, but several salient features are worth noting. Currently, about one-half of the states provide for hearings before a jury on demand by the alleged incompetent.[23] A smaller number of states have enacted legislation that specifically secures the right of the alleged incompetent to present evidence, to cross-examine witnesses, and to have the hearing closed from public view.[24] These same rights can be asserted in all states, notwithstanding an absence of specific statutory entitlement. Where a right is not granted by statute, it may be accorded by court rules, by case precedent, or by statutory interpretation.

Emergency Appointments

Almost every state permits expedited appointments of guardians and conservators in emergency cases. In many states, courts may appoint, solely on the basis of a petition, temporary guardians who are empowered to act on behalf of an alleged incompetent until full proceedings can be completed.[25] In others, courts may exercise the powers of a guardian pending a full hearing.[26] And in still others, temporary appointments lasting for specified durations (usually thirty or sixty days) can be made following preliminary hearings.[27] A number of states provide for appointment by more than one of these emergency methods, and others employ unique hybrids of these procedures.[28]

Appeals, Periodic Reviews, and Modification or Termination Hearings

Even after full hearings have been concluded and a guardian or conservator appointed, the doors to the legal system remain open to the ward. A court's determination of incompetency is, of course, appealable to a higher court, but for a variety of reasons—lack of money, counsel, and legal knowledge, for instance—wards very rarely press appeals.[29] Rather, court review generally occurs, if at all, some time after the initial appointment. At least ten states require periodic (usually yearly) court review of guardianships. In addition, every state but Virginia explicitly provides by statute for termination or modification hearings, usually commenced on petition by the ward, the appointed surrogate, or other interested party.

Periodic reviews are held without the necessity of a petition. At the review, the court inquires into the need for continued control of the ward's person or property and generally places the burden of demonstrating that need on the guardian or conservator.

Termination or modification hearings are quite different in two respects. First, a court may summarily deny the petition for termination or modification, thus depriving the ward of review altogether. Second, even if the petition is granted and a hearing is held, wards are then required in many states to bear the burden of proving their own competence, a burden that is extremely difficult to carry. Paternalism, caution, and faith in the soundness of the initial determination may cloud the court's view of the ward's condition. Worse still, wards will typically be at a loss for evidence in support of their claim of competency; since the guardians or conservators will have assumed responsibility for them, they will have had little opportunity to demonstrate their independent capabilities. The task will be the onerous one of disproving a self-fulfilling prophecy.

No doubt, the goal of normalization will prompt the clinician to allow clients under guardianship maximum control over their own affairs. When a client moves to terminate or modify the guardianship, however, the clinician may find it beneficial even to encourage the client to assume control. By taking this active role, the clinician can aid the client in first gauging, then developing, and finally proving competency. Moreover, the clinician can provide needed assistance in this regard by two other means. First, the clinician can submit the petition for termination or modification on the client's behalf; nearly every state allows clinicians to do so, and the strength it adds to the client's case is obvious. Second, the clinician may testify in support of the petition, offering insights into the client's condition which, because of the nature of the clinician's training and relationship with the client, should carry special weight in court.

The Competency Standard

The standard applied to test competency in guardianship proceedings is unavoidably vague. Most state statutes can be divided into two distinct parts: one enumerates the types of disability that can lead to legal incompetency, and the other loosely defines the extent of disability necessary to constitute incompetency.[30] Every state lists mental illness—termed "lunacy" or "idiocy" in some of the more antiquated statutes—as grounds for legal incompetency. When properly conducted, the major focus of a guardianship hearing will be not the nature of the subject's disability but the extent of it.

The standard under California law exemplifies the vagueness of guardianship statutes. It allows the appointment of a guardian for "any person who . . . is unable properly to provide for his own personal needs for physical health, food, clothing or shelter."[31] It is left to the court to decide what it means to provide "properly" for one's needs. The California statute does guide the court in its decision, however, and in this regard is exceptional. It explains that "the phrase 'incompetent person' . . . shall be measured by functional disabilities. . . . [It] shall not be measured solely by isolated incidents of negligence or imprudence."[32]

As the California statute indicates, the standard is a legal rather than a medical one. And it is one that must be applied by reference to functional disabilities. Plainly, it is necessary to determine precisely what one's needs are before inquiring into one's ability to meet those needs. And although courts look to psychiatric and medical professionals for guidance in defining the needs of alleged incompetents, the ultimate determination is for the court alone. As one court put it, "the testimony of the psychiatrists is evidence to be considered by the court, [yet] it is well settled that the court in the final analysis is not bound by such testimony, may disregard it and rely upon the court's own observations and evaluations of the patient's condition."[33]

In making its determination, a court will apply basically the same formula as that described in the earlier chapter on competency. It will evaluate more than the abstract mental ability of the alleged incompetent, it will examine all the factors and circumstances which bear on the person's need for protection as well. One such circumstance is the availability of informal supports, including friends, family, and social services that can mitigate or alleviate the need for court-ordered protection. Another relevant factor is the person's physical condition; one who is faced with serious and complex medical decisions may be found more in need of guardianship than a person of equal mental ability but better health. Likewise, when a conservator or a plenary guardian is sought, the size and nature of the person's estate will be a factor in the court's determination.

The list of factors that are potentially germane to a broad judgment of competency to care for oneself or one's property is virtually endless. Perhaps the only statement that can be made without qualification in describing the test of competency is that each case must be decided on its own particular facts, and the fact of mental disability is not alone determinative.

Public Guardianship

In a growing number of states, no less than thirteen at present, courts are authorized by statute to appoint public officials as guardians. One major distinction between personal and public guardians is the source of their compensation: although both are generally allowed to take fees from their wards, public guardians are subsidized, and in some states wholly funded, by state or county fiscs.[34] Hence, public guardians can serve a needed function for indigent incompetent persons who could not afford the services of a private guardian. Still, this is a function that would appear to be better, if more expensively, served by public financing of private, personal guardians.

Although public guardians are in some places local officials with only one or several wards, more often they are oversized and impersonal agencies. In Los Angeles, for instance, a 1977 study reported that the County Office of the Public Guardian served 1,400 wards with a staff of forty-four deputy public guardians. At public hearings, the director of that office testified that his deputies spent an alarming average of only two hours per year serving each ward.[35] Despite the apparent shortcomings of such bureaucratic services, public guardians are typically vested with powers identical to those of personal guardians. They are granted all the authority of parents over their wards. For obvious reasons, public guardians often prove to be unfit parents, too distant from those under their charge to make the intimate personal decisions for which they are ostensibly appointed. As one commentator has noted, "the public guardian serves mainly as a functionary, i.e., to give effective consent to involuntary psychiatric treatment and to authorize involuntary placements."[36]

Although no form of guardianship should be sought or imposed except as a last resort in extraordinary cases, one should be especially reluctant to seek public guardianship. It will be the rare case indeed where other protective services alone or in combination can not offer an adequate, less restrictive alternative to public guardianship.

Other Protective Services

Agreements of Agency

By an agreement of agency, otherwise known as a power of attorney or power of appointment, one may assign control of all or part of one's property to an agent, any person of one's choosing. The agent then acts much like a conservator, managing the property for the benefit of the assignor, the owner of the property. The salient advantages of this model over conservatorship are several: assignors enter the agreement voluntarily and thus avoid the stigma of court-ordered protection; they determine who shall manage the property, how much shall be managed, and for what general purpose; and finally, they can reserve the right to void the assignment and regain control of the property at will. There is one major disadvantage, however: in most states, one must have the legal capacity to contract to enter an agreement of agency or assign a power. If one lacks that capacity, either at the time of assignment or later, transactions conducted under the power are open to legal challenge and may be declared invalid.[37] Two separate pieces of model legislation would cure this present defect in the law by providing that assignments made with capacity shall not terminate in the event that the assignor becomes incapacitated.[38] One of these model statutes goes further, allowing one with capacity to assign a conditional power that will become effective only in the event that one loses capacity.[39]

Since the agency agreement offers a workable, and certainly less restrictive, alternative to guardianship or conservatorship, it seems likely that state laws will be reformed to make this service both more available and more appropriate for persons in need of protective assistance. One statutory change worthy of endorsement would be a requirement that assignments be approved by a court or some other impartial authority, so that assignors may be protected from artful or designing persons.[40]

Trusts

A trust operates much like an agreement of agency: it allows a person with capacity to assign the control of property to another. Although virtually any person may be made a trustee, trusts are most commonly managed by financial institutions, particularly banks and trust companies, which exact sizeable fees for their services. The most important difference between agency agreements and trusts lies in the degree of discretion granted to the party managing the property. Whereas an agent is given wide latitude within the basic mandate of serving the assignor, a trustee is required to manage the property according to a specific scheme that must be established by the person who creates the trust.

Owing to the usually high costs of trust services, this model may be less desireable than agency agreements. Still, where a rigid and detailed scheme of management is preferred, a trust presents the better option.

Public Benefits and Representative Payeeship

Persons who receive income-payment benefits from a government agency may voluntarily seek, or be involuntarily subjected to, representative payeeship. Payeeship is essentially the same as conservatorship except that a representative payee is appointed not by a court but by the agency that issues the recipient's benefits, and the authority of the payee extends only to the management of the benefits issued by that agency.[41]

Any person may file a request with an agency that issues public benefits asking that a recipient's fiscal competency be investigated. The agency may then institute proceedings and, if it finds that the recipient lacks capacity, it may appoint a representative payee. Like a court in search of a guardian, the agency will usually look first to family and friends of the recipient for a willing payee, but any competent person may be appointed. Payees may be removed by the appointing agency, but a recipient seeking to dissolve a payeeship will face the same obstacles in the process of removal that a legally incompetent person faces in a guardianship-termination hearing.

Case Management

Increasingly, state mental-health departments are adding case management to their client services. Case management may go under different names in different states, but its essential characteristics are well described by the term *management*. According to this model, a mental-health client is assigned to a case manager, who does not provide direct therapeutic services but rather assists the client in managing daily affairs. The case manager may counsel a client with respect to personal decisions, but his or her primary role is that of a service broker, acting together with the client to secure all the community services to which the client is entitled.

One noted authority has stated flatly that, "[i]f adequate community services are developed, guardianship should rarely be needed."[42] For many, the need for guardianship could be eliminated by already existing services. But in the labyrinth of human services, clients—especially clients of borderline competency—are often lost. For them, case management is a promising protective service. Merely by helping clients navigate their way through the system of housing programs, public-benefit agencies, vocational-training projects, and so many other service programs, case managers can alleviate the need for a coercive form of protective service.

Although case management is not to be confused with citizen advocacy nor with legal advocacy, described earlier in chapter 2, all three service models are similar insofar as they aid clients in gaining access to other services. In this respect citizen and legal advocacy are forms of protective services.

Protective-Services Offices

A fairly recent federal law provides for funding to states for the purpose of creating and operating protective-services offices to assist persons in "achieving or maintaining self-sufficiency . . . [and to prevent] inappropriate institutional care."[43] Offices funded under this law may provide "services related to the management and maintenance of the [client's] home, day care services for adults, transportation services, . . . training and related services, employment services, information, referral and counselling services, the preparation and delivery of meals, health support services [and more]."[44]

In short, a protective-services office is an interdisciplinary program providing an array of services on a voluntary basis. It is surely a less restrictive and potentially more protective model than guardianship or conservatorship. Although many states have yet to create such programs, one can expect that protective-service agencies will become increasingly available as the still-infant federal enabling law advances toward its goal of "preventing or remedying neglect, abuse, or exploitation of children and adults unable to protect their own interests."[45]

Conclusion

It cannot be overstressed that protective services are truly double-edged swords. However rightly and however slightly, each cuts away at personal liberties. The very determination that one requires protection from one's own poor judgment may be psychologically damaging. The protective sword, then, should not be drawn lightly. And many would insist that it not be drawn at all:

> The only freedom which deserves the name, is that of pursuing our own good in our own way, so long as we do not attempt to deprive others of theirs, or impede their efforts to obtain it. Each is the proper guardian of his own health, whether bodily, or mental and spiritual. Mankind are greater gainers by suffering each other to live as seems good to themselves, than by compelling each to live as seems good to the rest.[46]

Notes

1. *See, e.g.*, Cal. Prob. Code §1500 (West Supp. 1981); Mass. Gen. Laws Ann. ch. 201 §6 (West Supp. 1981); Wash. Rev. Code §11.92.040(3) (West Supp. 1981).

2. Staff of the Senate Special Committee on Aging, 95th Cong., 1st Sess., Protective Services for the Elderly: A Working Paper, app. 2, Model Guardianship, Conservatorship, and Power of Attorney Legislation §5-312 (a)(1) (Comm. Print 1977) (available through the Congressional Information Service, CIS MF S 142-3) [hereinafter cited as Senate Special Committee].

3. Gafford v. Oklahoma, 617 P.2d 886 (Okla. 1980).

4. *In re* Eberhardy, 294 N.W. 2d 540 (Wis. Ct. App. 1980).

5. *See, e.g.*, Bollen v. Zetterberg, 165 Cal. Rptr. 160, 106 Cal. App. 3d 524 (1980). *See generally*, Lippman, *The Least Restrictive Alternative and Guardianship, in* President's Committee on Mental Retardation, The Mentally Retarded Citizen and the Law 520 (Kindred, Cohen, Penrod & Shaffer, eds. 1976).

6. *See, e.g., In re* Estate of Mackey, 85 Ill. App. 3d 235, 406 N.E. 2d 226 (1980). See also, the Texas Limited Guardianship Act, which essentially incorporates the least-restrictive-alternative principle. Tex. Prob. Code Ann. §130A (Vernon Supp. 1980-81).

7. For a state-by-state listing of the legal disabilities that may result from a court determination of incompetency, see S. Brakel & R. Rock, The Mentally Disabled and the Law 315-40 (rev. ed. 1971).

8. For a complete state-by-state listing and synopsis of guardianship statutes, see Developmental Disabilities State Legislative Project, American Bar Association Commission on the Mentally Disabled, *Guardianship and Conservatorship: Statutory Survey and Model Statute* 9-74 (1979) [hereinafter cited as ABA Commission].

9. North Carolina law presently allows clerks of courts to decide guardianship cases. N.C. Gen. Stats. §33-1 (Supp. 1981).

10. Duncan v. Louisiana, 391 U.S. 145 (1968). No single criterion distinguishes serious from petty charges; however, the potential prison sentence is a major distinguishing factor. In the federal system, for instance, all charges carrying potential sentences of six months or more are termed "serious."

11. Some eleven states statutorily provide for different proceedings in conservatorship and guardianship cases. *See* ABA Commission, *supra* note 8, at 4. In other states, procedural differences have been created by judicial decisions or court rules. *See, e.g.*, Katz v. Superior Court, 73 Cal. App. 3d 952, 969, 141 Cal. Rptr. 234, 243 (1977) (appointments of parents as guardians over their adult children who had become "Moonies," that is, joined the Unification Church, vacated on appeal; distinction made between standards of proof applied in guardianship and conservatorship proceedings).

12. ABA Commission, *supra* note 8.

13. Senate Special Committee, *supra* note 2.

14. Notice is not required in Alabama, South Dakota, and in some instances in Texas.

15. ABA Commission, *supra* note 8, Model Statute §32.

16. Senate Special Committee, *supra* note 2, Model Legislation §5-309.

17. N.Y. Surr. Ct. Proc. Act §1750 (McKinney Supp. 1981); Conn. Gen. Stat. Ann. §45-78a (West 1981); Ky. Rev. Stat. §203.015 (Supp. 1980).

18. Ill. Ann. Stat. ch. 110 1/2 §11a-9(b) (Smith-Hurd Supp. 1981).

19. One source of support for the constitutional claim to appointed counsel in guardianship cases is a decision of the U.S. Supreme Court in a

case involving probation-revocation hearings. After noting that the right to appointed counsel is not limited to defendants in criminal trials, the Court decided that the right may extend to indigent probationers facing possible revocation but that its extension depends on the circumstances of individual cases. One circumstance that the Court suggested would require the appointment of counsel is "difficulty [on the part of the probationer] in presenting his version of a disputed set of facts where the presentation requires the examining or cross-examining of witnesses or the offering or dissecting of complex documentary evidence." Gagnon v. Scarpelli, 411 U.S. 778, 787 (1972). Since one who is subject to guardianship proceedings is, by legal definition, only questionably competent, and since the proceedings are surely complex, it seems axiomatic by this standard that one should be accorded the right to appointed counsel. *See* Petty v. Petty, 592 S.W. 2d 423, 425-26 (Tex. Civ. App. 1979) (state guardianship statute interpreted to require court-appointed counsel).

20. ABA Commission, *supra* note 8, Model Statute §31(a).

21. Senate Special Committee, *supra* note 2, Model Legislation §5-303(c).

22. For example, Indiana allows ex parte hearings where presence of the subject would be "injurious to his health." Ind. Code §29-1-18-19 (1976). Pennsylvania allows the same where "the physical or mental welfare [of the subject] will not be promoted" by attendance at the hearing. Pa. Stat. Ann. tit. 20 §511(a)(i) (Purdon 1975).

23. Several of the states that grant the right to jury hearings grant it only in cases where a guardian is sought and not in cases where a conservator alone is sought. *See, e.g.,* Ariz. Rev. Stat. §14-5303 (West 1975); Colo. Rev. Stat. §15-14-303 (1974).

24. These three rights are enumerated in the Uniform Probate Code (UPC), a model statute proposed by the National Conference of Commissioners on Uniform State Law. To date, no less than eleven states have adopted at least some portion of one or another of the several revisions of the UPC. *See* ABA Commission, *supra* note 8, 11-17.

25. *See, e.g.*, Mass. Gen. Laws Ann. ch. 201 §14 (West Supp. 1981).

26. *See, e.g.*, Ariz. Rev. Stat. §14-5310 (West 1975).

27. *See, e.g.*, Conn. Gen. Stat. Ann. §45-72 (West 1981).

28. *See generally*, ABA Commission, *supra* note 8, table II.

29. A survey of guardianship cases in New York illustrates the point: of the more than 600 cases studied, not one was appealed. G. Alexander & T. Lewin, The Aged and the Need for Surrogate Management 29 (1972).

30. As an example, the Uniform Probate Code, adopted in at least eleven states, authorizes guardianship for "any person who is impaired by reason of mental illness, mental deficiency, physical illness or disability, advanced age, chronic use of drugs, chronic intoxication or other causes (except minority) to the extent that he lacks sufficient understanding or

capacity to make or communicate responsible decisions concerning his person.'' UPC, *supra* note 24, §5-101.

31. Cal. Prob. Code §1751 (West Supp. 1981).

32. *Id.*

33. Matter of Roosevelt Hospital (Otis Simmons) (N.Y. Sup. Ct., N.Y. County, Jan 10, 1977) [reported in N.Y. Law Journal, Jan. 13, 1977, at 7, col. 1].

34. *See* ABA Commission, *supra* note 8, table V.

35. Mitchell, *Involuntary Guardianship for Incompetents: A Strategy for Legal Services Advocates,* 12 Clearinghouse Rev. 451, 463 (1978).

36. *Id.*

37. It should be noted that the capacity to contract is distinct from general competency to manage one's affairs. Cases have held that even one who is under conservatorship may enter a contract. Thus it is conceivable that a power of attorney will be upheld in any case where the assignor, despite his or her general incompetency, understands the consequences of the assignment. *See, e.g.,* Board of Regents v. Davis, 14 Cal. 3d 33, 533 P.2d 1047, 120 Cal. Rptr. 407 (1975). *See generally,* Weihofen, *Mental Incompetency to Contract or Convey,* 39 S. Cal. L. Rev. 211 (1966).

38. Senate Special Committee, *supra* note 2; Uniform State Law Commissioners, *Model Special Power of Attorney for Small Property Interests Act, reprinted in* Legal Research and Services for the Elderly and National Council of Senior Citizens, Legislative Approaches to Problems of the Elderly: A Handbook of Model State Statutes 157 (1971).

39. Uniform State Law Commissioners, *supra* note 38.

40. The Uniform State Law Commissioner's Act includes such a requirement. *Id.* at §1(2).

41. Details of representative payee systems in the administration of federal benefits are included in the following statutes: 42 U.S.C. §§401, 405(j)(1979) (social-security benefits); 42 U.S.C. §1383(a) (1974) (supplemental-security-income benefits); 38 U.S.C. §3202 (1979) (Veteran's Administration disability benefits).

42. Kindred, *Guardianship and Limitations upon Capacity*, President's Committee on Mental Retardation, The Mentally Retarded Citizen and the Law 62, 67 (Kindred, Cohen, Penrod & Shaffer, eds. 1976).

43. 42 U.S.C. §1397-1397f; Title XX of the Social Security Act, entitled Grants to States for Services, Social Service Amendments of 1974, Pub. L. No. 93-647, 88 Stat. 2351 (Oct. 1, 1975); 42 U.S.C. §1397(2), (4) (Supp. Pamphlet 1981).

44. 42 U.S.C. §1397a (a)(2).

45. 42 U.S.C. §1397 (3).

46. J.S. Mill, On Liberty (1859), quoted with approval in Lessard v. Schmidt, 349 F. Supp. 1078, 1084 (E.D. Wis. 1972).

10 Antidiscrimination Laws and the Promise of Equal Opportunity

Shocking stories of discrimination against mental-health clients are abundant. Variations on the fifteenth-century practice of setting the mentally different afloat on aimless ships can still be found in the contemporary United States. In New York City, for instance, officials recently considered proposals for housing former mental patients in abandoned buildings on islands in New York harbor.[1] To be sure, the mentally ill are no longer banished on "ships of fools," yet they remain too often excluded from the societal mainstream. As a class, they are still denied equal access to employment, housing, education, credit, loans, licenses, and a host of other basic necessities. One million disabled children are entirely excluded from schooling, and an even larger number lack appropriate education.[2] Discrimination on the basis of handicap costs U.S. society billions of dollars each year, part of the social cost of supporting mentally disabled but employable adults who find no welcome in the job market.

Against this dismal neglect, the struggle of the mentally handicapped for equality has made great advances in the last decade. Following the trail toward civil rights blazed by women and blacks, the handicapped and their advocates have secured legislative and judicial promises of equality. Much remains to be done, however, both in enforcing present antidiscrimination laws and in securing stronger guarantees of equal opportunity.

The term *handicapped*, as used here, is quite distinct from the term *disabled*. Handicap means the "cumulative result of the obstacles which the disability interposes between the individual and his functioning in society."[3] Thus, the legal disadvantages and the social stigma that result from disability are deemed a part of one's handicap. Accordingly, mental-health clients are generally far more handicapped than actually disabled. In a world free of discrimination, of course, the terms handicap and disability would be synonymous, but to the misfortune of us all, they are not.[4] Disabled persons are handicapped in the pursuit of services, jobs, and benefits as much by the prejudices of others as by their own disabilities.

In recognition of this stubborn fact, the federal antidiscrimination law, the Rehabilitation Act of 1973, protects not just persons with "physical or mental impairments," but also those who are "regarded as having such an impairment."

The Federal Rehabilitation Act

The Rehabilitation Act of 1973 arms federal agencies for a broad, but circumscribed, attack on discrimination against the handicapped. Although the act prohibits essentially all forms of discrimination against a wide class of handicapped persons, it is enforceable only against agencies or persons that, in one way or another, receive federal financial assistance.

Section 504

The act's antidiscrimination mandate is comprised of four primary sections. By far, the most significant of these is section 504.[5] As amended, section 504 states that:

> No otherwise qualified handicapped individual in the United States . . . shall, solely by reason of his handicap, be excluded from participation in, be denied the benefits of, or be subjected to discrimination under any program or activity receiving Federal financial assistance or under any program or activity conducted by any Executive agency or by the United States Postal Service.

The strong spirit of section 504 is clear, but the fine letter of the law is found not in the statute but in regulations. Authoritative regulations were first issued in 1977 by what was then the Department of Health, Education and Welfare (HEW). That department, of course, has since been divided into the separate departments of Education and of Health and Human Services. By now, every federal executive agency has either enacted or drafted its own regulations governing the implementation of section 504. Pursuant to an executive order intended to ensure uniformity, the regulations of each federal agency are identical in all important respects to those promulgated by HEW.[6] The HEW regulations have been assumed in their entirety by the Department of Health and Human Services (HHS), and reference will be made throughout this chapter to the HHS regulations, since they are now the model for all federal regulations implementing section 504.

The Scope of Section 504

The HHS regulations include definitions of "qualified handicapped person" and "federal financial assistance"; together, these define the basic scope of section 504. As noted earlier, "handicapped person" is broadly defined to extend the protection of section 504 to persons who are merely regarded as being disabled as well as to those who are disabled in fact. According to HHS regulations, "Handicapped person means any person who

(i) has a physical or mental impairment that substantially limits one or more major life activities, (ii) has a record of such an impairment, or (iii) is regarded as having such an impairment."[7] Thus any person who now has, once had, or is regarded as having any "mental or psychological disorder, such as mental retardation, . . . emotional or mental illness" that impairs "functions such as caring for one's self, performing manual tasks, . . . [or] working" is a handicapped person.[8] Moreover, any person who has been misclassified as having such a condition, even though never actually disabled and not presently regarded as being so, is nevertheless a handicapped person for the purposes of section 504. Finally, it is worth noting that alcoholism and drug addiction are expressly listed as "physical or mental impairments."[9]

This inclusive definition will allow most mental-health clients to claim the protection of section 504. To actually realize 504 protection, however, one must be not just a handicapped person, but a "*qualified* handicapped person." In other words, one can prove unlawful discrimination only if qualified for the service, benefit, or job at issue. Obviously, the requisites of a qualified handicapped person will differ from case to case depending on the essential requirements for obtaining the particular service, benefit, or job in question.

Section 504's prohibition of discrimination applies to virtually all persons and entities receiving federal funds in any amount or form.[10] Only three categories of recipients are exempted: ultimate beneficiaries of federal assistance programs, for example, social-security recipients; recipients of government procurement contracts (which, in return for supplying goods to the government, receive payments as opposed to financial assistance);[11] and recipients of insurance or guaranty contracts. It is worth noting that health-care providers reimbursed by Medicaid funds are recipients and therefore are subject to section 504, since Medicaid is explicitly defined as a form of federal financial assistance.[12]

The Prohibitions and Requirements of 504

Section 504 is more than an unequivocal proscription of discrimination, it is also a prescription of affirmative duties. It requires that recipients actively work toward the goal of equal opportunity for the handicapped. The specific obligations imposed by section 504 can only be determined on a case-by-case basis. The HHS regulations do provide general principles informing these determinations, and the principles can be separated into two categories: those applicable to providers of services and benefits and those applicable to employers.

Services and Benefits. Two basic principles define the obligations of service and benefit providers subject to section 504: equal opportunity and integration. Equal opportunity, the most fundamental promise of 504, means equal access to equally effective services. The regulations explain that to be "equally effective," a service must "afford handicapped persons equal opportunity to obtain the same result . . . or to reach the same level of achievement" as others receiving that service.[13] More specifically, it means, among other things, that buildings must be accessible to the physically disabled; that appropriate educational services must be available for the blind, deaf, and developmentally disabled; that public housing must be open to former mental patients. In short, it means that qualified handicapped persons must be allowed, to the utmost extent of their capabilities, to participate in and to benefit by all services available to others.

The second principle, that of integration, is already quite familiar as a clinical principle in the mental-health field, variously termed "mainstreaming" or "normalization." It requires that services and benefits to handicapped persons not be different or separate from those provided to others unless necessary to be equally effective.

Plainly, these broad mandates can impose very different, but very significant, obligations on different service providers. The affirmative duties frequently involve accommodations for the physically handicapped: elevators and ramps, interpreters and communication devices, special outreach efforts, and integration plans. But affirmative accommodations may be required for the mentally handicapped as well. A recent federal-court decision suggests the potential of section 504 as a means of effecting major systemic reforms in the provision of services to handicapped persons generally, and to the mentally disabled in particular.

The case is *Halderman* v. *Pennhurst State School and Hospital*, a class action brought by and on behalf of institutionalized developmentally disabled persons.[14] In *Pennhurst*, a federal district court in Pennsylvania held that 504 "imposes affirmative obligations on state and local governmental officials and that under section 504 unnecessarily separate and minimally inadequate services are discriminatory and unlawful." Relying only in part on section 504, the court ordered that individualized programs be developed for the approximately twelve hundred plaintiffs leading to their placement in less restrictive, community-based settings and to the eventual closing of the institution. In addition to section 504, the court based its order on the federal Constitution and on state law. When the decision was reviewed on appeal, the federal circuit court found it unnecessary to consider whether section 504 actually required the major reforms ordered by the district court: "we have found clear expression of a least restrictive alternative requirement in the Developmentally Disabled Assistance and Bill of Rights Act. . . . One clear federal statute announces the governing rule, and one is enough. Thus we decline to consider section 504 issues on this appeal."[15] The case was later reviewed by the Supreme Court, but because the circuit court had chosen not to consider section 504, the Supreme Court was not presented with those claims.[16] On remand by the Supreme Court, the circuit court once again upheld all relief but the institution's closing and once again sidestepped section 504 by relying this time on the state law. Consequently, the district court's ruling that section 504 confers a right to minimally adequate habilitation in a nondiscriminatory setting still stands, but its precedential value is debatable. It is dicta—something less than a definitive statement of the law. Yet other courts have followed its lead in ordering services to forestall institutionalization, thus demonstrating the use of section 504 as a means to improve the quality (under the principle of equal opportunity) and minimize the restrictiveness (under the principle of integration) of social services, including mental-health care. For instance, in a recent federal-district-court decision in Connecticut, a quadriplegic adult brought suit under section 504 and other statutes seeking to enjoin the state from terminating home health-care services and from refusing to authorize Medicaid payments for noninstitutional services, thus effectively compelling the plaintiff's institutionalization. The court issued a preliminary injunction, basing its order in part on section 504 and on its view that this law can, in the proper case, impose an affirmative obligation on states to provide treatment in the least restrictive environment.[17]

The potential of section 504 to effect major systemic reforms should not overshadow its more common, and perhaps ultimately more important, function: that of achieving simple equal opportunity for individuals. Many handicapped persons need and want nothing more than a fair chance to participate in services and to partake of public benefits. They require no special accommodations, they would impose no affirmative duties. For them section 504 represents a key to the door of personal opportunity. One mental-health client used this law to open the door to a prison vocational-training program[18] and another to get into a high-school athletic program.[19] Section 504 can make schools of all levels, programs of all sorts, and services of every type available to persons who would otherwise be discriminatorily rejected.

Employment. The door most frequently opened by 504 is that which leads to job opportunities. The HHS regulations on this subject are quite clear. They prohibit discrimination in every aspect of employment, from recruitment to layoffs, pay scales to promotions, fringe benefits to leaves of absence. As a guard against discrimination, the regulations expressly prohibit preemployment medical examinations and inquiries as to handicap.[20] The regulations do not prevent employers from applying bona fide medical criteria; employers may inquire into an applicant's ability to perform job-related functions and may condition an offer of employment on the results of a medical exam. They merely prohibit open questions that probe for unrelated disabilities or treatment histories and, by allowing medical exams only after job offers, they prevent employers from hiding discriminatory rejections under medical excuses.

By their own terms, the regulations impose affirmative obligations on employers. An employer must make "reasonable accommodations to the known physical or mental limitations of an otherwise qualified handicapped applicant" unless the accommodations would cause the employer to suffer "undue hardship." The standards—"reasonable accommodation" and "undue hardship"—are patently vague, but the regulations offer some examples of what might be required of an employer. These include architectural alterations and equipment modifications; job restructuring to allow handicapped persons to trade duties with other employees; and schedule changes to enable handicapped persons to work part-time.[21]

For qualified mental-health clients, special accommodations will rarely be necessary. Sometimes compliance requires only minor adjustments, such as flexible scheduling to permit an employee to keep therapy appointments, sympathetic supervision, or proper orientation to the new environment.[22] More often employers need give mental-health clients no more than a chance. At present, the extent to which section 504 can be used to secure even that, an equal chance, is in question. Until an ambiguous amendment was added to section 504 in 1978, it was well settled that the employment-related mandates applied to every program and person receiving federal assistance. The amendment has been interpreted by at least two courts as limiting the scope of the employment provisions to a small subclass of recipients, those whose federal financial assistance is appropriated primarily for the purpose of providing employment.[23] This restrictive interpretation has been explicitly rejected by the U.S. Senate Committee on Labor and Human Resources and by at least one federal court.[24] Until the matter is finally resolved, all recipients of federal financial assistance, including mental-health centers, would be well advised to conform their employment practices to the regulatory requirements of section 504. No "undue hardship" can result, and the benefit of compliance will be shared by employer and employee alike—and by the rest of us as well.

Before passing from the subject of employers' duties, it should be emphasized that mental-health centers are subject to the same rules of nondiscrimination as are other employers. In fact, the federal Office of Civil Rights has explicitly opined that section 504 prohibits mental-health facilities from refusing, as a matter of policy, to consider former clients for employment.[25] Indeed, if equality, like generosity, is to begin at home, mental-health centers might give clients more than consideration, they might give them preference, as prospective employees.

Administrative and Judicial Procedures for Enforcement

There are three basic avenues for resolving section 504 complaints: informal negotiations or internal grievances with the program complained of, possibly involving the federal agency that administers the program's assistance; formal administrative complaints filed with the federal agency concerned; and federal-court action. Countless other resolution methods may be pursued, but these few are generally the most availing.

Many service providers will be required by section 504 regulations to make formal grievance procedures available for persons alleging discrimination. These procedures may provide a good initial step, but it is not mandatory that complainants follow them. A complaint under section 504 may be brought directly to a federal agency whether or not the program complained of offers the alternative of internal grievance procedures.

Every federal agency providing financial assistance must establish a system for processing section 504 complaints. Any handicapped person, or any representative of his or her choice (a clinician, for instance), can file a complaint with the agency that administers assistance to the violating program. The complaint can be a simple letter, but it should include at least the following information:

1. the name and address of complainant (and representative) and of the program that is the object of complaint;
2. a statement that complainant is a "qualified handicapped individual" and that the program is a "recipient of Federal financial assistance"; and
3. a description of the discriminatory act or practice at issue, stated as specifically as possible.

Once a complaint is registered with a federal agency, the agency becomes responsible for investigating the matter and taking remedial action. Its primary tool for enforcement is the money it administers. Although rarely necessary, an agency can suspend or terminate financial assistance to programs in violation of section 504. Typically, the mere threat of defunding leads to voluntary compliance.

In more stubborn cases, individuals may sue in federal court. Before doing so, however, they may be required to pursue and exhaust available administrative remedies. But even after individuals succeed in bringing a private judicial action and proving a section 504 violation, they may be restricted from seeking damages, confined instead to pressing for an end to the discrimination at issue.[26] These and other enforcement questions will plague attorneys litigating section 504 claims, but they may be of little interest to the clinician.[27] The point to emphasize here is that section 504, with some qualifications, can be enforced in court.

In any of the three enforcement mechanisms described, a legal advocate can play a significant role on behalf of a complainant. Perhaps the first step a client or clinician should take in a 504 case is to contact a legal resource.

Although the exact contours of section 504 are yet uncharted, this sweeping prohibition against discrimination can help clients to obtain access to a wide range of services, benefits, and jobs. It is a potent remedy in the fight against unfair treatment of the handicapped, and clients and clinicians should assert it forcefully.

Other Rehabilitation Act Sections

The Rehabilitation Act of 1973 includes several antidiscrimination measures in addition to section 504. The following three provisions, for present purposes, are the most important.

Section 501. The law requires every federal agency and the Postal Service to take affirmative action to hire and advance qualified handicapped persons.[28] Section 501 concerns only employment practices of the federal government, but in that limited sphere its requirements are significantly more stringent than those of section 504. It seeks to make the federal government a "model employer of the handicapped."

Section 502. Under section 502, Congress mandates a federal Architectural and Transportation Barriers Compliance Board, comprised of representatives of various federal agencies.[29] The board's purpose is to enforce, through informal negotiations and formal hearings, the Architectural Barriers Act of 1968.[30] The object of that act is to make all buildings that are financed, constructed, owned, operated, or rented by the federal government accessible to people with mobility impairments.

Section 503. This requirement is an important extension of the employment-related provisions of section 504.[31] Through regulations promulgated by the federal Department of Labor (DOL) and enforced by DOL's Office of Federal Contract Compliance Programs, section 503 prohibits discrimination and, more importantly, requires affirmative action on the part of private employers supplying goods or services to the federal government by contract or subcontract of $2,500 or more.[32] It goes beyond section 504 in two important respects: first, it applies to a large number of employers who are exempt from 504; and second, it expressly requires affirmative action rather than just "reasonable accommodation."

In short, section 503 protects mental-health clients and others from discrimination and remedies past inequities by promising them special aid in gaining employment in businesses and corporations that provide the government with anything from pencils to highways to consultative services. It is enforced by methods much like those described for section 504. And like section 504, it is an empty promise if not enforced.

Other Legal Remedies for Discrimination

The Rehabilitation Act of 1973 represents only one of many legal recourses for clients stymied by discrimination. Another potentially useful recourse derives from the equal protection clauses of the Fifth and Fourteenth amendments to the federal Constitution. These amendments have traditionally been applied to protect people who fall within what are termed "suspect classes"; persons such as racial minorities and women who have suffered from longstanding patterns of unequal treatment. Persons not fitting within a suspect class may yet avail themselves of the equal protection clauses, but to a lesser extent than persons belonging to a suspect class. Discriminatory action will be subjected to a lower standard of judicial review and can be more readily justified if against persons who are not within a suspect class.

Suspect classes are defined by reference to such criteria as political powerlessness and the imposition of social and legal disabilities: burdens that often add to the afflictions of the mentally ill.[33] Recognizing the legal disadvantages and societal discrimination that have been heaped on the mentally ill, a recent federal court ruling characterized institutionalized mental patients as a "quasi-suspect class."[34] Thus, institutionalized clients (and possibly other mental-health clients as well) may be accorded special constitutional protection from government action that is discriminatory in purpose or effect. The case in which this ruling was issued, *Sterling* v. *Harris*, involved regulations of the Social Security Administration that denied supplemental-security-income allowances to certain recipients in public psychiatric hospitals, while granting the allowances to comparable recipients in other public institutions. The regulations were judged unconstitutional by a lower court for failing to provide the special degree of equal protection owed to the plaintiffs as a quasi-suspect class. The Supreme Court reversed that decision, but in doing so it expressly sidestepped the lower court's finding that residents of public mental-health institutions constitute a quasi-suspect class. Hence, the designation still stands, and the promise of special constitutional protection remains.

Finally, clients in many parts of the country can find protection from discrimination in local state law, both statutory and constitutional. In Massachusetts, for example, an amendment added to the state constitution in 1980 declares that "[n]o otherwise qualified handicapped individual shall, solely by reason of his handicap, be excluded from participation in, denied the benefits of, or be subject to discrimination under any program or activity within the commonwealth." This amendment, clearly patterned after section 504 of the Rehabilitation Act, seeks to accomplish at the state level what section 504 is intended to do on the federal level. State antidiscrimination statutes show considerable diversity, both in the forms of discrimination prohibited and in the means of enforcing the prohibitions. A 1978 survey of state antidiscrimination laws reported that fully forty-two states had enacted statutes outlawing various forms of discrimination on the basis of handicap.[35] Many of these laws, however, protect only the physically, and not the mentally, handicapped. Of thirty-six states prohibiting employment discrimination, for instance, the mentally disabled are covered in twenty-one states. Although twenty-eight bar discrimination in housing, only nineteen states accord this protection to persons with mental disabilities. And with respect to public accommodations, they are covered in only seventeen of twenty-nine state laws.

In general, state antidiscrimination statutes prohibit discriminatory practices in the areas of employment, housing, and public accommodations. Several states go further and expressly prohibit handicap-based discrimination in such areas as insurance and credit transactions.[36]

The laws and regulations on this subject vary so much from state to state that they cannot be described accurately with generalizations. The reader interested in more specific information on local discrimination law should consult such agencies as state human-rights commissions or protection and advocacy offices. And state law should be consulted even if one of the federal remedies previously described is available, for state law may offer several distinct advantages: it generally applies to a wider range of private persons and businesses; it usually applies to state-funded or state-assisted programs beyond the reach of the federal Rehabilitation Act; and the state enforcement mechanisms, whether judicial or administrative, may prove faster and more convenient than federal procedures. In sum, when a client can potentially seek a legal remedy under any of several different laws, state and federal, there is no reason to arbitrarily discriminate between them. State law always should be considered.

From all the particulars described in this chapter, it is evident that Congress and the states have demonstrated a strong commitment to ending the cruel segregation and impoverishment of handicapped persons. That goal necessarily involves substantial costs and unyielding efforts on the part of both the federal and state governments and all those persons working on behalf of the disabled. The promise of equal opportunity embodied in antidiscrimination laws can be realized only if all concerned invest the effort necessary to enforce those laws. And that investment is actually far less than the incalculable economic, social, and psychological costs of discrimination exacted from society as a whole as well as from the handicapped themselves. The costs become all the more apparent when discrimination is viewed for what it is: a major obstacle in the path of normalization, of deinstitutionalization, and even of individual therapy.

The law cannot alter stubborn attitudes nor correct misconceptions about mental illness. But perhaps by forcing an end to discriminatory practices, it will enable clients to demonstrate their capabilities. If so, we will all be the better for it.

Notes

1. A description of these proposals, part of a powerful exposé of the plight of mental-hospital dischargees in New York City, can be found in Baxter and Hopper, *Pathologies of Place and Disorders of Mind: "Community Living" for Ex-Mental Patients in New York City*, 11 Health Pol'y Advisory Center Bull. 1, 11 (1980).

2. *See* 20 U.S.C. §1400(b)(3)-(4) (Supp. 1982).

3. TenBroek & Matson, *The Disabled and the Law of Welfare*, 54 Cal. L. Rev. 809, 814 (1966).

4. The annual social cost of supporting disabled but employable adults has been estimated at $100 billion. Disabled white males alone lost an estimated $4.5 billion annually in potential earnings because of discrimination. Senate Comm. on Labor and Human Resources, Equal Employment Opportunities for Handicapped Individuals Act of 1979, S. Rep. No. 316, 96th Cong., 1st Sess. 5 (1979).

5. 20 U.S.C. §794 (Supp. 1981).

6. Exec. Order No. 11914, 41 Fed. Reg. 17,871 (1976), *reprinted in* 29 U.S.C. §794 (1980).

7. 45 C.F.R. §84(j)(1)(1981).

8. *Id.* at §84.3(j)(2).

9. *Id.* at §84.3(j)(2)(i), and app. A(A)4 (analysis of regulations).

10. For the HHS definitions of "recipient" and "Federal financial assistance," see 45 C.F.R. §§84.3(f), 84.3(h).

11. Recipients of procurement contracts in excess of $2,500 are subject to section 503 and its prohibition of handicap-based employment discrimination. *See infra*, notes 31, 32 and accompanying text.

12. 45 C.F.R. §84, app. A(A)1 (1981). Medicare, as distinct from Medicaid, is not a form of federal financial assistance; rather, it is, as the regulations define it, "basically a program of payments to direct beneficiaries." Hence, facilities and practitioners receiving reimbursements under

Medicare are not subject to section 504 by virtue of those reimbursements. Other assistance, however, including Medicaid, may bring them within the ambit of section 504. 45 C.F.R. §84, app. A(A)2 (1981).

13. *Id.* at §84.4(b)(2). For an explanation of the obligations of service providers under section 504, see Cook, *The Provision of Health and Rehabilitation Services to Disabled Persons under the Federal Rehabilitation Act*, 12 Clearinghouse Rev. 693 (1979).

14. 446 F. Supp. 1295 (E.D. Pa. 1977), *aff'd in part, rev'd and remanded in part*, 612 F.2d 84 (3rd Cir. 1979), *rev'd in part and remanded*, 451 U.S. 1 (1981).

15. 612 F.2d at 108. In a comparable case, Johnson v. Solomon, 484 F. Supp. 278 (D. Md. 1979), the civil commitment and treatment of juveniles in a Maryland mental institution, and the lack of less restrictive alternatives, were challenged under various constitutional and statutory provisions including 504. The federal court in that case refused to consider 504 issues because they were not raised until the eve of trial, some three years after the suit began, and because, as in *Pennhurst*, the court's order of major reforms was adequately supported by other legal bases. 484 F. Supp. at 311-12.

16. Pennhurst State School and Hospital v. Halderman, 451 U.S. 1 (1981). The Supreme Court considered only a single question: whether the Developmentally Disabled Assistance and Bill of Rights Act, the federal statute on which the circuit court rested its decision, imposed on the defendants an obligation to provide care and treatment in the least restrictive setting appropriate to each mentally retarded person's needs. The Court ruled in the negative, holding that the act is "a mere federal-state funding statute," and that the act's bill of rights "is simply a general statement of 'findings' and as such is too thin a reed to support the rights and obligations read into it by the court below."

17. Lynch v. Maher, 507 F. Supp. 1268 (D. Conn. 1981).

18. Sites v. McKenzie, 423 F. Supp. 1190 (N.D.W.Va. 1976) (elderly man confined for forty-five years in prisons and mental hospitals excluded from prison vocational program on basis of mental disability; exclusion held unlawful under section 504).

19. Doe v. Marshall, 459 F. Supp. 1190 (S.D. Tex. 1978) (high-school student placed in new school for psychiatric reasons excluded from school's football team under a rule barring transfer students from interscholastic athletics; exclusion held unlawful under section 504).

20. 45 C.F.R. §84.14 (1981). Preemployment exams and inquiries are permissible only if conducted as part of one or another specified affirmative-action plan.

21. *Id.* at §84.12(a) and (b). *See generally*, Lehr, *Employer Duties to Accommodate Handicapped Employees*, 31 Lab. L.J. 174 (1980).

22. For a discussion of job adaptation and ways of avoiding unnecessary stress, see V. Grossman, Employing Handicapped Persons: Meeting EEO Obligations 56-60 (1980).

23. Trageser v. Libbie Rehabilitation Center, Inc., 590 F.2d. 87 (4th Cir. 1978), *cert. denied*, 442 U.S. 947 (1979); Zorick v. Tynes, 372 So.2d 133 (Fla. Dist. Ct. App. 1979).

24. S. Rep. No. 316, 96th Cong., 1st Sess. 13 (1979); Hart v. Alameda County, 485 F. Supp. 66 (N.D. Cal. 1979).

25. HEW Office of Civil Rights, Office of Standards, Policy, and Research Memorandum (June 6, 1979).

26. *Compare* Meiner v. Missouri, 498 F. Supp. 944 (E.D. Mo. 1980) (no private right of action for monetary damages under 504) *with* Patton v. Dumpson, 498 F. Supp. 933, 937-39 (S.D.N.Y. 1980) (private right of action for monetary damages is available under 504).

27. There are two major questions clouding the enforceability of 504 in federal court. First, is there a private right of action, that is, can an individual sue under 504 for a personal remedy? The question is discussed extensively in Rogers v. Frito-Lay, Inc., 611 F.2d 1074, 1083 (5th Cir. 1980) (§504 does provide a private right of action, citing seven other federal decisions that reached the same conclusion). Notably, however, the Supreme Court, in Southeastern Community College v. Davis, 442 U.S. 397, 404-05 n.5, reserved that question but nonetheless allowed the individual plaintiff in that case to press her section 504 suit to the end, and in doing so made a tacit ruling in favor of a private right of action. The second question concerns exhaustion of administrative remedies prior to court action. The courts are divided on this issue. *Compare* Boxall v. Sequoia Union High School Dist., 464 F. Supp. 1104 (N.D. Cal. 1979) (administrative remedies must be exhausted prior to court action) *with* Patton v. Dumpson, 498 F. Supp. 933, 939-41 (S.D.N.Y. 1980) (exhaustion of remedies unnecessary).

28. 29 U.S.C. §791 (1981 Supp.). Regulations implementing §501 have been promulgated by the Department of Labor. 29 C.F.R. §1613 (1980), 41 C.F.R. §60-741 (1981).

29. 29 U.S.C. §792 (1981 Supp.).

30. 42 U.S.C. §§4151-57 (1977).

31. 29 U.S.C. §793 (1981 Supp.).

32. 41 C.F.R. §60-741 (1981). In each regional office of the Department of Labor is a branch of that department's Office of Contract Compliance Programs, which processes complaints under §503.

33. *See*, Burgdorf & Burgdorf, *A History of Unequal Treatment: The Qualification of Handicapped Persons as a "Suspect Class" under the Equal Protection Clause*, 15 Santa Clara Law., 855, 905-08 (1975); Note, *Mental Illness: A Suspect Classification*, 83 Yale L.J. 1237 (1974).

34. Sterling v. Harris, 478 F. Supp. 1046 (N.D. Ill. 1979), *rev'd on other grounds sub nom.* Schweiker v. Wilson, 450 U.S. 221 (1981). The Supreme Court was able to bypass the quasi-suspect-class issue by deciding that the challenged regulations were sufficiently reasonable to satisfy even the highest level of judicial scrutiny applied in cases of discrimination against true suspect classes.

35. Developmental Disabilities State Legislative Project, American Bar Association Commission on the Mentally Disabled, *Prohibiting Discrimination against Developmentally Disabled Persons* 5-23 (1978).

36. *E.g.,* Ill. Ann. Stat. ch. 68 §1-102(A) (Smith-Hurd Supp. 1981).

11 Taking Patients' Rights Seriously

This chapter deals with two intertwined questions: Why should mental-health professionals take the rights of their patients seriously? What can they do to honor those rights in their clinical practices? Indeed, the central problem of the 1980s is not the granting of new rights but the protection of old rights.

Responsible Professionalism

The role of mental-health professionals as advocates is too often overlooked. Yet this field has produced many professionals and paraprofessionals willing to struggle for the rights of persons identified as mentally ill. The origin of the concept of the right to treatment is credited to Dr. Morton Birnbaum, a physician and attorney. He not only produced the seminal paper setting forth the right but his years of tireless advocacy exposed the two-tiered system that leaves the most disabled and deprived with the least access to adequate mental-health resources. Under those circumstances, it is not only the patients but their care providers as well who are devalued by the deficiencies of public mental-health care.

When the Bryce State Hospital workers obtained judicial review of the inhuman levels of care and treatment, they adopted the logic of many civil-rights movements. But, in less conspicuous ways, countless interventions on behalf of patients' rights occur daily. For example, the staff of the Massachusetts mental-health department is working to create a network of psychiatric care that has the potential of allowing patients to receive adequate treatment in their own communities. Yet only a few years ago, Massachusetts, like so many other states burdened with large, outdated state hospitals, spent 80 percent of its mental-health budgets on institutions and only 20 percent on community programs.[1] Now a majority of that budget is allocated to community services. With private and voluntary community hospitals increasingly accepting state-hospital patients, less restrictive alternatives are being realized.[2]

In earlier times less congenial to reform and civil rights, pioneering voices still spoke out. David Vail, while responsible for the care of the mentally disabled of Minnesota, wrote *Dehumanization and the Institutional Career*, a searing indictment of the conditions bred by convenience and political indifference.[3] Israel Zwerling, psychiatrist, psychologist, and hospital director, testified in the *Wyatt* case on the standards necessary for adequate treatment. As long ago as 1958, Dr. Harry C. Solomon, in his presidential address to the American Psychiatric Association, warned that the large mental hospital is "antiquated, outmoded, . . . bankrupt beyond remedy." He urged that it be "liquidated as rapidly as can be done in an orderly and progressive fashion."[4]

Today, mental-health workers need be neither sages nor heroes to help vindicate the rights of those entrusted to their care. Our generation finds many examples of principled conviction: clinicians like Loren Roth, who would face imprisonment rather than betray a patient's confidence, or William Bronston, who would suffer the harassment of his bureaucratic superiors rather than remain silent to the indignities suffered by the residents of one of the largest custodial warehouses. Yet, for the most part, being serious about patients' rights is more a matter of common sense than uncommon moral aspiration.

Defending Human Rights as a Professional Value

Heightened concern for mental patients' rights is part of a global upsurge in civil and human-rights expectations. The United Nations' proclamation of 1981 as the International Year of Disabled Persons signifies this trend. As with other disabled persons and minorities, the mentally ill increasingly lay claim to equality and to full participation—the very themes of the International Year.[5] But the rights they demand—rights increasingly recognized under law—are patterned after the rights granted to any patient in a health-care facility.[6] Specific statutory guarantees of patients' rights in general and of mental patients' rights in particular reflect society's concern for, and investment in, protecting the lives and liberties of its citizens.

Protecting the rights of mental patients also has its unique difficulties. As a group these persons are not politically popular and are relatively unable to mobilize support. At times satisfying their rights poses conflicts with other groups competing for a piece of the rapidly diminishing human-services pie: old people, women, the physically handicapped, not to mention racial minorities, and civil-service employees.

Prominent leaders also recognize the potential for abuse from within the mental-health field. This flows from the great imbalance of power, information, and status between clinician and patient.[7] The use of psychiatric power to silence political dissidents in the Soviet Union, or to control the poor or the criminal offender can serve to raise the human-rights sensitivities of all who are involved in the mental-health enterprise.[8]

In this country, perhaps the most serious threat to patients' human rights lies in the highly bureaucratized settings in which mental-health care is often organized. As a former mental-health commissioner put it, judicial action would "never have been necessary if our system of care and treatment had not deteriorated to inhuman levels."[9] But even if those systems were in proper working order, it cannot always be guaranteed that patients' human and legal rights will be respected or eagerly guarded:

> They must be implemented in day-to-day actions at the interpersonal interface between attendants, nurses, social workers, rehabilitation workers, doctors, and patients. Eternal vigilance must be built into the system to insure a continuing human climate for the respect of patients as human beings. Working against this in any institution is the tendency for the burdensome duties and routines of ward life to lower the sensitivity of personnel to the needs of others. Too often the training and education of staff persons in closest contact with patients are not sufficient to keep up with the turnover of employees.[10]

Set against these bureaucratic realities, protecting a patient's rights is surely not the sole concern of the mental-health administrator. But it is a central value. This is true even for the administrator also charged with preserving physical health, improving the patients' mental functioning, maintaining organizational viability, and balancing the budget. And since the clinician owes a primary allegiance to the patient, the clinician has even greater reason to respect the legally defined rights of the patient as a major guidepost in carrying out ethical and professional responsibilities.[11] If clinicians are not vigilant, can they justifiably expect the trust and understanding of their patients or the society that must support and fund their work? The notion of rights, as Ronald Dworkin explains, is crucial because it represents the majority's promise to the minorities that their dignity and equality will be respected. This is surely what distinguishes law from "ordered brutality."[12] Although mental-health professionals have enormous power to deny certain rights of their patients, they must ponder these decisions gravely or forfeit their trust.

Reconciling patients' rights with other societal interests is the major conceptual challenge facing the mental-health field. Providers of services have enumerated lists of rights, but often there is no sense of the priority accorded various rights or the specific grounds for their abridgement, periodic review, and restoration. For example, the Vermont State Hospital lists thirty specific patients' rights, but only four are absolute (right to counsel, right to apply for a writ of habeas corpus, right to communicate by sealed mail with attorney, judge, or officials, and right to humane care and treatment). All the rest may be limited under the broad rubric, "medical welfare or needs of the patient or the hospital."[13] Under these circumstances, it is not rights that can create an adversarial atmosphere but the breadth of the discretion setting such ill-defined needs above individual rights.

Responsible professionals do have a moral obligation to speak out against the injustices inflicted against patients and pseudo-patients both here and abroad. The American Psychiatric Association, to its credit, sent a distinguished group of psychiatrists to South Africa to investigate alleged abuses of blacks in psychiatric facilities and to recommend specific improvements in the care of the ten thousand blacks in those mental hospitals.[14] The Association's president also served as a member of the diagnostic team that found General Pyotr Grigorenko, a prominent Soviet dissident, neither mentally ill nor in need of hospitalization.[15] But when will professional associations bring the same objective scrutiny to bear on the abuses and imperfections of mental-health care in the United States?

Dr. Donald G. Langsley, past president of the American Psychiatric Association, has expressed support for a right to health care and the equally important right to refuse treatment. "We are concerned," he wrote for his profession, "that patients have the right to set their own goals and not simply to accept those of the psychiatrist."[16] But how, in practical terms, will the mental-health profession take steps to implement these rights, to reinforce patient autonomy, and to provide the eternal vigilance that all agree is necessary when the integrity, dignity, privacy, and physical well-being of vulnerable people are at stake? As the following pages suggest, safeguarding the patient's legal and human rights is wholly consistent with the clinician's goals of fostering autonomy and reintegration into the community.

Steps to Promote Patients' Rights

Keeping informed of the legal rights of mental patients is surely the keystone of other responsible action. Despite the law's increasing regulation of mental-health care, workers in this field are, to a surprising degree, unclear and misinformed about patients' rights.[17] This certainly raises the risk of malpractice and other unlawful behavior. Surveys have reported that although mental-health workers have generally favorable attitudes toward patients' rights, those rights are likely to be seriously jeopardized by a lack of initiative and knowledge among those workers who must take the necessary action to protect those rights.[18]

Courses and clinical experiences dealing with forensic and other social-welfare-rights issues are only part of the answer. For example, at Columbia University, medical, social-work, architecture, and law students and faculty have pooled their talents in an interdisciplinary clinical course designed to assist the residents of SRO (single-room occupancy) hotels on New York's Upper West Side. As a result of a policy of deinstitutionalization, ten thousand former state-hospital patients live in this area and comprise 25 to 30 percent of those SRO residents. In providing direct services to them, students will learn to better understand their rights and needs at both the client and policy levels. Their field experiences are also expected to provide the basis for new interdisciplinary-training materials for professionals to assist a multiproblem population and to avoid their reinstitutionalization.

If the topic of patients' rights is to be included in licensure requirements (as it should), universities should offer academic course work on the basic substance and reasoning underlying those rights. Since these rights are fast-changing and professionals already in practice have only limited familiarity with those changes, this subject matter should be included in continuing-education programs, professional meetings, employment orientation, and inservice training. Some mental-health professionals may also wish training in advocacy skills to equip themselves for new roles.

This guidebook can help to structure the topics to be covered by such educational ventures. Specialists supplementing these readings with lectures, discussion, and other materials specific to the state law and local conditions should adapt presentations to audience needs. Law schools, bar committees on mental-disability law, protection and advocacy systems, and mental-health associations may be of assistance in identifying those specialists and organizing appropriate workshops and panel discussions. Other meetings might be jointly sponsored by bar and mental-health professional groups. Recently, for instance, the New York State Bar Committee on Mental Hygiene held a multidisciplinary panel session entitled "Deinstitutionalization—the Community and the Rights of the Mentally Disabled—a System in Conflict?" No only did the physician participants receive continuing-medical-education credit but they also had a chance to share clinical, legal, and research perspectives on this topic.

There is an even more challenging educational assignment ahead: Finding better ways of informing and training patients to know and exercise their rights as citizens and mental-health-care consumers. Despite the obvious importance of this task, woefully little has been done in most states. For example, a legislative mandate was required in 1977 before New York mental-health officials prepared and distributed such a manual in "clear, concise and easily understandable language." Only then did mental patients in state psychiatric centers have a readily available description of their rights.[19] Patients as well as persons authorized to act on their behalf are now provided at the time of admission with a 16-page manual in clear English, dealing with such topics as rights to individual-service plans, to appropriate treatment, and to legal assistance. For members of the Hispanic community it is also available in Spanish. According to the mental-health commissioner, the manual has a therapeutic as well as a civil-rights aim: "It is hoped that a full explanation of your rights will give you a secure feeling and enable you to cooperate fully in a treatment program to which you have the right to consent or object."[20]

Words alone may not be enough to convey this message. California's Department of Mental Health has produced a pocket-sized patients'-rights handbook that combines illustrations and texts describing essential rights.[21] A copy must be given to all patients at admission and to their authorized representatives with a signed receipt kept in patients' records. If patients are unable to read or understand the list of rights, staffs must note in the record that the patients were not given a copy of their rights "for good cause" and that an appropriate effort was made to explain the listed rights.[22] In fact, the first of the twenty-nine rights enumerated is that each client admitted to a facility is: " . . . to be fully informed in writing of his or her rights and responsibilities as a client and of all rules and regulations governing client conduct and responsibilities. Information shall be provided prior to or at the time of admission or in the case of clients already in the facility, when this facility adopts or amends client rights policies. Its receipt shall be acknowledged in writing and witnessed by a third person."[23]

Ideally, this rights-notification provision should be explained by someone well versed in the relevant law and social policy to avoid meaningless, high-speed, mumbled laundry-list recitations. Otherwise the risk of ignorant or uninformed waiver of rights is too great, as often occurs where facility staff view this responsibility as unimportant or burdensome.[24] Although a partial solution is to make specialized, internal patients'-rights advisors accountable for the integrity of this process, a more efficient method—and one involving fewer risks of conflict of interest—is to request the services of an external advocacy organization for these notifications. This suggestion is most practical when those organizations maintain regular offices within the facility. Such groups may also be willing to collaborate in more extensive client-training efforts. Some may also have experience in supporting self-help groups of patients and ex-patients to be their own advocates and to recognize and protect their own rights. Even for clients who have serious intellectual deficits, audio-visual materials are now available that offer a reading-free, self-instructional program on rights, responsibilities, and decision making.[25]

It is not enough merely to post lists of rights on facility walls or to distribute booklets. By their own observation of staff, patients will soon learn whether a facility gives concrete form to the concept of human dignity and teaches patients how to respond to the rights and responsibilities in their own lives. For instance, staffs could organize programs to help psychiatric inpatients to vote, to claim their welfare entitlements, or to understand the consequences of bizarre or antisocial behavior that can lead to conflict with the criminal-justice system.[26]

In one sense, clinicians must serve as the front-line advocates in securing the claim and liberty rights of their patients. Clinicians who have good working relationships with independent legal advocates can be more confident of their ability to fulfill that function. This is especially true as efforts are made to avoid or minimize hospital stays and as discharged patients confront neglect and discrimination in the community. As one leading clinician acknowledges, implementing the patients' full civil rights is one of the ten commandments to successful deinstitutionalization.[27] This can occur in innumerable professional contexts, as when determining what constitutes least restrictive treatment or protective-service alternatives as part of service-plan reviews, or when safeguarding patients' assets, or when negotiating with other agencies for services. But in its most basic form, it happens through extended conversations with patients aimed at finding services that satisfy both their aspirations and needs. Decent treatment and a decent regard for human rights both require every effort at such consultation. This contractual approach may well offer the "optimum chance for therapeutic gain."[28]

Inevitably some conflicts may not be resolved through face-to-face compromise. In those instances, respect for the personhood of the client requires that the mental-health system offer the aggrieved client the opportunity to receive a fair and full hearing. One of the basic rights outlined in recent federal legislation is the right of patients and their representatives to have access to a "fair, timely and impartial grievance procedure."[29] Michigan, Wisconsin, and a few other states have taken strides to set up such procedures,[30] but, for the most part, grievance procedures are unsatisfactory or nonexistent.[31] Even where viable mechanisms are functioning, greater effort is needed to secure their adoption by community service providers and to encourage their use by minorities and nonliterate or non-English-speaking clients.

The development of human-rights committees offers a quasi-external forum for resolving some individual and systemic problems of rights compliance. Those committees now operate in many states under a variety of mandates. Some are authorized by statute, such as the Florida Statewide Human Rights Advocacy Committee. This model involves a predominantly problem-solving approach by district committees, with opportunities for appeal to a seven-member state committee and ultimately to the governor. Others are created by state regulations and mental-health departments. As in Massachusetts, such committees may be called on to investigate complaints, monitor the use of restraints, and oversee the means used by community programs to "inform clients and staff of the clients' rights; to train clients served by the residence or program in the exercise of their rights; and to provide clients with opportunities to exercise their rights to the fullest extent of their capabilities and interests."[32] Courts have also been responsible for creating human-rights committees to review behavior-modification programs, research involving human subjects, and other forms of hazardous or experimental treatment.

Committees that are staffed by volunteers, let alone internal complaint procedures, often have real limits on their scope and effectiveness. At their best, these committees may serve useful roles as watchdogs of human-rights compliance and as agents in raising staff consciousness of the importance of these issues. The cynical administrator may see this as an appeasement device, but those genuinely interested in citizen input will approach such committees with an open mind, a desire to provide reasoned explanations for questionable practices and policies, and a willingness to adopt recommendations that promise a greater measure of client exercise of rights. Unless these channels for outside consultation and oversight are allowed to work, more intrusive forms of review are likely to be demanded—and obtained—by the public.

Clinicians must be free to refer their patients to sources of legal and other outside-advocacy assistance. This requires both a knowledge of those sources and an ability to rise above the pressures that sometimes inhibit such referrals. It may involve developing personal relationships with advocates in this field to gain either their acceptance of new cases or their aid in referring cases to knowledgeable and competent practitioners. As an aid to locating these specialists, the appendix to this book calls attention to directories of national, state, and local legal advocates with expertise in the mental-disability field.

For the general civil- and criminal-defense problems of poor people, there is also a nationwide network of legal-aid and public-defender offices. An annual directory listing their city-by-city locations and identifying programs providing specialized legal services in forty different areas of law is also available.[33] The Legal Services Corporation (LSC) and its 320 local programs provide federally funded legal assistance to indigent persons in a wide range of civil-law matters. Within their service areas, they are frequently the most knowledgeable and active advocates in resolving problems of low-income housing, domestic relations, welfare and food-stamp payments, and other poverty-related matters. In recent years, those programs have become increasingly aware of the need to provide mentally disabled persons with greater access to their services.[34] Some have begun to expand their efforts in this field and to hire specialists in the problems of institutionalized people. But whether or not special units exist, all LSC offices are barred from discriminating against mental patients or other disabled persons in the provision of their services. However, unless confronted with the needs of specific, individual clients, legal workers are unlikely to take the initiative to ensure that mental patients receive their fair share of admittedly scarce legal aid. The Reagan administration's sharp cuts in the LSC budget will place added pressure on clinicians and advocates to search for this assistance elsewhere.

In every state, protection and advocacy (P&A) systems now provide information and referral to enable developmentally disabled persons to secure their rights. Although their direct services are limited to persons with a developmental disability (mental retardation, cerebral palsy, epilepsy, autism, and related severe and chronic conditions), P&A staff can generally identify the mental-health-advocacy resources within their states. The passage of the Mental Health Systems Act, with its provisions for a nearly parallel advocacy program for recipients of mental-health services, offered promise of increased direct, outside advocacy services. Unfortunately, that section of the act has now been repealed, and the fate of like programs has been jeopardized by recent political shifts.

Some clinicians have persuasively argued that patients need immediate and continuing access to legal services to resolve certain socioeconomic problems. This might well relieve real sources of anxiety beyond the reach of other therapies, thereby improving the efficacy of treatment. It has been suggested that a staff lawyer would be an important adjunct to any psychiatric facility as counsel to patients and as a consultant to mental-health clinicians informing staff of the patients' legal rights. These psychiatrists conclude:

> What may appear to be depression with psychogenetic roots deep in a patient's past may hinge on the reality of his being unjustly and illegally abused of his rights or economically exploited. In such cases the appropriate treatment for his depression may not be antidepressant medication or psychotherapy but rather referral to a lawyer so that the issue involved may be clearly defined and his rights defended.[35]

This need seems manifestly clear, but it is doubtful that a lawyer who serves as the facility's part- or full-time consultant can at the same time be the zealous champion of its patients' rights vis-à-vis mental-health care. The conflict becomes more apparent when the issue involves petitions for involuntary treatment or allegations of overreaching discretionary authority. In such instances, a patient's legal advocate should avoid not only a conflict of interest but also the appearance of one. An increasingly popular solution is the establishment of independent legal-advocacy projects that are on-site in central facilities and whose advocates regularly visit clients in community day and residential programs.[36]

Mental-health professionals cannot simply leave to others the protection of civil rights and the correction of wrongs. At times, the clinician must "blow the whistle" on neglect or more subtle human- and civil-rights encroachments. In many states there is already a legal duty to report instances of cruelty, maltreatment, or abuse.[37] The abuse-reporting statutes often immunize the facility employee or other person reporting from retaliation, including legal protection against reprisal or libel suit.[38]

For the timid, reluctant person there may also be possibilities for anonymous reports or confidential-source information, laying the foundation for further official investigation. Indeed, many oversight agencies and outside advocacy groups rely heavily on leads from insiders who may not feel able to go on the record with their charges or misgivings.

However, there are limits to the usefulness and reliability of the information gained behind the veil of confidential background investigations. Sometimes the informant must go public or see abuse perpetuated. For this reason, recent civil-service-reform legislation protects the whistle-blowing federal public employee from retaliation.[39] The use of the subpoena power by courts and administrative agencies may also shield the apprehensive or reluctant witness from official displeasure. If necessary, the courts can—and have—safeguarded the employment rights of public mental-health workers who exercise their free-speech rights to criticize care standards, even for statements that were erroneous but were reasonably believed to be true.[40] If judges can protect mental patients from punitive action for criticizing hospital conditions,[41] they can offer some legal immunity for the professionals and others who dare to speak out for their patients.[42] Moreover, those who suffer either discharge or less formal reprisals for having followed the tenets of their code of professional ethics should be able to look to colleagues in the profession for both moral and legal support and to the profession's organizations for practical aid.

At times, more than conscientious individualism is demanded. Especially in this period of conservatism and social-welfare retrenchment, mental-health professionals should stand together to work toward distributive justice and the removal of barriers to their clients' participation in open society. For example, only eight years ago the representatives of the country's community mental-health centers were forced into court before then-HEW Secretary Weinberger would release $52 million of impounded funds needed for operating those centers.[43] The demands of now-Defense Secretary Weinberger's swelling military appropriations have already been linked to calls for cuts in mental-health and other social-welfare budgets. Even if the supplemental-security-income and other welfare payments that undergird community care were to remain at their current levels, the steady erosion of inflation will leave economically marginal patients in increasingly desperate straits. If clinicians are not actively and publicly supporting a group that by itself possesses little political clout, who will preserve present and former patients from majoritarian indifference and systemic discrimination? Inevitably, coalitions at state and national levels will seek the aid of lawyers, courts, and legislators in efforts to safeguard existing rights and to ensure the provision of decent standards of care. As even a traditionalist clinician must concede, law and the mental-health professions have common enemies to combat: "The judiciary has tried to fill a vacuum created by public apathy, executive indifference, and legislative do-nothingness."[44] In the 1980s, the urgency of trying even harder to fight these foes will soon be apparent.

Incentives for Preserving Rights

At the heart of reform movements promoting deinstitutionalization and patients' rights is a fundamental moral, social, and legal vision: mental patients should be able to satisfy their basic needs without sacrificing their basic rights. Although many mental-health professionals share this philosophy, it is questionable whether society offers enough positive incentives for taking this principle seriously. Few salary or promotion decisions, for example, hinge on a record of demonstrated respect for clients' rights.

Fortunately, progress is occurring as professionals with a commitment to human rights advance within their organizations. One illustration is a Florida multiservices-delivery system in which three successive staff-liaison professionals to a human-rights committee have all gained management promotions. Similarly, professional recognition and honors are increasingly bestowed on clinicians and administrators who have forged careers at the law and mental-health interface. One of the most famous psychiatrists in the United States, Thomas Szasz, became prominent through advocacy of rights and freedom for mental patients. Less dramatically, public esteem, favorable press reports, and good community relations often accompany programs marked by conscientious regard for their patients' individuality and dignity. Such programs find it easier to retain accreditation and federal funding as well as to attract government grants, private gifts, and highly competent staff. They are also the programs that can secure the mental-health advocates, legal and laypersons alike, who will fight to preserve their financial base in a time of inflation, will lobby increasingly cost-conscious government entities, and will support competitive salaries for recruiting qualified staff. But the most compelling reasons are personal: the satisfaction that comes from working for the rights and needs of others; the increased feelings of competence in becoming an effective patient advocate; and the sense of harmonizing professional goals and personal ideals.

The costs and consequences of neglecting patients' rights are even clearer. Where patients are not respected, staff forfeit respect as well. Arbitrary denials of rights erode trust and produce adversaries. The range of negative consequences may be severe: criticism by peers and the public; adverse publicity; disciplinary action; suspension of public funding; loss of accreditation; suits for malpractice and/or civil injunction; and even criminal prosecution where fraud or patient abuse is involved. The indirect effects of any or all of this heightened scrutiny can be devastating. Paper work multiplies, morale plummets, defensive postures predominate, and staff turnover and "burn-out" escalate. The lesson of the nursing-home scandals is a reminder to those who fear a so-called transinstitutionalization of patients from one large wretched institution to many small deplorable ones: failing facilities can be forced to "clean up their act" or to close their doors.

Will increased emphasis on the patient's legal rights drive the good practitioners out with the bad? Some argue that patients' rights restrict the clinicians' discretion and burden their time. Yet the entire field of medicine has witnessed a wide expansion in legal regulation without significant decline in either the indices of health care or the number of medical-school applicants. Rights do not stand in some artificial contradistinction to needs. A generation of advocates has pursued the right to education, the right to treatment, and an array of other socioeconomic-welfare rights with at least as much vigor as the right to liberty or the right to be left alone. Preserving mental patients' rights to optimum freedom and care serves values higher than mere convenience or efficiency.

The fight for patients' rights is not a transitory phenomenon. It is here to stay. The direction and content will, of course, be shaped by an informed exchange among the public, the lawmakers, and the mental-health profession. But any counterrevolt or nostalgia for the so-called good old days of unfettered paternalism seems futile. Fortunately, the profession has achieved some accommodation with patients' movements and other diligent advocates and the lawyers who represent them. It has come away from that experience determined to hone its own advocacy skills and sharpen its own perceptions of what the mental-health field does best and what it ought to leave for others to do. If this contributes to the decline of coercive psychiatry and the divestiture of social-control functions, then mental-health professionals will reclaim their historic mission as healers, not jailers. That result will certainly benefit the broad profession. In fact, pleas for this redemption increasingly come from within the professions. As social-welfare concerns sink lower on political priority lists, mental-health professionals, consumers, and advocates must join together in fighting to protect human rights and to satisfy human needs.

Notes

1. Goldman, *Change in a State Department of Mental Health: A View from Within*, 4 Ad. Mental Health 2, 6 (Fall 1976).

2. McLaughlin, *Revolution with Promise: Hospital Network of Psychiatric Care Taking Shape*, Boston Globe, May 29, 1980 at 17, col. 3.

3. D. Vail, Dehumanization and the Institutional Career (1967).

4. Solomon, *The American Psychiatric Association in Relation to American Psychiatry*, 115 Am. J. Psychiatry 1, 7 (1958).

5. Schuster-Herr & Herr, *Human Rights and Disabled Persons: An International Perspective*, 5 Amicus 14 (Feb. 1980). With little fanfare, the United States has declared 1982 as the National Year of Disabled Persons.

6. *See* Massachusetts Gen. Laws Ann. ch. 111, §70E (West Supp. 1980) (patients' rights in hospitals, clinics, and other health facilities).

7. Robitscher, *The Uses and Abuses of Psychiatry* (*The 1976 Isaac Ray Award Lectures*), J. Psychiatry & L. 331 (1977); J. Robitscher, The Powers of Psychiatry (1980).

8. Robinson, *World Congress Condemns Abuse*, Psychiatric News, Oct. 7, 1977, at 1, col. 1 (collaboration of psychiatrists and Soviet state in hospitalization of non-mentally-ill persons to suppress political dissent); S. Bloch & P. Reddaway, Psychiatric Terror: How Soviet Psychiatry Is Used to Suppress Dissent 31 (1977).

9. M. Greenblatt, Psychopolitics 73 (1978).

10. *Id.* at 92.

11. President's Commission on Mental Health, Report of the Task Panel on Legal and Ethical Issues, *reprinted in* 20 Ariz. L. Rev. 49 (1978). *See* Shestack, *Psychiatry and the Dilemmas of Dual Loyalties*, 60 A.B.A. J. 1521 (1974); Powledge, *The Therapist as Double Agent*, 11 Psychology Today 44 (July 1977).

12. R. Dworkin, Taking Rights Seriously 205 (1977).

13. G. Brooks, Superintendent, Vermont State Hospital, Patients' Rights (Aug. 1979)(memorandum). Reprinted with permission.

14. *Report of the Committee to Visit South Africa*, 136 Am. J. Psychiatry 1498 (1979).

15. Onesti, *Alan A. Stone, 108th President, 1979-80*, 137 Am. J. Psychiatry 895, 898 (1980).

16. Langsley, *Response to the Presidential Address*, 137 Am. J. Psychiatry 892, 893 (1980).

17. *See* Danflevicus, *Legal Rights of Psychiatric Patients*, 224 J. A.M.A. 1645 (1973).

18. Laves & Cohen, *A Preliminary Investigation into the Knowledge of and Attitudes toward the Legal Rights of Mental Patients*, 1 J. Psychiatry 328 (1972); Tancredi & Clark, *Psychiatry and the Legal Rights of Patients*, 129 Am. J. Psychiatry 328 (1972); Kahle & Sales, *Attitudes of Clinical Psychologists toward Involuntary Civil Commitment Law*, 9 Prof. Psychology 428 (Aug. 1978) (national survey shows general support for trend toward greater concern for legal rights of individuals being committed).

19. 1977 N.Y. Laws, ch. 16.

20. Prevost, *Preface* to N.Y. State Office of Mental Health, Rights of Patients in Psychiatric Centers of the New York State Office of Mental Health at 1 (n.d.).

21. California Dept. of Mental Health, Patients' Rights Handbook (1978).

22. Cal. Health Facilities and Referral Agencies Regulations, Cal. Admin. Code tit. 22, R76525(f)(1981).

23. *Id.* at R76525(a)(1).

24. For example, in Massachusetts, the law requiring prior notice of the rights of voluntary patients to receive legal counsel before admission is often ignored, or given in such a perfunctory way that no such requests are ever made.

25. Project Independence, Social Planning Services, Inc., Rights Now! A Learning Program on Rights and Responsibilities (published by the National Institute on Mental Retardation, P.O. Box 5019, Downsview, Ontario, Canada).

26. *See* Thompson & Hall, *Helping Psychiatric Inpatients Exercise Their Right to Vote*, 25 Hosp. & Community Psychiatry 441 (1974).

27. Talbott, *Deinstitutionalization: Avoiding the Disasters of the Past*, 30 Hosp. & Community Psychiatry 621 (1979).

28. Morse, *A Preference for Liberty: The Case against Involuntary Commitment of the Mentally Disordered*, 70 Cal. L. Rev. 54, 103 (1982).

29. Mental Health Systems Act, 42 U.S.C. §9501(1)(L) (1981 Pamphlet).

30. Coye & Clifford, *One-Year Report on Rights Violations under Michigan's New Protection System*, 29 Hosp. & Community Psychiatry 528 (1978)(of the 1,034 complaints filed, half filed by the retarded and one-fourth filed by the mentally ill clients against state and community mental-health agencies were substantiated); Government Studies & Systems, 2 Evaluation of Models of Advocacy Programs for the Mentally Ill and Developmentally Disabled: Final Report at 4-7 (Client Advocacy Program of the Wisconsin Dept. of Health and Social Services established four-tier procedure, with 70 percent of 212 clients resolving grievance at the stage of informal settlement).

31. *See* New York Mental Health Information Service, Report on the Adequacy of the Current Grievance and Disciplinary Procedures of the Department of Mental Hygiene in Safeguarding the Rights of Patients Involved in Incidents of Abuse and Mistreatment (1976).

32. Mass. Regulations on Mental Health Community Residential Alternatives, Mass. Admin. Code tit. 104 §14.03(11) (1979).

33. National Legal Aid & Defender Association, 1981 Directory of Legal Aid and Defender Offices in the United States (1981) (available from NLADA, 1625 K Street, N.W., 8th Floor, Washington, D.C. 20006).

34. Legal Services Corporation, Special Difficulties of Access and Special Unmet Legal Problems of the Elderly and Handicapped: Summary (May 1980); S. Herr, The New Clients: Legal Services for Mentally Retarded Persons (1979).

35. L. Tancredi, J. Lieb & A. Slaby, Legal Issues in Psychiatric Care 146 (1975).

36. S. Herr, Advocates for People with Mental Disabilities: A Report to the United States District Court Monitors on Advocacy Needs and Models for Massachusetts Class Clients (Sept. 1980).

37. *See, e.g.*, Fla. Stat. Ann. §827.09 (West Supp. 1982) (any professional employee, parent, or other person who has reason to believe a mentally ill or other disabled person has been subjected to abuse must report it to the health and rehabilitative-services department).

38. Fla. Stat. Ann. §827.09(9) (West Supp. 1982): "No resident or employee of a facility serving disabled or aged persons shall be subjected to reprisal or discharge because of his actions in reporting abuse pursuant to the requirements of this section."

39. 5 U.S.C. §2302(8) (Supp. 1980) (federal employees or job applicants may not be subjected to personnel-action reprisals for a disclosure of information that the employee "reasonably believes evidences a violation of any law, rule, or regulation, or mismanagement, a gross waste of funds, an abuse of authority, or a substantial and specific danger to public health or safety").

40. Donahue v. Staunton, 471 F.2d 475 (7th Cir. 1972), *cert. denied*, 410 U.S. 955 (1973). In a decision restoring the full employment rights of a mental-health chaplain who publicly criticized a facility, the district court upheld the state employee's free speech as in "the interest of society in 'uninhibited and robust debate' on matters of public concern, such as mental health care, and plaintiff's individual interest in being free to speak out on matters of concern to him, outweigh those of the State as an employer." *Id.* at 481.

41. On judicial protection for mental patients criticizing hospital conditions, see Brown v. Schubert, 389 F. Supp. 281 (E.D. Wis. 1975) (patients writing letters to local newspaper and Urban League have First Amendment right to restoration of privileges and ward assignment and to injunction against any restrictive transfer or other disciplinary action).

42. *E.g.,* Lynch v. King, No. 78-2152, Order and Memorandum (D. Mass. March 8, 1982)(contempt citation upheld against social-service commissioner who forced area director's resignation following his testimony; public employees entitled to participate in civil-rights case "without sanction or reprisal of any kind").

43. National Council of Community Mental Health Centers, Inc. v. Weinberger, 361 F. Supp. 897 (D.D.C. 1973).

44. Lebensohn, *Defensive Psychiatry or How to Treat the Mentally Ill without Being a Lawyer*, Law and the Mental Health Professions 19, 40 (W. Barton and C. Sanborn, eds. 1978).

Appendix: Directories to Advocacy Services

The best sources of information on the exact nature of mental patients' rights in the various states are the legal and other advocates who specialize in this field. Because the lists of organizations and individuals active in this field are rapidly changing, we provide the names of the following organizations and the titles of their directories, if any, as a starting point in locating various types of advocacy services.

American Bar Association
Commission on the Mentally Disabled
1800 M Street, N.W.
Washington, D.C. 20036

The American Bar Association Commission on the Mentally Disabled compiles and periodically revises a useful directory, entitled *Mental Disability Advocates: A General Listing*. This provides names, addresses, and phone numbers of national organizations, legal services/legal-aid mental-disability units, developmental-disabilities protection and advocacy projects, private attorneys, state-agency advocates, and those whose activities in this field are part-time or through consumer groups, law clinics, bar associations, or other public-interest programs.

Human Interaction Research Institute
10889 Wilshire Boulevard, Suite 1120
Los Angeles, Cal. 90024

The most recent and comprehensive national survey of mental-health-rights protection and advocacy programs is published in the *National Directory of Mental Health Advocacy Programs* (1982). The Institute, a grantee of the National Institute of Mental Health, conducted its survey in May 1981, with a brief follow-up survey in February 1982. The *National Directory* contains profiles on 417 programs in forty-seven states and the District of Columbia. Approximately one-fourth of the programs surveyed are classified as legal-services organizations, one-fourth as mental-health associations, and one-fourth as internal advocacy programs, with the remaining programs consisting of patient/ex-patient groups, parent/family groups, and other organizations.

National Legal Aid and Defender Association
1625 K Street, N.W., 8th Floor
Washington, D.C. 20006

The National Legal Aid and Defender Association publishes an annual directory of legal services available primarily for poor persons. It is entitled *Directory of Legal Aid and Defender Offices in the United States*. In addition, the Association has a section on mental-disability law.

American Civil Liberties Union
132 West 43rd Street
New York, N.Y. 10036

The American Civil Liberties Union, primarily through its network of state affiliates and volunteer counsel, assists clients raising civil-liberties and civil-rights issues, particularly in cases implicating novel constitutional or other law-reform issues.

United States Department of Justice
Office of Special Litigation
Civil Rights Division
10th and Pennsylvania Avenue, N.W.
Washington, D.C. 20530

The Office of Special Litigation maintains a docket of federal class-action suits posing major mental-disability-law issues. Under S.10 passed by Congress in 1980, the Department of Justice is also empowered to initiate litigation in highly selective cases involving "a pattern or practice of resistance to the full enjoyment" of the constitutional and statutory rights of institutionalized persons.

By far, the major share of advocacy in the mental-disability field is performed by those working at state and local levels. The diversity and richness of those efforts are not fully captured by any of the existing directories. Some states, such as Massachusetts with its Coalition of Advocates for the Legal Rights of the Disabled, have a ready means for identifying those programs and individuals. Other states have bar committees that may be able to assist with referrals to experienced practitioners. In New Jersey and elsewhere, state-funded agencies have been created to provide legal and other advocacy services to eligible clients within mental-health systems. Consumer groups, self-help and self-advocacy groups, human-rights committees, and other public and nonprofit associations and agencies may also provide support and assistance to persons with legal and human-rights-related complaints in the mental-health field.

Index

About the Authors

Stanley S. Herr is associate professor of the University of Maryland Law School. He has previously been a visiting scholar at Harvard and Columbia law schools, an associate of the Columbia University Center for the Study of Human Rights and senior adjunct associate at the Hastings Center, Institute of Society, Ethics and Life Sciences. He received an undergraduate degree from Yale University, the J.D. from Yale Law School, and the D.Phil. in law from Balliol College, Oxford. A member of the District of Columbia Bar, he has been extensively involved in mental-disability law as a public interest lawyer, clinical teacher, consultant, lecturer, and professional-association officer. Dr. Herr is the author of *The New Clients: Legal Services for Mentally Retarded Persons* (1979) and *Rights and Advocacy for Retarded People* (Lexington Books, 1983).

Stephen Arons is associate professor and former chair of the Legal Studies Program of the University of Massachusetts at Amherst. He received the B.A. from the University of Pennsylvania and the J.D. from Harvard Law School. He is a former director and cofounder of the Mental Patients Advocacy Project, located on the grounds of the Northampton State Hospital in Northampton, Massachusetts. Professor Arons is the author of *Compelling Belief: The Culture of American Schooling* (1982), coauthor of *Before the Law* (1974), and a past contributing editor to the *Saturday Review*.

Richard E. Wallace, Jr., is an associate in the Washington law office of White & Case. He received the B.A. in legal studies from the University of Massachusetts at Amherst and the J.D. from Harvard Law School. He previously worked as an advocate supervisor of the Mental Patients Advocacy Project and led its community-education program. Mr. Wallace is chair of the American Bar Association Y.L.D. Committee on the Delivery of Legal Services to the Disabled.